With Wings Like Eagles

MICHAEL KORDA

WITH
WINGS
LIKE
EAGLES

A History of the Battle of Britain

BOOKS

First published in Great Britain in 2009 by
JR Books, 10 Greenland Street, London NW1 0ND
www.jrbooks.com

First published in paperback, 2010

A catalogue record for this book is available from the British Library.

ISBN 978-1-907532-07-8

1 3 5 7 9 10 8 6 4 2

Printed in the UK by CPI Bookmarque, Croydon CRO 4TD

For Margaret, who was there,
with all my love

And for my dear friend Jay Watnick,
whose wisdom, financial acumen, sound judgment,
and unfailing friendship, I have treasured
for more than thirty years

And in fond memory of Flying Officer Philip Sandeman, RAF,
friend, mentor, generous role model—

Oh! I have slipped the surly bonds of earth
And danced the skies on laughter-silvered wings;
Sunward I've climbed, and joined the tumbling mirth
Of sun-split clouds—and done a hundred things
You have not dreamed of—wheeled and soared and swung
High in the sunlit silence. Hov'ring there
I've chased the shouting wind along, and flung
My eager craft through footless halls of air.
Up in the long delirious, burning blue,
I've topped the windswept heights with easy grace
Where never lark or even eagle flew—
And while with silent lifting mind I've trod
The high untrespassed sanctity of space,
Put out my hand and touched the face of God.

—*"High Flight," by Pilot Officer Gillespie Magee, Jr.*
No. 412 Squadron, RCAF, killed December 11, 1941

Never in the field of human conflict
was so much owed by so many to so few.

—Winston Churchill, House of Commons,
August 20, 1940

Per ardua ad astra.

—Motto of the Royal Air Force

They shall mount up with wings as eagles;
they shall run, and not be weary;
and they shall walk, and not faint.

—Isaiah, 40:31

CONTENTS

With Wings Like Eagles

CHAPTER 1

"The Bomber Will Always Get Through."

—Prime Minister Stanley Baldwin,
House of Commons, 1932

Few moments in British history are so firmly fixed in people's minds as the summer of 1940, when, after the fall of France, fewer than 2,000 young fighter pilots seemed to be all that stood between Hitler and the victory that was almost within his grasp. Like the defeat of the Spanish Armada and Nelson's victory at Trafalgar over the combined fleets of France and Spain, it is etched deeply into the national consciousness as a moment of supreme danger when Britain, alone,* courageous, defiant, without allies, defeated a more powerful and warlike enemy in the nick of time.

Today, nearly seventy years later, the Battle of Britain—as it rapidly came to be called, after a phrase in one of Winston Churchill's

---

* Except for its Empire and Commonwealth, which were very distant and even less well prepared for war than "the mother country."

greatest war speeches*—unlike many other great events of World War II, has lost none of its luster. As modern warfare goes, it was, up to a point, both glamorous and gentlemanly (though, as we shall see, it involved plenty of horrors, atrocities, and suffering), and it was fought by fairly "dashing" young men on both sides (and on the ground, on the British side of the Channel, also by young women, the WAAFs of the Women's Auxiliary Air Force who operated the radar plotting stations and took their full share of casualties).

Of course there is, among the victors at any rate, a natural tendency to glamorize the past, but even allowing for that, the Battle of Britain still retains a certain glamour, and not just in the United Kingdom—even the Germans, who lost the battle, are still fascinated by it, to judge by the number of German-language books and Web sites on the subject, as are the Japanese, who were not even in the war at that time. In Britain it is still commemorated annually on Battle of Britain Day, September 15. Until 1959, the events of the day included the "fly past," of a carefully preserved Spitfire and Hurricane, the two principal British fighter aircraft of the battle, flying low over London, weather permitting, the unfamiliar low-pitched, throbbing roar of their twelve-cylinder Rolls-Royce Merlin engines music to the ears of those old enough to have heard it before, as they passed over Buckingham Palace and climbed swiftly away. For a time, they were flown by aces who had taken part in the Battle of Britain, but soon they were too old to fly anymore.

Given time, all historical events become controversial. That is the nature of things—we question and rewrite the past, glamorizing it or diminishing it according to our own inclinations, or the social and

---

* In his speech in the House of Commons on June 18, 1940, on the fall of France, Churchill said, "What General Weygand called the Battle of France is over. I expect that the Battle of Britain is about to begin."

political views of the present. Historians—indeed whole schools of history—have made their reputation by casting a jaundiced eye on the victories, heroes, and triumphs of their forefathers. Nobody in academe gets tenure or a reputation in the media by examining the events of the past with approval, or by praising the decisions of past statesmen and military leaders as wise and sensible.

Not surprisingly, the Battle of Britain has come in for its share of revisionary history and debunking, though given its special standing as (let us hope) the last in the series of great battles in which Britain stood alone against a tyrant threatening invasion (and seeking at the same time hegemony over the European continent), it has not come in for the kind of sharp criticism directed toward British motives and generalship in, for example, the American Revolutionary War, the Crimean War, or World War I. There is no equivalent here of General Burgoyne's surrender at Saratoga, or the Charge of the Light Brigade, or the First Battle of the Somme. As at Trafalgar, the British got it triumphantly right—RAF Fighter Command made up for years of dithering, pessimism, and appeasement among the politicians between the wars (the "locust years," as Churchill called them), and also of doubt in the Air Ministry that fighters could defend Britain against air attack, since the conventional view was not only that "the bomber will always get through," a phrase Prime Minister Stanley Baldwin had borrowed from an immensely influential book by the Italian theorist of aerial warfare Giulio Douhet, but that the only defense lay in having a bomber force big enough to deter any continental enemy. "The only defense is in offense," Baldwin warned the House of Commons darkly in 1932, "which means that you have to kill more women and children more quickly than the enemy if you want to save yourselves."[1] This was a grim prospect, which the prime minister, like most members of the House, wanted to eliminate or discourage altogether, rather than to prepare for; indeed, he was arguing *against* increasing military expenditure at the time.

Throughout the 1920s and the early 1930s, Fighter Command (as it eventually came to be called) was the Cinderella of the Air Ministry. Such money as was made available to the RAF by the politicians was used, according to the prevailing orthodox doctrine of air power, to build up Bomber Command. In theory, money spent on fighters was money down the drain, since the only real protection was thought to be a force of bombers large enough to scare off the Germans.

Reluctant as the British government and the air marshals were to develop an effective fighter force, it remained unclear what the role of the RAF was to be in the event that a diplomatic policy of "appeasing" Germany failed to prevent a war. The roots of many of the various controversies that surround the Battle of Britain may be found, as we shall see, in the prejudice against building fighters and the mistaken belief that bombers (theirs and ours) would always "get through." In addition to this, there is a more recent, and growing, tendency to question whether the Battle of Britain in fact played the decisive role in discouraging Hitler from attempting to invade Britain when to his surprise the opportunity to do so suddenly presented itself after Dunkirk.

This is a difficult question to answer. The "what ifs" of history are always problematic and of course by definition unanswerable, but they usually involve supposing an alternative outcome to a historical event. What would have happened if Lee had won the Battle of Gettysburg? What would have happened if Admiral de Robeck had not heeded his fears and instead had pushed the British fleet on through the Dardanelles to take Constantinople in March 1915, as he came very close to doing? What would have happened if Hitler had released Panzer Group West on June 6, 1944, and Rommel had returned from his leave in time to destroy the Allied troops on the beaches at

Normandy? Since these things did *not* happen, we can only speculate, and speculation is a bad habit for anybody writing history. As the old saying goes, "If my aunt had balls, she'd be my uncle."

The speculation about the Battle of Britain is of a different kind. Nobody denies that we won it; but we simply do not know how serious Hitler was about invading Britain—or, of course, whether such an invasion would have succeeded. The mere fact that the *Kriegsmarine* assembled a large quantity of barges and tugs for *Fall Seelöwe* ("Operation Sea Lion") as the German cross-Channel invasion was known, does not necessarily mean that the Führer had made up his mind on the subject, nor do the German army's relatively makeshift exercises in getting tanks, guns, and horses onto and off these makeshift landing vessels, or the hastily printed guidebook to England for the use of German troops, or even the Gestapo's long and often inaccurate printed booklet listing people who were to be arrested (and presumably murdered) once Britain was taken.* As we shall see, the German invasion plans were elaborate but ambivalent, and in a very untypical way much in them was left to chance or luck.

No doubt too there was an element of bluff. Hitler had taken Poland and defeated France, and was astonished at his own success. His opinions about the British were formed by those who, like former prime minister David Lloyd George, the duke of Windsor, and the marquess of Londonderry, had come to pay homage to him before the war and to assure him that the British desired peace at any price, and by Foreign Minister Joachim von Ribbentrop's self-deluding impression— Ribbentrop was a victim of extreme vanity, snobbery, and tunnel vision—of those of the British upper class who had invited him to their homes when he was German ambassador to the Court of St. James's.

---

* The author's uncle, Sir Alexander Korda, was on the Gestapo's list. In his case they had his correct business and home address.

Hitler was not wrong in thinking that many people in England, on the left as well as the right, would still have preferred a compromise peace to a continued, all-out war. As late as May 26, 1940, more than two weeks after Churchill took office as prime minister, Lord Halifax, the British foreign secretary who George VI and most of the Conservative Party had hoped would replace Neville Chamberlain as prime minister instead of Churchill, revealed to the War Cabinet that he had been talking to the Italian ambassador in London about the possibility that "Signor Mussolini" might agree to inquire of the Führer what his terms would be for peace with Britain. This démarche dismayed Churchill when he heard of it—his own opinion, as expressed later to the members of the larger cabinet, was, "We shall go on, we shall fight it out here or elsewhere, and if at last the long story is to end, it were better it should end, not through surrender, but only when we are rolling senseless on the ground."[*2] Halifax's chat with the Italian ambassador, however much it alarmed and displeased Churchill, must have kindled optimism in Berlin. Hitler himself had thrown the British what he intended to be an olive branch, in the form of a long speech in which he offered to guarantee the continued existence of the British Empire and fleet in return for a free hand for Nazi Germany in Europe. So far, the results of this were disappointing, to be sure, but who could be certain that in the face of invasion the British might not come to their senses and replace Churchill with, say, Halifax or Lloyd George, and agree to sit down at the bargaining table like sensible people? The British were defeated, Hitler believed—the fact of their defeat had simply not sunk in on them yet.

Many people, most recently Derek Robinson, the author of *Piece of*

---

[*] Others remember this as ". . . when we are lying on the ground choking on our blood," but either way Churchill's view of the situation was dramatically different from that of his foreign minister, Lord Halifax.

Cake, a splendid BBC series about a fictional fighter squadron in the Battle of Britain, have argued that the invasion was a sham, that what prevented it was not the RAF's victory in the air but the Royal Navy's ability to send several cruisers and as many as forty destroyers into the Channel, if need be, to destroy an invasion fleet, and that even if the Germans had managed to get ashore the British were sufficiently prepared and armed by midsummer to defeat them on the ground.*

There is nothing intrinsically impossible about this scenario—the Royal Navy would certainly have done *something*, and it had at least ten times as many destroyers available to attack the German invasion fleet as the Germans had to defend it, and certainly the flow of rifles from across the Atlantic was putting thousands of American Enfield .30-06-caliber rifles into the hands of the "Local Defense Volunteers," later to be renamed more inspiringly the Home Guard by Winston Churchill, releasing their Lee-Enfield .303 service rifles to rearm those troops who had lost theirs at Dunkirk.

Still, all war is chance. Given good luck and good weather, the Germans might have gotten on shore in substantial numbers with some of their heavy equipment, and had they done so, the Home Guard, despite the affection with which we now look back on it, would very likely not have proved a serious obstacle to the German army; and after Dunkirk the British regular army was woefully deficient in guns, tanks, mortars, and machine guns. As for the Royal Navy, the sinking of HMS *Repulse* and *Prince of Wales* by Japanese bombers off the coast of Malaya a year and a half later would demonstrate just how vulnerable even heavily armored modern battleships were to determined air attack, particularly when close inshore—and at its narrowest point the English Channel is only twenty-one miles wide.

* Robinson, *Invasion 1940*, Carroll and Graf, New York, 2005.

Much has been made by historians of the notion that Hitler was a "land animal," ill at ease on the subject of naval warfare. Certainly, in one of the few photographs of Hitler visiting the German fleet in a naval launch he looks out of place and uncomfortable, and his hair is strangely windblown. Did he suffer from seasickness, one wonders? In any case, his view of the world remained that of an Austrian, and Austria is not by any stretch of the imagination a nation of bold seafarers. On the other hand, he did not hesitate to use the German navy in April 1940 in a daring, and successful, amphibious assault on neutral Norway that took the Allies by surprise. Admittedly, this assault cost the German navy most of its destroyers, and that became a matter of serious concern two months later as Sea Lion was being contemplated, but in the meantime he had extended German power to the Arctic circle, protected Germany's supply of iron ore from Sweden, and handed the British a significant defeat. There is, therefore, no reason to suppose that Hitler suffered a prolonged attack of nerves on the subject of the invasion of Britain.

To be sure, he was no fool. General von Brauchitsch's breezy characterization of Sea Lion as a *grossen Flussüberganges*, a "giant river crossing," while comforting to his fellow generals who knew all there was to know about river crossings, created dismay among the German admirals, who had a more realistic view of what the English Channel was like even in good weather, and was no doubt taken with a grain of salt by the Führer. Hitler did not doubt that Sea Lion would be a difficult and risky operation, and although he allowed the preparations to proceed, it is telling that he took very little interest in them, and he seems to have thought of the operation as something that might take place *after* a change of government in Britain, or even that the mere threat of Sea Lion might be enough to bring the

British to their senses and make them sue for peace. Thus, the date for Sea Lion was repeatedly moved forward in the expectation of good news from London. In the meantime, however, the one thing that was clear to everybody—Hitler, the admirals, and the generals—was that before Sea Lion could take place the Royal Air Force would have to be crippled, in the air and on the ground, and German air supremacy established over the English Channel and the southeastern coast of England in the area where the German army would cross and land.

This was nothing more than common sense. It would be hard enough to transport 250,000 German troops (and more than 50,000 horses, for the German army's artillery was still largely horse-drawn), as well as quantities of field artillery and tanks—and this would constitute merely the first wave of the invasion—across the Channel in flat-bottomed river barges towed by tugboats, without their being constantly strafed by Fighter Command and bombed by Bomber Command on the way over. More important, the *Luftwaffe* could hardly concentrate on the vital task of sinking British cruisers and destroyers attacking the invasion fleet in the narrow waters of the Channel if the skies were full of RAF Spitfires and Hurricanes. When it came to Sea Lion, the German armed forces were involved in an "After you, Alphonse" situation. The army was ready to go as soon as the navy was prepared; the navy would go the minute the *Luftwaffe* had destroyed the RAF; and it was therefore left to the *Luftwaffe* to make the first move.

In normal circumstances, any air force might have hesitated before accepting this responsibility, but Germany was not a normal place. The *Luftwaffe* was commanded by Hermann Göring, then still regarded as the second most important man in the Reich and as Hitler's closest collaborator. In addition to the fact that Göring ran the *Luftwaffe* as a personal fiefdom, it was also the youngest and the most authentically Nazi of the three armed forces. The navy and the army had traditions that went back into the eighteenth and nineteenth centuries, and many of their senior officers regarded the Führer as an upstart and the Nazi Party as a collection of social misfits, clowns, and sinister thugs, but the *Luftwaffe* had been created by the Nazis in 1933—secretly, because at the time the Treaty of Versailles forbade Germany to have an air force. The *Luftwaffe* owed its existence to Hitler, and as a young man's service it represented his modernistic and futuristic ambitions. Like the autobahns; the Volkswagen; the streamlined record-breaking silver race cars from Mercedes-Benz and Auto-Union; the huge, spectacular Nuremberg rallies and the Berlin Olympic Games; and the sleek zeppelins carrying passengers across the Atlantic to Brazil and New York, the *Luftwaffe* was intended to show the world that Nazi Germany was the unstoppable power of the future.

Because Göring was its founder and commander in chief, the *Luftwaffe* never suffered from the kind of cheeseparing economies that the British Treasury inflicted on the RAF. What Göring wanted, he got, and that was that, much to the displeasure of the army and navy. Nobody would deny Göring's energy, intelligence, courage, or ruthlessness, but the *Luftwaffe* also suffered from the flaws in his ample character. First of all, his view of air warfare was ineradicably fixed by his experience in the 1914–1918 war as one of Germany's leading air aces and winner of its highest and most coveted decoration for valor, Pour le Mérite, known as the "Blue Max." Second, despite his expansive powers he was abjectly subservient to the Führer. Third, self-indulgence on a grand scale and prodigious vanity were beginning to destroy a character that in any case had always been more receptive to flattery and adulation than to reasoned argument—he was Hitler's yes-man and wanted his own yes-men around him. Fourth, he collected high offices as avidly as he collected the awards and decorations that made him resemble, in full uniform, a stout, walking Christmas tree. He was not only commander in chief of the *Luftwaffe* but also Hitler's appointed successor; head of the German four-year plan, with wide-ranging powers over Germany's economy and industry; aviation minister; founder of the Gestapo; the smiling, cheerful face of Nazism to the outside world, which tended to contrast his girth and luxurious tastes with the abstemious habits of the Führer; and *Jagdmeister* of the Reich— that is, he controlled all hunting and was in charge of what we would now call game and forest conservation. The list of his offices goes on and on—no one person, even someone who was deskbound day and night, could have discharged all of Göring's duties; and unlike his rival SS Reichsführer Heinrich Himmler, whose *Sitzfleisch* even his numerous enemies did not deny, Göring did not have a deskbound nature. He was Germany's biggest and most aggressive collector of art; he built on a huge and ambitious scale; his lifestyle bore a resemblance to that of the more flamboyantly corrupt later Roman emperors; and he intruded shamelessly and sometimes brutally into the realm of every other minister of the Reich. Under the circumstances, his attention was not necessarily fixed on the *Luftwaffe* twenty-four hours a day. To be sure, Göring delegated much of his workload, but he was not, as it happened, a particularly gifted delegator, and tended to favor people who agreed with him (or at least said they did), and old flying comrades from World War I. He could be autocratic in his own bluff, outspoken way—when it was pointed out to him that General Erhard Milch, whom he had plucked from Lufthansa to play a leading role in the creation of the *Luftwaffe*, was half Jewish, Göring replied angrily, "In Germany, it is *I* who will decide who is a Jew and who is not!"*[3]—but his patience and his attention span were fatally limited.

He was also boastful. When the British Expeditionary Force retreated to Dunkirk, he had assured Hitler that there was no need for the army to attack them there—the *Luftwaffe* would strafe them on the beaches and sink any ships that were sent to take the troops home to Britain. He had been unable to deliver on this promise—the British, using 1,000 ships of all kinds, from yachts and pleasure steamers to destroyers, managed to take more than 300,000 men off the beaches and out of the besieged port of Dunkirk, and in the air battles above Dunkirk the Germans for the first time found themselves confronted with the metropolitan squadrons of Fighter Command (as opposed to the relatively small number of British Hurricanes that had been stationed as part of the RAF Advance Air Striking Force in France, and were flown from makeshift fields without the benefit of a sophisticated fighter control system on the ground), and they were taken aback by the quality and the number of British fighter planes. Admittedly, there were mistakes, surprises, and disappointments on both sides, but the *Luftwaffe* could hardly claim a victory.

As a result, however, Göring was all the more determined to show that his beloved *Luftwaffe* could, by itself, bring the British to their knees. This was no small task, as a glance at the map should have told him. Before they could even begin it, the Germans would have to move two *Luftflotten* ("air fleets") to air bases in northeastern France, the Netherlands, and Belgium, and a third to Norway, together with all the men, equipment, communications, supplies, and

---

* Göring exaggerated his powers in this instance. In the end Milch, whose father was Jewish, was obliged to persuade his mother to swear that he was actually the child of an Aryan with whom she had had an extramarital affair.

fuel needed to maintain the nearly 3,000 aircraft involved. Runways at most of the existing military airfields (*Luftflotte* 2 alone would require more than thirty operational airfields spread out from Amsterdam to Le Havre) would need to be lengthened and reinforced for the use of heavily loaded bombers, and protected with flak (antiaircraft) batteries (which in Germany, unlike the United Kingdom, came under the control of the *Luftwaffe* rather than the army); huge numbers of vehicles of every size and type would need to be assembled quickly; and sophisticated repair and service facilities would have to be put in place. Admittedly, this was the kind of thing the Germans excelled at—Milch was a gifted organizer, who, unlike several of his rivals in the *Luftwaffe*, surrounded himself with skilled technicians—but it was still a big job. Then too, although the French air force had not put up much of a fight, the *Luftwaffe* had suffered substantial losses in the Norwegian campaign and in the attacks on Poland, Norway, the Netherlands, Belgium, and France. More than 1,500 German aircraft were lost—most of them, inevitably, to accidents—and although a substantial number of the aircrews survived and returned to their units to fight again, there was, unavoidably, a certain amount of wastage, confusion, and delay.

Though nobody was about to bring it to Göring's attention, the *Luftwaffe*, in fact, had not been built with this kind of task in mind. Its successes in Spain, Poland, Norway, and the attack on France had been won against weaker air forces or none, and with the *Luftwaffe* acting in support of the German army, in the role of flying artillery, rather than as a long-range strategic weapon in its own right. The bombing of Guernica, Warsaw, and Rotterdam had brought a chill to the hearts of those who believed the bomber would always get through, but none of these cities had a first-rate, modern, technologically advanced air defense system, or fighter squadrons equipped with aircraft that were as good as those of the *Luftwaffe*. In contrast, Britain had a modern air defense system, and its fighter aircraft were in some respects better than those of the *Luftwaffe* and flown by pilots whose morale, skill, and spirit were second to none.

Göring was, in fact, about to launch a new kind of war; and it was a war for which the British were better prepared than he (or anyone else) supposed. Over the past decade they had devoted an astonishing amount of thought, innovation, and preparation to it.

The story of how that came to be is perhaps the least appreciated part of the Battle of Britain, for ironically the RAF's victory was made possible only by the far-reaching and courageous decisions of the same governments that would be later reviled as consisting of "appeasers," "guilty men" (in the words of a best-selling polemic),[4] and "the men of Munich."

CHAPTER 2

**"To England, All Eyes Were Turned.
All That Has Gone Now. Nothing Has
Been Done in 'the Years That the
Locust Hath Eaten.'"**

—*Winston Churchill, House of Commons,*
November 12, 1936

Victory against the *Luftwaffe* in 1940 came about neither by luck nor by last-minute improvisation. In photographs of the period, the fighter pilots tend to look like young, carefree, happy warriors, if there is such a thing, but the reason they won the Battle of Britain was above all that Fighter Command was prepared for it.

The architect of this victory was Air Chief Marshal Sir Hugh Dowding, who took over as Air Officer Commanding-in-Chief of RAF Fighter Command on its formation in 1936. The fighters, such as they were—for they were then all biplanes with an open cockpit, two guns, and fixed landing gear—had been part of a more amorphous organization, Air Defence of Great Britain (ADGB), which everybody agreed was inadequate to its task. Dowding had transferred from the Royal Artillery to the infant Royal Flying Corps during World War I, had commanded ADGB in 1929 and 1930, and since then had served as Air Member for Research and Development on the Air Council, the RAF equivalent of the army's General Staff. In that capacity, Dowding, a man who had the patience to listen to scientists and engineers, and to ask questions until he understood exactly what they were proposing, learned more about the technology of air defense than any other senior air officer in the world, particularly in two areas that were then in their infancy: the "black art" of radio direction finding, and high-frequency ground-to-air communication. Dowding, in fact, had early on in his flying career been the first man to send a radio signal from an aircraft to the ground, an innovation in which nobody at the time was interested.

Dowding was, in many respects, a remote, stubborn, difficult man with strong opinions—it was not for nothing that his nickname was "Stuffy"—and he could never charm politicians or his fellow air marshals, an inability that would eventually be his undoing; but on the subject of air warfare he knew what he was talking about. He had in his head an airman's three-dimensional sense of how to fight a battle in the sky over southern England, and he understood that it would involve combining the newest and most radical scientific ideas about radio direction finding* on a grand scale with the latest kinds of radio communications equipment and a totally new breed of fighter airplane into an efficient, tightly controlled, well-led organization,

---

* The term "radar" was coined later, in the United States, and became universally used. Its birth in the United Kingdom came about in 1935, when the Air Ministry, informed erroneously that the Germans were developing a radio beam "death ray" that could destroy airplanes in midair, asked scientist Robert Watson-Watt to look into the matter. Watson-Watt dismissed the notion of the death ray, but suggested the use of radio beams to locate aircraft. He first tested such beams successfully at Daventry on February 26, 1935. Although Prime Minister Stanley Baldwin has been accused of lacking interest in defense and technology, he was kept fully informed of Watson-Watt's progress, in which he showed great interest. He understood at once the vital importance of radar, and pushed hard for the development of the "Chain Home" radar network along Britain's southern coast. It became operational in 1937, and it enabled Fighter Command to detect the number, height, and course of enemy aircraft at ranges of up to 100 miles.

linking fighters, antiaircraft guns, and ground observers into a single unit involving thousands of people and technology which did not as yet exist. With those who did not share his vision or sense of urgency he could be bloody-minded indeed.

Dowding was a lonely man, a widower with one son (who would become a fighter pilot under his father's command in the Battle of Britain), humorless, exacting, somewhat inarticulate except about the things that seemed really important to him, given to various crank ideas (in his old age he would devote himself almost entirely to spiritualism), and perhaps for that reason unafraid of new or seemingly crackpot scientific schemes and of challenging authority—indeed, as we shall see, he probably saved Britain by standing up to Winston Churchill during the great crisis of France's defeat, and paid a stiff price for his blunt, outspoken refusal to be bullied, persuaded, silenced, or coerced by the prime minister. In his own gruff, shy way Dowding was strangely sentimental about his fighter pilots, whom he sometimes referred to as "my chicks," and in his official farewell letter to them on giving up his beloved command, he addressed them, like a Mr. Chips in uniform, as "My dear Fighter Boys."

It would be difficult to imagine a person less like Göring or Göring's commanders. So far as one can tell, Dowding had no hobbies or recreations—to a remarkable degree, he felt the hot wind of war at his back, urging him on to prepare Fighter Command for battle, despite doubt, interference, and hostility, and, as it would prove, he succeeded just in time. His technical expertise and his imagination on the subject of air warfare were the impetus that produced radar, the eight-gun Hawker Hurricane and the Supermarine Spitfire, and the "brain" of Fighter Command, a centralized Fighter Control, the futuristic Operations Room at Fighter Command Headquarters, which was in constant communication with the radar plotters and

the fighter squadrons, and from which the battle could be systematically observed, controlled, and led.

Above all, in 1936 Dowding was perhaps the one man of consequence in the United Kingdom—perhaps in the world—who did *not*
believe that the bomber would "always get through."

Stanley Baldwin's statement in the House of Commons represented
accepted wisdom in the 1920s and 1930s. Toward the end of World
War I the Germans had made a major effort to bomb London and
coastal cities in the south of England, first using zeppelins, then using big Gotha biplane bombers with twin Mercedes motors and a
seventy-seven-foot wingspan, hoping to weaken British resolve by the
application of *Schrecklicheit* (frightfulness), always the fallback position of German policy. Though compared with what happened in the
next world war the damage and the number of deaths were small
(835 British civilians were killed and 1,990 wounded), the bombing
campaign, not surprisingly, made a huge impression. Unfortunately
for the Germans, however, the net effect was merely to increase British determination to win the war.

Once the war was over, and aircraft gradually started to become
larger and more powerful (by very small degrees—in 1932, when
Baldwin made his remark about the bomber, the bombers of the
world's air forces still resembled those of 1917 and 1918 much more
than they did those of 1939), the belief grew that the next war, if there
was one, would begin with huge bombing raids that would annihi-
late great cities on the first day. This illusion was in part the work of
military propagandists for "strategic bombing," such as General Giulio Douhet in Italy and General "Billy" Mitchell in the United States,
and in part the work of senior air force officers, who promised the
politicians that a big bombing force would serve as the best deterrent

to war, and would be much cheaper to build up and maintain than a big army—an argument that appealed both to those who sought peace and to those who sought economy in governmental spending.

Of course, nowhere did these fleets of bombers exist: the United States, for instance, was thousands of miles away from any country it might possibly need to bomb, and in any case was in the middle of the Great Depression and was resolved never to fight another war. But strangely enough, the idea of the bomber as the inevitable, ultimate weapon of the future became more widely accepted in Britain than in any other country, to the dismay of the admirals, who still believed the answer was more and larger battleships. The French were not much interested in bombers (perhaps because they lived in fear that their beloved Paris would be bombed), or indeed in military aircraft of any kind; Marshal Foch himself had said, "Aviation is a sport—for war it's worth zero." To protect itself from the Germans, France continued to rely on a mass army of citizen conscripts, trained by fulfilling, with whatever reluctance, their annual period of military service; and on immense, elaborate fortifications, particularly the famous Maginot Line. The Germans, forbidden by the terms of the peace treaty to rearm, dreamed first of all of rebuilding their army. The Soviet Union relied, as always, on its millions of conscript peasant soldiers. During World War I the British had put off conscription for as long as they could, as a deeply un-English notion, and the moment the war ended they swiftly demobilized their army—conscription, obligatory military service, and a large army went against every tradition of British life; and the idea of a small regular army of long-term professional soldiers, commanded by officers who were so far as possible members of the upper class or the younger sons of the landowning aristocracy, was deeply treasured. In the circumstances, the idea of a powerful bombing force whose very existence would prevent war, and which would involve a comparatively small number of professional airmen, was undeniably attractive. Nobody in the United Kingdom, from King George V down, wanted to repeat the experience of World War I, in which more than 750,000 Britons had been killed and more than 2 million seriously wounded, most of them in the mud of Flanders.

The idea of the bomber as the weapon of the future—even the near future—moved rapidly from the quiet places in Whitehall where British military policy was somewhat lackadaisically discussed—for it was not one of the subjects in which Baldwin showed much interest—to make its way into the mind of the public, thanks to the immense power of the popular press, and was reinforced by the growing power of what was beginning to be called popular culture, i.e., radio, magazines, popular fiction, and above all films. In 1936, my uncle, Alexander Korda, a friend and admirer of H. G. Wells, produced an ambitious, immensely successful futuristic film based on Wells's novel *The Shape of Things to Come*, which began with the destruction of a major European city (recognizably London) by a huge fleet of bombers darkening the sky, without a declaration of war. Designed by my father, Vincent Korda, *Things to Come* held audiences breathless, presenting them with a convincing picture of a world in which war would come, literally, out of the blue, wiping out whole cities in one blow with bombs and poison gas. Alex and my father were not, to be sure, attempting to buttress the arguments of the air marshals for more money, or to instill fear in the public; they were merely attempting to brings Wells's ideas to the screen as faithfully (and dramatically) as possible. But the film (which deeply impressed Hitler) nevertheless had an immense effect on the public, and indeed on the government.

For despite the phlegmatic, calm, peace-loving appearance of Prime

Minister Stanley Baldwin—a man who looked exactly like a character
in a novel by R. F. Delderfield about the English countryside, puffing
contentedly on his pipe and determined to avoid full-scale rearmament and war, or even *talk* about full-scale rearmament and war—
some radical notions were quietly being put into preparation. Baldwin,
a cousin of Rudyard Kipling, had a somewhat inflated reputation for
sagacity, blunt talk, and plain common sense, thought to be part of his
heritage from a family of wealthy, tough-minded West Midland iron-
masters.* It was also his misfortune to be almost comically uninterested
in foreign affairs and foreigners at a time when nothing was more important, and even his most sympathetic biographer, G. M. Young,
notes that Baldwin "would ostentatiously close his eyes [in cabinet
meetings] when foreign affairs were under discussion. 'Wake me up,'
he would say, 'when you are finished with that.'" Foreigners "made
him peevish, or sent him to sleep."[1] He liked to give the impression
that there was nothing much on his mind except keeping the Conservative Party in power, and long, quiet country weekends of taking
walks and reading Trollope, but in fact he was a shrewd, devious politician, who deftly managed the House of Commons—the Labour
members liked him as much as the members of his own party did—
and easily outflanked Churchill during the abdication crisis. Nobody
understood the British public of the 1930s better than Stanley Baldwin, or was more trusted by the public. In Young's words, "They
trusted him, they believed in him, less for anything he had done or
was likely to do, than for being himself." Unlike Churchill, whose reputation was badly singed by his outspoken, belligerent support for "the
King's matter," as Baldwin tactfully called Edward VIII's determination to marry Wallis Warfield Simpson, Baldwin had instantly

---

* This was perhaps balanced out in Stanley Baldwin's character by his mother, who was a
successful author of fiction about rural life and a book of ghost stories.

understood that however much the British might like their young king, they were not about to put up with his marrying a twice-divorced American adventuress from Baltimore.

Baldwin, though he was notoriously indolent and often never bothered to read the papers that were sent to him—a failing that was to backfire on him with regard to the air estimates—in his own way faced unpleasant facts once they could no longer be avoided, whether they were on the subject of Mrs. Simpson or Hitler. He not only said, "The bomber will always get through"; he *believed* it, and drew the consequences. First of all, there must be no war, and British policy should above all be directed toward giving the Germans no reason to start one, and of course toward avoiding the awkward, misplaced continental entanglements that had dragged a reluctant, appalled, divided Liberal government into war against Germany in 1914. Second, steps should be taken—without alarming the public, of course—to deal with the consequences if Hitler was mad enough to start a war. Behind the scenes, in the staid world of the civil service, bureaucrats would soon be drawing up plans to have hundreds of thousands of cheap plywood coffins made and stored in strategic locations, to supply the entire population of Britain with gas masks, to dig trenches in the treasured lawns of London's parks as emergency air-raid shelters, and, even more alarmingly, to identify convenient sites for mass graves, should they be needed.

This dark view of the future, though concealed from the public, was echoed in Winston Churchill's speeches calling for rearmament and a stronger air force, in which he painted a picture of future war in startling, if somber colors for the House of Commons.* "We may . . . ,"

---

* Curiously, Baldwin—like his predecessor, Ramsay MacDonald, and his successor, Neville Chamberlain, the other two major apostles of appeasement—allowed Churchill to have access to British intelligence estimates about German air strength and to information

he said, "be confronted on some occasion with a visit from an ambassador, and may have to give an answer in a very few hours; and if that answer is not satisfactory, within the next few hours the crash of bombs exploding in London and the cataracts of masonry and fire and smoke will warn us of any inadequacy which has been permitted in our aerial defences."[2]

Addressing what he took to be Baldwin's reluctance to spend more money on the RAF, Churchill predicted that no "less than 30,000 or 40,000 people would be killed or maimed" in a German bombing attack on London, and that as many as "3,000,000 or 4,000,000 people would be driven out [of London] into the open country around the Metropolis." This apocalyptic vision, not unlike that of H. G. Wells, was not something most members of Parliament, on either side of the House, wished to contemplate—nor, as it happened, was the vision, for the moment, a likely one—and did almost as much harm to Churchill's political reputation as his support for Edward VIII's marriage. To the general public, his talk of "cataracts of masonry and fire and smoke" made Churchill seem like a "wild man," and also something of a warmonger, and to most people Baldwin seemed an even more steady and reliable figure by comparison.

The dispute on rearmament between Baldwin and Churchill became so bitter that when, later, during the war, Churchill was told that the Baldwin family's ironworks had been bombed by the Germans he remarked grumpily, "How ungrateful of them," and after being congratulated by Harold Nicolson on his eulogy for Neville Chamberlain in the House of Commons, he replied, "That was not an

about the RAF's strength, perhaps on Lyndon B. Johnson's theory that it was "better to have him inside the tent pissing out than outside the tent pissing in." If so, the theory didn't work. It was not just the accuracy of the numbers that Churchill protested, but the interpretation of them, and the failure to react to them by increasing British air strength dramatically.

insuperable task, since I admired many of Neville's great qualities, but I pray to God in his infinite mercy that I shall not have to deliver a similar oration on Baldwin—that would indeed be difficult to do."3 But their disagreement was misleading in the sense that both of them were talking about the *number* of aircraft available to the RAF and the *Luftwaffe*, rather than about type and quality, which were harder to define.

The argument was further muddled in most people's minds by an artificial distinction between "frontline aircraft" and those "in reserve," and the confusion was made worse by the Germans' habit of exaggerating their air strength when they wanted to frighten people, and playing it down when they wanted to claim that they sought no more than "parity" with the United Kingdom and France. That the Germans were building military aircraft faster than the British was obvious enough to most people, though Baldwin and his supporters in the House of Commons continued to deny it soothingly, despite ample evidence to the contrary. But were they building fighters or bombers, and in what proportion, and how effective were the latter? These were the critical questions, and for the most part they remained unanswered, or even unasked.

The truth is that despite Göring's bombast, the one task the *Luftwaffe* was *not* prepared for in 1936, or even in 1939, was bombing London, let alone destroying the city in the kind of surprise raid that Churchill had described and that so many people feared, particularly those who had seen *Things to Come*. Between 1933 and 1936 the Germans, like the British, were infatuated with the idea of the *Schnellbomber* ("fast bomber")—faster than the fighters that would be available to intercept it. In England the eccentric millionaire Lord Rothermere, owner of the newspaper the *Daily Mail*, and an aviation enthusiast, ordered for himself from the Bristol Aircraft Company the fastest private transport plane in the world—a twin-engine all-metal monoplane, called, a typical Rothermere touch, *Britain First*, which would carry six passengers and a crew of two at the then unheard of speed of almost 300 miles per hour. When it was delivered to him in 1935 he gave both the aircraft and the blueprints of the design to the Air Ministry as a patriotic gesture; the ministry then modified the plane to create the Bristol Blenheim Mark I bomber.

The Blenheim was faster than any fighter then existing, as were its rivals the Dornier (Do) 17, the Heinkel (He) 111, and the Junkers (Ju) 88 in Germany.* The problem with all these aircraft, however, was that they carried a relatively light bomb load, made up of fairly small bombs; even the largest of them, the He 111, could carry only eight 500-pound (250-kilogram) bombs, held nose upward in a modular rack like eggs in an egg container. This seemed like a reasonable bomb load in the mid 1930s, but to put the matter in perspective, only six years later RAF Bomber Command would be sending deep into Germany at night hundreds of four-engine Avro Lancasters that were able to carry a "Blockbuster" bomb of up to 12,000 pounds, and eventually, with some modifications, the enormous 22,000-pound "Grand Slam" bomb.

By one of those curious strokes of good fortune for their enemies, the Germans started the mass production of bombers too early, and stuck with the idea of the *Schnellbomber*. Also, since Göring was above

---

* Like the Bristol Blenheim, the German bombers He 111 and the Do 17 (called the "flying pencil" because its fuselage was so narrow) were originally designed and built as fast civilian passenger aircraft—in their case because Germany was forbidden to build military aircraft under the terms of the Versailles peace treaty. All these aircraft became slower when converted into bombers, since they then were heavier and sprouted drag-producing gun turrets, radio antennas, bomb aimer positions, etc. Only the Ju 88 was designed from scratch as a fast bomber, and not coincidentally it proved the best and most adaptable of all. It gained a new lease on life in 1942 as a very effective radar-equipped night fighter.

all interested in quantity rather than in efficiency—when those around him pointed this out, he replied that the Führer would ask him only how many bombers he had, not how big they were or how far they could fly—the Germans continued to produce the same types to the end, whereas the British Air Ministry took a hugely expensive leap in the dark, quietly abandoned the "fast bomber," and instead set about drawing up ambitious plans to design and produce, on a huge scale, a whole family of big, four-engine bombers, intended to carry heavy bomb loads over very long distances—to Berlin, for example.

In any case, by 1938, as we shall see, the leap in the performance and armament of the new generation of fighters, represented in Britain by the Hurricane and the Spitfire, and in Germany by the Bf 109, abruptly invalidated the whole idea of "fast bombers." These new fighters would easily fly 100 or even 200 miles per hour faster than the fastest bomber, and could reach much higher altitudes. The Germans faced another problem, too—since the more a bomb load weighs, the less can be spared for fuel, their "fast bombers" designed in the 1930s had a fairly limited combat radius. Reaching targets in England from airfields in Germany would put them at the extreme limit of their range, and well beyond the ability of German fighters to accompany them. Of course in the 1930s neither the Germans nor the British anticipated that the *Luftwaffe* would be attacking Britain from airfields in the Netherlands, Belgium, or northern France, much closer to British targets, making possible an aerial campaign that would have been unimaginable before June 1940.

Thus, although the Germans were certainly producing military aircraft at an alarming rate in 1935, the situation was in fact less critical than Baldwin's detractors, led by Churchill, liked to make it out. The solution was not simply for the British government to build more aircraft than the Germans—least of all bombers, which then had neither the range nor the bomb capacity to deter Hitler from war—but to start thinking rationally about the possibility of defending the United Kingdom against aerial attack, and investing in the advanced technology and complex ground organization that would be needed to detect and destroy enemy bombers.

Baldwin, who did not share Churchill's enthusiasm for military matters, seems to have stumbled on the idea of defense rather than deterrence by some mysterious thought process of his own. It may be that threatening to bomb German civilians—or, worse still, actually having to *do* it—in order to keep the peace struck him as morally indefensible, and as a blind alley, since the Germans under Hitler would very likely retaliate. It may also have been a dose of realism on his part, since by the mid-1930s, despite the firm belief of the Air Ministry in the principle of deterrence as the keystone of British strategy, there was still no sign to the layman that RAF Bomber Command would be able to make good on any such threat in the near future. The majority opinion of the "bloody air marshals," as Lord Beaverbrook would later take to calling them, was that every fighter built meant further delay in creating the all-important bomber force on which the safety of Britain really depended. Another factor in Baldwin's mind was that fighters were easier to sell to the House of Commons than bombers. Even the Labour members—who were, in general, against increased armaments of any kind, in favor of "collective security," and strong believers in the League of Nations as the equivalent of labor-management negotiations between nations— were less offended by spending money on fighters than by spending it on a bomber force. At least fighters were by definition for defense, not attack, and it was hard even for Labour's pacifist fringe to argue that having the ability to defend oneself if attacked was morally wrong.

Baldwin seems to have been moved by the same idea. As a business-man, he saw fighters as a kind of insurance policy against the failure of diplomacy or the remote possibility that Hitler might actually mean what he said, or worse still what he had written in *Mein Kampf*. Bombers offended Baldwin's moral scruples; fighters did not.

He spoke movingly of his belief that "since the day of the air, the old frontiers are gone. When you think of the defense of England you no longer think of the chalk cliffs of Dover, you think of the Rhine." What appeared to horrify him was the idea that England could defend itself only by dropping bombs on the men, women, and children of the Rhineland (since this was the only major target in Germany that the current generation of RAF bombers could reach). Whether the victims were British, French, or German, the prime minister rejected the notion that "two thousand years after Our Lord was crucified, [we] should be spending our time thinking how we can get the mangled bodies of children to the hospitals and how we can keep poison gas from the throats of the people," and worried (prophetically) about the future, when "the bomb no bigger than a walnut"[4] might blow up whole cities. (Can he have been imagining nuclear weapons, or reading H. G. Wells instead of Trollope?) Sincere and sympathetic as this kind of speech was, it was hardly a rousing call to arms.

Baldwin had other, more practical concerns about the cost of rearming the RAF. The projected cost of building a single modern fighter plane was estimated at between £5,000 and £10,000 each, whereas one big four-engine bomber was expected to cost more than £50,000, and perhaps twice that. In addition, fighters could fly from grass strips at what were then still called aerodromes, whereas bombers, because of their heavier weight, required long, expensive concrete runways and hardstands, much bigger hangars, and of course bigger aircrews, all of which would cost enormous sums of money. In the war of numbers that was going on between Baldwin and Churchill, it seemed possible that the latter might be silenced at much less expense by building fighters rather than bombers.

The argument about numbers was in any case complicated by the fact that both men counted "frontline airplanes" and reserves separately. What most politicians, including those in France, Italy, and the Soviet Union, meant was that "frontline airplanes" would be of the latest type, whereas the "reserves" would consist of older but still usable machines. What the air marshals meant, but did not always say, was that *all* their airplanes must be of the latest type, the "frontline" planes being those delivered to combat-ready squadrons, the "reserves" held back to supply new squadrons as they were formed or to replace machines that had been lost in combat or in accidents. As war would prove, when it finally arrived, only the latest and most up-to-date aircraft were useful in combat. Each side would work incessantly to improve the performance and armament of its aircraft and to bring in new types at a dizzying rate, so that the machines with which Britain and Germany began the war in 1939 were already rendered obsolete by 1940 (those of the French were, unfortunately for them, already obsolete in 1939). This was a hard point to get across—the majority of the Royal Navy's battleships had either served during World War I or been completed and updated shortly after it ended; the British Army, like the German, was still using a slightly modified version of the same rifle its soldiers had carried in World War I*; and most of the field artillery in both armies would have

---

*The British Lee-Enfield .303 rifle of World War II had a slightly longer barrel than the Lee-Enfield rifle of World War I (and a different, less effective bayonet). The Mauser 98K of the German army was merely a slighter shorter version of the World War I Mauser rifle. In both armies the pistols, hand grenades, and helmets were identical to those of the earlier war, as were the British Army's machine guns.

been familiar to a veteran of the 1914–1918 war. In the air, however, obsolescence was such a rapid process that it was hard to avoid— once war broke out ground crews would be struggling night after night to carry out the latest "modifications" from the Air Ministry, changes and additions to their aircraft that arrived in the form of end- less mimeographed pages and diagrams. Aircraft that were not "front- line" would be swept out of the air by those that were. Counting older aircraft as part of a nation's air strength, as the French (and the Rus- sians) did, was like including old, lame horses in the fighting strength of a cavalry corps.

In the end, Baldwin's long political career would eventually fall victim to the numbers in which he took so little interest. As long ago as 1933, already under pressure from those who wanted Britain to rearm, he had announced to the House of Commons that in the event no agreement could be reached between the European nations on restricting the size of air forces or, better yet, abolishing them, Brit- ain would accept "No inferiority to any country within striking dis- tance."[5] In 1934 he had announced that German air strength was "not fifty per cent of our strength,"[6] although many people suspected that the truth was otherwise. In 1935, he unwisely repeated this pledge, only to have Hitler reveal that Germany had already reached parity with the United Kingdom, and was approaching parity with France—which would, of course, mean that the *Luftwaffe*'s strength would soon exceed that of France and Britain combined.

If Baldwin had been reading the intelligence analyses produced for him by the Air Ministry and MI6 he would have seen that the fa- mous pledge he had given in 1933 to allow "no inferiority to any power within striking distance" had already been swept aside by the rapid increase in German aircraft production since then, and even his devoted friend and biographer, Young, complains of "his indolence"[7] in this respect. In any case, in 1935 Baldwin had the unpleasant task of explaining to an uneasy House of Commons that he had been wrong. Being Baldwin, he did not attempt to justify himself by complaining that he had been duped by Hitler, or by explaining to the House that Britain was already developing a sophisticated air defense system—he took full responsibility for his mistake, but this did him very little good.

His proposal to speed up the program for rearming the RAF so that the target for aircraft strength planned for 1939 would be reached in 1937 brought down on his head both the objections of Labour members, who wanted no increases in armaments, and those of Conservatives who supported Churchill and thought that Baldwin was proposing to produce too little, too late, as well as an outcry from industrial leaders, businessmen, and the chiefs of the army and navy, who argued that attempting to produce so many aircraft so quickly would disrupt British industrial production.

Even so, it would still take the Hoare-Laval crisis, in which the British foreign minister Sir Samuel Hoare appeared to have agreed with the crafty French foreign minister (and future collaborationist) Pierre Laval to let Mussolini get away with the conquest of Abyssinia; the abdication crisis, which exhausted an already weary Baldwin; and Hitler's bold move to remilitarize the Rhineland to finally persuade Baldwin to resign in 1937 and advise the new king to send for Neville Chamberlain, the chancellor of the exchequer, to form a government.

Honors rained down on Baldwin—he was made a knight of the Garter and an earl—but he got no credit for the most important accomplishments of his political life. For by 1937 the "Chain Home" (CH) radar network was already in place and operating, silently and secretly, and the first Hurricanes were reaching RAF Fighter Command squadrons, to be followed a year later by the first Spitfires; Dowding had been appointed Air Officer Commanding-in-Chief of Fighter Command almost a year ago; and Dowding's special brainchild, the central Operations Room at Fighter Command Headquarters, was completed and functioning. There were problems, of course—not surprisingly, considering the amount and variety of revolutionary science and technology involved—but one by one they were being solved.

Whatever else might happen, Britain would no longer be completely undefended in the air.

CHAPTER 3

"I Can't Understand Why Chicago Gangsters Can Have Bulletproof Glass in Their Cars, and I Can't Get It in My Spitfires!"

—Air Chief Marshal Sir Hugh Dowding,
KCB, 1937

The decision to place Dowding in command of the newly named Fighter Command was made while Baldwin was still prime minister, and was already clouded by the low esteem in which Dowding was, even then, held by the other members of the Air Council, and by the enmity, going back to their days as army subalterns in India, which existed between himself and the next Chief of the Air Staff Air Chief Marshal Sir Cyril Newall—an enmity made stronger by Dowding's belief that *he* had been promised the post of Chief of the Air Staff, and that because he was senior to Newall it should have been his. To say that Dowding was a difficult colleague would be putting it mildly—he was impatient not only with fools, but also with people who did not agree with him, whatever their rank; he was also, despite a forbiddingly conventional appearance, a man of vision and imagination, always open to unorthodox new ideas, and although generally uncommunicative, he was argumentative when it came to things that mattered to him, and not easily open to compromise. The members of the Air Council were happy to be rid of him and his crank ideas, and since they believed that fighters were a distraction from the all-important task of building up the bomber force, Dowding's new command was not, in their eyes, a promotion—on the contrary, they felt they had rid themselves of a uncongenial nuisance and sidelined him to a place where he could presumably do little or no harm until his retirement. The notion that Fighter Command would become the "first eleven," to use a cricket term for the top players, and the fighter pilots rather than Bomber Command the glamour boys of the RAF had not yet occurred to Dowding's colleagues. The duration of his command and the date of his retirement were already abrasive issues long before the Battle of Britain, and Dowding knew it—a skilled military bureaucrat himself, he was always obliged to fight on two fronts, one against the *Luftwaffe* and the other against his enemies on the Air Council; and although he would prove victorious in the first battle, he was defeated in the second.

As Air Member for Research and Development on the Air Council, Dowding had laid the groundwork for Fighter Command, often against stiff opposition. He had backed Watson-Watt's experiments in radar, and helped to transform scientific theory into a solid chain of radar transmitters along the southern coast of England. He had been instrumental in laying down the Air Ministry's specifications for a new generation of revolutionary eight-gun, all-metal monoplane fighters, with an enclosed cockpit and retractable undercarriage, and encouraged Rolls-Royce in its private venture to develop a super-charged twelve-cylinder aero engine, called the PV XII and eventually named the Rolls-Royce Merlin. He had insisted that future fighters be equipped with high-frequency wireless sets, enabling the pilots to talk to each other and to communicate with the ground, and even foresaw the need to link the radar operators to an operational center that would transmit to the fighter pilots the information they needed in terms they could understand in order to intercept the enemy in what we would now call "real time." Like all visionaries, he was impatient, and he also intuitively understood that great change would meet with suspicion and hostility even from those who would most benefit from it. The aircraft industry was not at all sure that the Air Ministry's specifications could be met, or that it would be possible to mass-produce any design that could meet them. Fighter pilots who had been brought up in the Biggles tradition* of aerial lone wolfsmanship were appalled at the notion that they would be told where to fly and what to do over the radio by young women—for Dowding had already guessed that the only way to provide the number of people who would be needed to transmit the endless flow of information from the radar stations to Fighter Command's Operations Room, and from there "filtered" to the operations room of each group, and on from there to the squadrons and the pilots in the air, would be to employ large numbers of young women. Maintenance units were aghast at the new tasks the ground crews would have to learn and the sheer quantity of unfamiliar new tools and spare parts they would need to deal with. An air force in which repairs to fuselage and wings still involved sewing and doping fabric patches, and air-to-air communications consisted of the flight leader sticking his arm out of the open cockpit of his aircraft and making hand gestures, was going to have be dragged into the mysteries of stressed, flush-riveted aluminum skin and high-frequency wireless, and there was bound to be some kicking and screaming, much of it directed at Dowding.

---

* In the 1930s "Biggles" was the pilot hero of a hugely successful series of what we would now call young adult novels; he was young, daring, and preternaturally brave.

. . .

Fighter Command Headquarters had moved into its new home, Bentley Priory, only two months before Dowding's appointment.[1] Not far from Harrow and Stanmore, and only ten miles from London, Bentley Priory was a huge but architecturally uninspiring eighteenth-century house, originally the property of the marquess of Abercorn, which had been converted first into a hotel, then into a girls' boarding school. Finally it ended up in the hands of the RAF in 1926, another of those stately homes, fallen into ruin, which only the government could afford to maintain. Bentley Priory sprawled all over, the original eighteenth-century house dwarfed by less harmonious structures that had been added to transform it first into the hotel and then into the school. Inside, much of it was a rabbit warren of rooms and passageways, but it retained a magnificent entrance hall, a grand staircase, a ballroom, two billiard rooms, a picture gallery in the form of a rotunda, a library, a gymnasium (added on during its days as a school), and, perhaps its strongest asset, a beautiful garden in the eighteenth-century classical Italian style that provided a serene and imposing view from the rear of the house. In the mid–nineteenth century it had been the home of the dowager queen Adelaide, widow of William IV; for her bedroom, an ornate Italianate ceiling was painted, which was for a time regarded as one of the architectural wonders of England. Among those who had visited the house in its grander days were Queen Victoria, the duke of Wellington, and Nelson and Lady Hamilton. Visitors coming up the drive who had business at Fighter Command sometimes remarked that it looked like a lunatic asylum, and it might have become one had the air force not bought it cheap, for less than £25,000.

Dowding's office, nowadays preserved as it was in 1940 as a kind of shrine, looked out through floor-to-ceiling French windows over the Italian garden, and like the man himself it was, apart from the view, spare—a Ministry of Works desk; a few uncomfortable, nondescript chairs that may have been part of the headmaster's furniture when the house was a girls' school; a conference table; a telephone. There were no personal photographs or souvenirs, and the surface of the desk was kept uncluttered. Dowding, while not a martinet, was a model of military propriety—other officers at Bentley Priory walked around indoors without wearing their caps, since capless they didn't have to be saluted or to salute back, but every time Dowding left his office he put his cap firmly on his head, the gold-braided visor dead straight and exactly parallel to the ground. Not for Dowding, either, a cap worn at the jaunty angle favored by popular admirals, or a cap with the top crushed like those of his pilots. Dowding's headgear, like Dowding himself, was uncompromisingly correct, to the extent that in photographs of Dowding and George VI together, the king looks more casual in RAF uniform than Dowding does. The Air Ministry acquired Montrose, a large, ugly, mock-Tudor house in suburban Stanmore, for Dowding's use, and he moved his sister Hilda in to look after him, then set about building the kind of organization he had in mind.

With a clairvoyance exceeding that of his fellow air marshals, let alone of the government, Dowding had a good picture in his mind of the battle to come, and what it would take to win. Fighter Command Headquarters, he had already determined, would not just control the fighter squadrons; it would have to control the entire battle. Thus, from the very beginning, he set out to fill the vast space of Bentley Priory with the people he needed. There would have to be a naval liaison officer, for example, to keep track of naval and merchant marine movements and to warn the navy of raids aimed at its home ports; there would have to be integrated control of the army's antiaircraft (AA) guns and searchlights, requiring the presence of senior officers of the Royal Artillery to ensure that the AA gunners shot down Germans, not Dowding's pilots. There would also have to be barrage balloons, the Observer Corps (volunteers—spread out across southern England and equipped with binoculars, military telescopes, compasses, and direct telephone lines to Fighter Command—whose task it was to count enemy planes and calculate their direction), civil authorities responsible for sounding the air raid sirens in each town and district as air raids approached them, and so on. All these elements, many of them not part of the RAF at all, had to be firmly unified under a single command, responsible for the total air defense of the United Kingdom. That, as Dowding saw it, was his job, and it says much for his energy, his determination, his sense of urgency, and the sheer sweep of his ambitious plan that he was able to deflect most of the Air Council's attempts to hamper him by rejecting or scaling down his requests, and the natural tendency of the Civil Service, the police forces and fire brigades, the army and the navy, and the civilian Observer Corps (which had hitherto been the responsibility of the Home Office) to resist being told what to do by an air marshal.*

Among the many things that Dowding demanded and the Air Council tried to reject were laminated armored-glass windscreens for his fighters; buried, concrete-shielded telephone lines from Bentley Priory to the radar sites and the Fighter Command airfields; all-weather concrete runways, which had hitherto been thought necessary only for bombers; an underground bombproof Operations Room at Fighter Command Headquarters; eight guns for the Spitfire and the Hurricane (the Air Council thought four were plenty); and the rapid formation of

---

* Starting in 1941, as the Germans came under increasingly heavy attack from Bomber Command, they instituted a very similar system of nationwide, integrated air defense, linking radar, fighters, night fighters, antiaircraft guns, searchlights, police, fire police, municipal authorities, and the Nazi Party's public assistance organizations under a single command. More ambitious (and authoritarian) than the British system, it was amazingly efficient. There is an excellent description of it in Len Deighton's novel *Bomber*.

the Women's Auxiliary Air Force (WAAF) to provide him with the radar operators and plotters he needed.

Dowding won most of these bruising fights, but not without making further enemies. The younger air marshals, such as Air Marshal Sir William Sholto Douglas, KCB, DFC, MC, thought Dowding was out of touch—it had been too long since he had flown an airplane, and he failed to appreciate that bombers, not fighters, would be what mattered in the war to come. As for the older air marshals, they had learned to fly on grass fields in aircraft with open cockpits, and were impatient with such frivolous, expensive, pie-in-the-sky notions as bulletproof glass. Even the idea of burying a fighter's battery of guns in its wings struck some of them as foolish. They had fought when a fighter aircraft mounted two machine guns above the engine, placed so the pilot could clear a jam or a frozen breechblock by pulling back on the cocking lever from his open cockpit, and if that failed, lean forward out of his seat and give the breech mechanism a sharp blow with a rubber mallet, which most pilots carried in the cockpit for just that purpose. For that matter, Fighter Command's inventory of aircraft still consisted mostly of biplanes with an open cockpit, fixed undercarriage, and two guns, not very different from those of the last war. They objected to the transparent sliding cockpit canopy, arguing that the pilot would be unable to turn his head and look behind him, and were unconvinced by the fact that Dowding had insisted on the provision of a perfectly ordinary rearview mirror, like that of a car, for just that purpose.*

It should not be assumed from all this that Dowding was invariably right and the Air Council always wrong, or that the air marshals who

---

* The first versions of the Hurricane and the Spitfire to reach service did not yet have this, and squadron commanders were obliged to buy up the local supply of car rearview mirrors from garages and have the mechanics fit them above the windscreen.

opposed him were foolish. Their mandate was to devise ways to use air power to win a war—defense of the homeland, or what Dowding liked to call the "Home Base," was a secondary issue—and to do so on very tight budget, over which Treasury watched with the eyes of a hawk. What is more, they were charged with projecting British air power over the whole empire, a worldwide commitment, which they were expected to carry out on a shoestring budget with obsolescent aircraft. Both they and Dowding himself recognized that whatever else they might do, fighter aircraft could never *win* a war; only bombers could do that. (Some of the members of the Air Council, including Newall, had been instrumental in drawing up the specifications for the new generation of fighters—it was not so much the fighters they objected to, it was Dowding's single-minded fixation on them.) The difference between Dowding and his colleagues, however, was that Dowding understood that without modern fighters Britain might lose the war the moment it began.

Across the North Sea, the Germans were having the same kind of arguments. When Willy Messerschmitt first demonstrated his revolutionary new all-metal monoplane fighter, the Bf 109, both Göring and his old squadron mate and fellow ace from Richthofen Squadron, Ernst Udet—the daredevil aviator and bon vivant who was in charge of the *Luftwaffe*'s development and research, a position rather similar to that of Dowding when he had been on the Air Council—remarked that it might make a pretty nice fighter if Messerschmitt took the cockpit canopy off and gave the pilot an open cockpit he could see out of; they showed no concern that the original prototype called for an armament of only two machine guns mounted in front of the pilot, just as it had been on the Fokkers and Albatrosses they had flown during the war. Udet at least was finally converted when Messerschmitt pointed out that at a speed of 350 to 400 miles per hour there was no way a pilot could stick his head out and turn it in the slipstream, but Göring remained deeply suspicious of the whole idea. It was not only on the British side of the North Sea that radical change in aircraft design and technology was being resisted.

Still, miraculously, Dowding got most of what he wanted, starting with the construction of the radar sites, each with four 300-foot-tall steel lattice transmitter masts and four 240-foot-tall wooden receiver masts (there was great concern at the Air Ministry over their effect on birds, and bird shooting) long before it was clear that radar was reliable. At this time, radar still gave many false readings, failed to accurately determine height, was an unreliable indicator of the number of aircraft in a formation (hence the importance of the 1,400 Observer Corps outposts, to count them visually once the enemy formation was in sight), and could not yet distinguish between enemy and friendly aircraft.[*]

The radar sites were to be placed so that they overlapped, giving complete coverage of the eastern and southern coasts of England, and were easily able to pick up signals from aircraft in the skies over the Netherlands, Belgium, and northern France, though of course nobody on either side in the mid- to late 1930s had any reason to suppose that the Germans would one day have bases there. By 1937 the first of these sites was in operation, and by 1939 there would be fourteen more—an immense job of construction and a huge expense for a scientific will-o'-the-wisp that might not work, all of it initially authorized by the supposedly lethargic Stanley Baldwin, and carried forward by his successor as prime minister, Neville Chamberlain, who is better remembered for Munich.

. . .

---

[*] This last problem was eventually solved just before the Battle of Britain by installing in all British aircraft a small wireless transmitter called "identification, friend or foe" (IFF). It sent out a constant coded signal identifying the aircraft to the radar operators as one of ours.

Looked at in this light—as it seldom is—the policy of appeasement, which was later to come in for such scorn, may be seen, at least in part, as a successful effort to buy time. The CH radar network would not be fully operational until 1939, and the government knew it; nor would Fighter Command begin to receive its Hurricanes until 1937 or the first of its Spitfires until 1938. Given the fear of bombing and the widespread belief that a modern war would begin with an effort by the Germans to destroy their enemies' major cities from the air in one blow (a belief shared by the left and by the right, and by such very different personalities as H. G. Wells, Stanley Baldwin, and Winston Churchill), it is hardly surprising that Neville Chamberlain, who was also faced with a succession of French governments even more determined not to be bombed by the Germans than the British were, chose to propitiate the Führer rather than to threaten him with war. We know now, of course, that a knockout blow against London or Paris was the last thing Hitler had in mind, and that the *Luftwaffe* was in any case in no position to carry it out, but at the time nobody could be altogether certain of that. Since the general public was unaware of the existence of radar, or of what would be its vital importance in protecting Britain, most people still believed, as Baldwin did, that "the bomber would always get through," and hardly anybody argued otherwise. Dowding's towers were in fact the first step in making that assumption false.

Interestingly, the towers aroused very little curiosity or comment at the time they went up, beyond the concerns of bird lovers; nor do they appear to have kept anybody in the *Luftwaffe* awake at night. Radar was not in itself a secret—like nuclear physics, it was a well-known, if specialized, area of scientific research, and it was being experimented on, with varying degrees of enthusiasm and success, in the United States, Germany, and the Soviet Union as well as Great

Britain. It was not so much that the British had made a scientific breakthrough as that—unlike anybody else—they had taken the experimental equipment out of the laboratory and placed it in the field. At first it was literally in *a* field, where it was tested against an RAF bomber. Then the British worked out by trial and error how to make practical use of it as a long-range early warning system; began to train operators—not scientists, but ordinary airmen (and soon airwomen)—to read and interpret the amorphous blips and squiggles as they appeared and pulsated on a radar screen; and drew up ambitious plans to put the whole system in place as rapidly as possible, and on a huge scale. The Germans had nothing like it; nor did the Americans; and neither did the unfortunate French—in fact, the lack of radar would be one reason for the total failure of the *Armée de l'Air* in May 1940. The French had no radar, no central fighter command, no strategy for using the fighters they had in abundance; even the far superior British Hurricanes sent to France to support them were wasted, just as Dowding had grimly predicted they would be, since without ground-based radar and fighter control their pilots were no better equipped to find the German aircraft or concentrate against them than fliers had been during World War I.

As for the Germans, although they sent the last great dirigible, the *Graf Zeppelin*, out to cruise the British coastline in bad weather in order to analyze the signals from Dowding's radar towers, they were thwarted by the fact that the radar operators, who could hardly fail to miss an object as large as the *Graf Zeppelin*, stopped transmitting during its flight around the coastline. The Germans failed to understand the means by which these signals were transformed into an orderly system of command and control. Yet, it was not radar that would escape their attention; it was the neat, methodical mind of Sir Hugh Dowding.

· · ·

Throughout 1936 and 1937 Dowding painstakingly built the foundations of his strategy to protect England, putting the pieces together
like those of a gigantic three-dimensional jigsaw puzzle. Almost as
soon as he took command he sent in a modest request for £500 to
construct his Operations Room at Bentley Priory, and chivvied archi-
tects, builders, the General Post Office (the GPO, which in the United
Kingdom controlled and installed telephone lines), and the Office of
Works to give him something that had existed before only in the form
of sets for a futuristic film like *Things to Come.*

Today, of course, all this is old hat, familiar from countless movies
and from innumerable televised rocket launches at Cape Canaveral,
but in the mid-1930s it was the only thing of its kind in the world.
Dowding moved fast, transforming the ballroom of Bentley Priory
into a big, crowded amphitheater for a new kind of war, and using
the graceful rotunda next door for the necessary teleprinters and
switchboards. On the floor of the ballroom, he built an enormous,
irregularly shaped table to represent the southern coast of England,
the English Channel, and the northern coast of the continent, "from
Edinburgh to the French coast, to Cherbourg, and from the Welsh
border to the East of Belgium."[2] The surface of the map table was
divided into squares, each one marked and identified with a letter of
the alphabet. This was the "Filter Room." Around the table would sit
or stand a dozen or so young airmen and airwomen (at first the
women were the wives of officers serving at Fighter Command Headquarters who had volunteered for the job, but by 1939 most of the
"filterers" would be young women in the blue-gray uniform of the
WAAF, who would soon be known, predictably, as the "beauty chorus"),
each supplied with a box of counters, rather like those used in playing chemin de fer or roulette in a casino, and long stick with a bar at the
end like that used by the croupier at the roulette table. Each "filterer"

wore earphones, and some of them also wore a microphone suspended around the neck. Above the filterers was built a "gallery," where the whole table could be observed from above by the officers charged with warning each Fighter Group of the situation as it developed on the board below, as well as by the naval liaison officer, a senior Royal Artillery officer with a direct line to the headquarters of the antiaircraft gunners and searchlight operators, and officers linked by direct lines to the Observer Corps, the police, the fire services, and those in charge of sounding the air-raid alarms. The filterers received information as it came in from the operation room in each Fighter Group, from the radar plotters on the coast, and from the observers on the ground; and once an enemy raid had been identified, they set up an identifying marker for it, showing its present position, the projected course of the raid, the height, and the number of enemy aircraft it contained, moving the marker with their long sticks as it progressed from the "enemy" coast, across the Channel or the North Sea, and toward one of the four Fighter Groups, each defending its own "Sector." From the very beginning it was assumed, correctly, that the *Luftwaffe* attacks would not follow a straight, predictable course—there would be feints, sudden changes of direction and altitude, "phantom" attacks intended to draw the British fighters away from the intended targets and to create the maximum confusion. All this would have to be recorded instantly on the board, and analyzed.

Behind the table, on the wall facing the gallery, there was another big board with rows of colored lights on it, known, inevitably, as the "Tote Board" (after the board at a race track that shows the horses competing in a race and the latest odds on each one), that displayed the readiness of each fighter squadron (on standby, available, refueling and rearming, or in the air). A large, prominently placed clock, with time segments marked in different colors, allowed the filterers to instantly plot the exact position of a raid—for everything would be taking place in real time at 200 to 300 miles an hour, and the fighter squadrons in the air would need to know where the enemy they were approaching was *now*, not where it had been two or three minutes before. Equally important, they would need to be "scrambled" in time to climb, if possible, to a height above the enemy's and to attack from behind. (The Spitfire, when it came into service in 1938, would require just under eleven minutes to climb to 25,000 feet, and complex and precise mathematical calculations would need to be made in split seconds to bring fighter squadrons to exactly where they had to be for successful "interception.")

The senior Fighter Command officer present could tell at a glance from his seat in the gallery down to the board below how many air raids were forming up, how big they were, and what their course was, as well as how many fighter squadrons were available, and at what state of readiness, to attack them. An innovation that Dowding quickly introduced was to place experienced fighter pilots in the Filter Room for a tour of duty alongside the filterers, so the pilots would gain confidence in the system (which they could then spread when they returned to their squadrons), and also so they could explain to the filterers what the pilots could and could not do, and what they needed to know, the object being that the fighter pilots must have absolute trust in the instructions they received from the ground, even if the voice was that of a young woman who had never been up in an airplane in her life.

Dowding's genius was to have built a system that economized on his fighter strength—there would be no wasteful "patrols" of fighter aircraft searching for, or trying to intercept at random, groups of enemy aircraft, and losing sight of them in the clouds. Dowding was not a romantic, at least on the subject of air warfare—he sought efficiency.

The fighter squadrons nearest to each raid as it passed through their Group could be scrambled at the last possible moment to attack the enemy as he drew close to them; this procedure would also help to conserve the amount of fuel they had for combat at full power. In effect, the system acted like a multiplier to Fighter Command's strength, as well as imposing the firm control of Fighter Command Headquarters over the whole air battle (a matter which was to cause great and bitter controversy in Fighter Command later on), for Dowding correctly foresaw that the German raids would come from many different directions simultaneously, at different heights, and attacking different targets spread out all across Britain, and that the only way to beat them was to look at the "big picture," then decide where, when, and in what strength to intercept them.

By definition, no air battle can be static—the RAF could not defend every city, port, factory, and airfield in the United Kingdom. Instead, the British fighters would have to attack in relatively small formations, perfectly timed so that as one squadron ran low on fuel and ammunition, another could take its place as it landed to refuel and rearm, thus inflicting on the *Luftwaffe* a constant, and in the long run unacceptable, rate of loss. This concept, too, would become a major issue between Dowding and his critics during the battle.

Ambitious as Dowding's Operations Room was, it was more in the nature of an experiment, or trial run. Almost before it was up and working Dowding was seeking more funds to duplicate it underground at Bentley Priory so that it could not be put out of action by German bombing, and in view of the increasingly aggressive foreign policy of Nazi Germany he was eventually authorized to proceed, despite the Air Council's continuing skepticism on the subject of fighters. His new Operations Room was to be deep underground, built of reinforced concrete (ferroconcrete), and the GPO placed the innumerable telephone lines leading to it in deep trenches, protected by concrete. It was as secure as possible against a direct enemy attack and would be in full operation early in March 1940, just three months before it was needed. By that time, the system had proved itself again and again, through experimentation, trial and error, and constant refinement and improvement.

But of course all this would have been no use without the right fighter aircraft.

If there was one thing that prime ministers Ramsay MacDonald, Stanley Baldwin, and Neville Chamberlain had in common, it was that each was a "belt and braces man," an English phrase used to describe somebody so cautious that he wears both a belt and suspenders to hold his trousers up, thus avoiding potential embarrassment in case one of the two should fail. Whenever the current Minister of State for Air had been consulted about Britain's air defense, the Air Council's reply had always come back that the only effective defense was a bomber force so powerful that no country within striking range would dare to attack. No British government in the 1930s had been eager to fund such a bomber force (and none would have been eager use it, had it existed), but each government was bound to accept the professional advice of the air marshals, albeit with a grain of salt. Once Hitler came to power and the European situation began to deteriorate into a succession of nerve-racking crises, exacerbated by the panicky demands of the French for support and assistance, each prime minister pressed the Air Ministry for some credible scheme of home defense, if only as a way to reassure the public.

The Air Ministry remained stubbornly wedded to RAF dogma, but in order to soothe the increasingly nervous politicians—who were, after all, its masters and provided the funding for the armed services—it took a few reluctant steps in the direction of ordering more modern fighter planes, at first more in the spirit of window dressing than as a serious change in strategy. Still, although the initial intention was to soothe the politicians (and the public) while continuing to plan for the construction of more and bigger bombers, in part thanks to Dowding and a few other visionaries the fighter airplane soon captured the attention of the public, and took several rapid giant strides ahead of the bomber in technology and performance.

It has to be added that quite apart from the glamour that had attached to fighter pilots from the very beginning of aerial warfare, people in the late 1920s and the 1930s were also attached to the glamour of speed. The wealthy British daredevil Sir Malcolm Campbell, who broke the world's speed record on land nine times between 1924 and 1939 in his famous Bluebird race cars, and on water four times in his hydroplanes, was an international celebrity. Streamlining, introduced into design by Raymond Loewy, became the fashion not only in cars, railway locomotives, and ships, but even in stationary objects like toasters, radio sets, furniture, and blenders, which hardly needed to be streamlined. Even in the relatively conservative circle of the Air Council the irony that British fighter planes were still fabric-covered biplanes with fixed landing gear, their wings braced with struts and wires, and slower than the bombers they were supposed to shoot down, was difficult to ignore—not that other air forces were more advanced in this regard during the 1920s and early 1930s.

Also ironically, the world's fastest airplanes at the time were British, though they were not warplanes. Throughout the period, the British dominated the expensive, esoteric, and even more glamorous sport of seaplane racing. Winning the biennial international Schneider Trophy race* was, between the wars, the ambition of every nation with an aviation industry worth mentioning (the Germans were excluded in the aftermath of the war, and as time passed did not at first wish to attract attention to the fact that they even had an aviation industry), and it was, in the eyes of many, the world's supreme speed event. The seaplanes were as beautiful and graceful as the America's Cup racing yachts, were even more costly—the manufacturers were mostly subsidized by their own governments—and flew at speeds that were phenomenal for the day.

The Schneider Trophy—a large art deco sculpture of a winged, naked nymph, *The Sprit of Flight*, kissing a wave—was the brainchild of Jacques Schneider, of the wealthy French industrialist family, an early aviation enthusiast who believed that the future of aviation lay in seaplanes, since more than 70 percent of the world's surface consisted of water. This belief, like that in the zeppelin, did not altogether die out until the late 1930s. The Schneider Trophy, intended to encourage the design of seaplanes, was first offered in 1912 by the Aéro-Club de France as the prize for a speed event, flown over a course of 150 miles. It began as an annual event, but in 1928 the organizers decided to hold it once every two years instead, in view of the increasing complexity of the designs, and the growing world economic crisis. If any nation should win the trophy three times in a row, it would go to that nation in perpetuity.

By the mid-1920s the major contestants were Britain, the United States, and Italy, and the fastest British planes were often those designed by a young Englishman, Reginald J. Mitchell, chief designer of the Supermarine Aviation Works, near Southampton, a firm that

---

* Offcially La Coupe d'Aviation Maritime Jacques Schneider.

concentrated largely on seaplanes. Then, starting with a victory in the 1927 race in which Mitchell's Supermarine S.5 set a new world's speed record for seaplanes and landplanes and ending in 1931, Mitchell's small, sleek, futuristic, monoplane designs, powered by Rolls-Royce aero engines, and largely constructed of aluminum instead of wood and fabric, succeeded in capturing the Schneider Trophy in perpetuity for Britain. They also set new world speed records—his S.6 floatplane reached 357 miles per hour in 1929; and in 1931, the S.6B, which took the trophy outright for Britain, went on to take the world air speed record as well, at 407 miles per hour—this at a time when the fighter planes of the major powers were hard pushed to reach 250 miles per hour, and despite the fact that a seaplane, however sleek, carried the additional drag of two floats on struts beneath its wings.[3]

From the very beginning, the RAF took a close interest in Mitchell's Schneider Trophy seaplanes, which were, among other things, flying test beds for advanced aeronautical design and for the latest and most advanced experimental aero engines from Rolls-Royce. For the last series of Supermarine Schneider Trophy planes, Rolls-Royce was producing engines of more than 1,900 horsepower, perhaps three times the power of most current military aircraft engines. The RAF also discreetly removed the prohibition against serving officers' competing in flying races or in attempts at speed records. Without a government subsidy and the help of the RAF, Supermarine could never have built and fielded a team for the Schneider Trophy races through the 1920s—indeed, when this subsidy for building the aircraft was finally withdrawn before the 1931 race, because of catastrophic economic conditions and widespread unemployment in Britain, the day was saved at the last minute only because a patriotic, wealthy widow, Lady Houston, made an unsolicited contribution of

£100,000, an immense sum at the time (and the equivalent of at least $8 million today).[4]

As Air Member for Research and Development on the Air Council from 1930 to 1936, Dowding watched Mitchell's work with special interest, for good reason. Mitchell was confronting, one by one, the problems of designing and building modern high-speed monoplanes, from wing flutter to flush head riveting to eliminating the drag of a radiator by means of evaporative steam cooling pipes buried in the sides of the fuselage. Oddly, Mitchell had begun his working life at the age of sixteen as an apprentice in a company that manufactured steam locomotives in Stoke-on-Trent—it is hard to imagine a machine more different in every way from a high-speed aircraft than a locomotive, but it taught him a lot about metal, and made him a first-class practical engineer, as well as teaching him everything there was to know about steam. In later years, when Leslie Howard played him in the film *The First of the Few*, he was portrayed as a soulful dreamer who got his ideas about the Spitfire's graceful elliptical wing from watching seabirds soaring over the beach while he was picnicking with his family, but in fact Mitchell was a hardheaded engineer, more interested in his drawing board and his slide rule than in birds. He once told one of his aerodynamicists about that perfect, famous (and impossibly difficult to manufacture) wing, "I don't give a bugger whether it's elliptical or not, so long as it covers the guns."[5] When told that the chairman of Supermarine's parent company, Vickers (Aviation), had decided to call his new fighter plane the Spitfire, Mitchell remarked, "It's just the sort of bloody silly name they would give it."[6]

In the meantime, after the Schneider Trophy had been won and the world speed record achieved, Supermarine and Mitchell were looking for something more interesting—and profitable—to do than continuing to build big, slow, twin-engine seaplanes for the RAF. Their attention was naturally drawn to the Air Ministry's Specification F.7/30, issued in October 1931, calling for a new "Single Seater Day and Night Fighter" for the RAF, which asked aircraft companies to "consider the advantages offered . . . by low wing monoplane or pusher." The idea of a "pusher"—that is, an aircraft with the engine and the propeller mounted behind the pilot (i.e., "pushing" it rather than "pulling" it through the air)—was either revolutionary or a bizarre, nostalgic return to the days of the old Farman "Shorthorn," in which people had learned to fly in 1914, but fortunately most of the manufacturers ignored it.

Mitchell and Vickers were eager to put to good use his experience of designing record-breaking monoplanes, but curiously, of the eight fighters built to meet the Air Ministry's specifications, his Type 224 monoplane, an ungainly all-metal gull-wing aircraft, though innovative, was one of the least successful designs, with a performance inferior to the very conventional biplane that was finally accepted by the RAF, the Gloster Gladiator.* The Type 224 was powered by the Rolls-Royce Goshawk engine, with evaporative cooling built into the leading edges of the wings; test pilots complained that the red warning light signaling an overheating engine came on before they were even off the ground, and ground crews got burned every time they touched the wings after a flight.

Mitchell was not a man who took criticism well, even from test pilots (he was already suffering from colon cancer, which would kill him), but in this case, he seems to have sat down at his drawing board and gone back to the basics willingly enough. In 1934, while

---

* Gloster Gladiators were still in service at the beginning of the war, and were not only robust but surprisingly effective. At one point in 1940 the air defense of Malta was reduced to three apparently unconquerable Gladiators nicknamed Faith, Hope, and Charity.

the Type 224 was still being flight-tested, he and Vickers undertook to redesign it as a "private venture" (that is, at Vickers's own expense). Mitchell began by getting rid of the gull wings, making the undercarriage retractable, and enclosing the cockpit, the result being a very modern-looking fighter, with squarish wings and the cockpit rather far forward. He was still stuck with the Goshawk engine and its evaporative cooling system, which he liked because it eliminated the drag of an external radiator. The Air Ministry was interested, but not overly enthusiastic, so Mitchell further refined the design, in which the lines of the Spitfire first begin to appear. The most radical part of Mitchell's design was its wing spars, made of "square concentric tubes which fitted into each other," and which were at once lightweight, extremely strong, and very flexible. As a result, the Spitfire's wings would flex like those of a bird in flight, to the delight or alarm of the pilot, and demonstrating the value of Mitchell's apprenticeship in locomotive construction, which had given him an instinctive feel for metal.

At this point, another private venture entered the scene: in the Rolls-Royce PV (for private venture) XII, a twelve-cylinder aero engine of twenty-seven liters (to put this in perspective, the largest twelve-cylinder automobile engines produced by Mercedes-Benz and BMW today have a cubic capacity of *six* liters) intended to produce more than 1,000 horsepower. The Rolls-Royce PV XII was almost "a third heavier than the Goshawk," so inevitably Mitchell's design changed. He moved the cockpit farther back to compensate for the added weight of the engine, and made the wing thinner and broader in chord. Working with a very thick, soft lead pencil, he rounded out the lines of his fighter on the drawings provided by his draftsmen, endlessly streamlining it until it began to "look right": harmonious, balanced, elegant, as his Schneider Trophy planes had been. By January 1935 his wing had achieved the graceful shape that was to make the Spitfire instantly recognizable—the thinnest possible wing that could contain two guns and the retractable undercarriage and its mechanism, perfectly elliptical, without a single straight line. On paper, this design impressed the Air Ministry enough that it wrote a new specification around it— events in Germany, although the British government played them down, were increasing the sense of urgency in the Air Council.

Under Dowding's aegis a study was undertaken of what it would take to shoot down one of the new all-metal German bombers. The speeds at which aerial combat would now be taking place were calculated, and it was determined that a fighter pilot would have only two seconds in which to fire a burst that would destroy a German bomber. Also, to provide a sufficient "weight of metal" to do the job a fighter plane would require at least six and if possible eight guns of .303 caliber—although only three years earlier, two guns had been considered sufficient. Mitchell was unfazed—his elliptical wing, he said, could carry four guns as easily as two, and he quickly made the necessary alterations, at the same time eliminating the evaporative cooling system in the interests of simplicity. Dowding altered the Air Ministry's specifications to match those of Supermarine's new fighter, and in June 1935 the Air Ministry placed an order for the aircraft even though it was still on the drawing board and Fighter Command was still waiting for its Gloster Gladiator biplanes.

On March 5 or 6, 1936 (the log of Vickers's chief test pilot, Captain "Mutt" Summers, is unclear), the Spitfire prototype made its first flight, and on March 15 Dowding inspected it. It was apparent to everyone that Mitchell had succeeded beyond anybody's expectations, perhaps including his own. Anxious to gain more speed, and perhaps also moved by pride in his fighter, he asked the Rolls-Royce engineers how they got such a perfect finish on their cars, and they sent painters down from Derby to sand down the prototype, apply numerous coats of blue-gray lacquer, and polish it until it shone like a mirror—or like one of their cars. By July it had demonstrated, in a service trial flight at RAF Martlesham Heath, that it could take off in 235 yards, climb to 25,000 feet in just under eleven minutes, and fly at 350 miles per hour; that it had a ceiling of 30,000 feet; and, most important of all, that it was "simple and easy to fly and has no vices." Even before that test flight the Air Ministry had ordered 310 aircraft at a total price of £1.395 million (about £4,500 each), excluding guns, radios, instruments, and all other "service equipment," the largest order ever given for an airplane in Britain to that date.[7] The first production Spitfires reached RAF squadrons in 1938, a year after Mitchell's death from colon cancer at the age of forty-two,* so he never saw the vital role his aircraft would play in Britain's survival in 1940, but it would not have surprised him.

It had first flown in 1936, the year Hitler reoccupied the Rhineland; and it began to reach service squadrons in 1938, the year of Munich. In the air, at least, the governments of Stanley Baldwin and Neville Chamberlain were better prepared than they have been given credit for—or than the Germans believed at the time.

Perhaps even stranger was the fact that unlike the Germans, the British spread their bets, and built two very different fighters instead of just one. At the same time as the Spitfire was being developed, one of Mitchell's rivals as an aircraft designer, Sydney Camm of Hawker Aircraft, was designing the Hawker Hurricane. In 1933 Camm, a forceful

* One measure of Reginald Mitchell's fame in the United Kingdom is that he was voted "the greatest Midlander of all time," in a poll conducted for BBC Midlands Today in 2003. Mitchell received 25 percent of the votes cast; William Shakespeare came in second, with 17 percent.

and energetic man, had tried and failed to interest the Air Ministry in building a high-speed monoplane fighter to replace the aging Hawker Fury biplane he had designed.[8] Objections had been raised regarding the weight, cost, and practicality of the Hurricane, but Hawker decided to continue the project as a private venture, and by 1935 the Air Ministry was sufficiently alarmed by the rapid growth of the German aviation industry to place an order with Hawker for a prototype. The Hurricane was easier to build than the Spitfire—Camm used the existing Fury as the starting point for his fighter, with fabric for some of the surface (which also made it quicker and easier for ground crews skilled in the use of fabric, dope, and glue to repair, and reduced the cost), and it would eventually be powered by the same Rolls-Royce Merlin engine as the Spitfire. Camm developed a thick, sturdy wing, in which there was no difficulty finding room for four machine guns and an undercarriage that retracted inward, toward the fuselage, rather than outward, thus giving the Hurricane a notably wide, stable track, unlike the Spitfire, with its dangerously narrow track. (Another benefit of Camm's robust wing design was that the Hurricane would later adapt easily to carrying four twenty-millimeter cannon and even two forty-millimeter cannon in its role as a "tankbuster" in the Western Desert of North Africa, and to carrying bombs under its wings as a Hurribomber. It could also be flown off carrier decks or fitted with skis for operating in Norway.) The Hurricane took its first flight in 1935, a year before the Spitfire, and it proved to be so easy to fly that when the Hawker test pilot, P. W. S. Bulman, who wore a snappy fedora hat for the flight, stepped out of the cockpit afterward, he turned to Camm and said, "It's a piece of cake—I could even teach you to fly her in half an hour, Sydney."[9]

By 1937, production Hurricanes were reaching RAF squadrons in quantity. Camm would always regret not having designed a thinner wing, but no pilot ever complained about that—the Hurricane could absorb enormous punishment and still get you home in one piece; and although it was slower than the Spitfire and had a lower ceiling, its thick wings and the grouping of its guns close together (that roomy wing again!) made it a steadier gun platform. Both aircraft were at least the equal of the Bf 109E in 1939 and 1940, and would remain in production, in updated versions, until 1945. Dowding fussed over the details of both his fighters, as he fussed over the details of everything, finally persuading the Air Ministry, after an epic struggle, to order the manufacturers to put a thick piece of laminated, optically flat, bulletproof glass in front of the pilot in 1939, just in time for the war, and to install hot-air ducting into the wings to keep the breeches of the guns from freezing solid at high altitudes.

With radar in operation, the details of fighter control worked out, and two different types of eight-gun monoplane fighters in service, Dowding had good reason to feel confident that he could meet the enemy on equal terms, if the politicians and the Air Council let him do his job.

CHAPTER 4

"The Other Side of the Hill"

—*The Duke of Wellington**

Across the North Sea, in Germany, the *Luftwaffe* was develop-ing in a very different way, and under a radically different lead-ership. The contrast between the two air forces was remarkable. The RAF as the junior of the three British services suffered from something of an inferiority complex, which manifested itself in a combination of bravado—an example, later in the war, was Air Chief Marshal Sir Arthur Harris's stubborn belief that RAF Bomber Command could win the war all by itself, if given the resources— and a prickly relationship between officers and "other ranks," which Len Deighton captured perfectly in *Bomber*, and whose spirit per-vades T. E. Lawrence's famous book on the RAF in the early 1920s, *The Mint*. Because the RAF lacked the ancient regimental traditions

* "All the business of war . . . is to endeavor to find out what you don't know by what you do; that's what I called 'guessing what was at the other side of the hill.'"

and identity that were the backbone of the British Army, and the sense of being shipmates sharing the same risks and dangers that made shipboard discipline in the Royal Navy more tolerable, the gulf between officers and "other ranks" was in some ways wider than in the other services. The fact was that the "other ranks" thought of themselves (and were officially described) as "tradesmen," unlike soldiers or sailors, and brought with them into the service some of the sullen attitude toward authority of skilled workers and union members in civilian life; while the NCOs in the more specialized trades took on something of the role of union shop stewards in a factory, becoming in effect intermediaries between management and labor. Eight weeks of "square bashing" and polishing his boots were seldom enough to turn a skilled engine mechanic into an obedient soldier-in-blue who accepted the authority of commissioned officers as natural.

A certain respect for pilots (and, to a lesser degree, for aircrew in general) pervaded the RAF, but flying was also a trade. Almost half the pilots in the RAF were NCOs, not officers (in the Battle of Britain 42 percent of the fighter pilots would be sergeants, flight sergeants, or warrant officers), as were many of the navigators, bombardiers, flight engineers, and wireless operators, and all of the air gunners—indeed, it was only the war that put stripes on the sleeves of many of these men, partly because flying duties made their mealtimes erratic and the sergeants' mess was better suited to flexible mealtimes, and partly because RAF aircrew would be afforded better treatment by the enemy as sergeants if they became prisoners of war.

Traces of old-fashioned class-consciousness pervaded the organization of the RAF, despite the fact that it was the most "modern" and technologically minded of the three services. An example was the so-called Auxiliary squadrons. In order to permit rapid expansion in the event of war, the RAF relied on three separate and distinctly different schemes. The first was the RAF Reserve, consisting of regular officers who had retired from the service, or had completed their term of service ("short-term" commissions were then for four years). The second consisted of the Royal Auxiliary Air Force squadrons, intended to be the equivalent of the army's "Territorials," many formed by adventuresome aviation enthusiasts. One of the earliest of such squadrons, No. 601 (County of London) Auxiliary Air Force Squadron, based at RAF Tangmere, had been founded in the bar at White's Club in 1924 by Lord Edward Grosvenor, a son of the fabulously rich duke of Westminster; its pilots were predominantly wealthy City stockbrokers and wine merchants, and it quickly became known as the "millionaires' squadron." The No. 615 (County of Surrey) Auxiliary Air Force Squadron was almost as exclusive, and furthermore had as its Honorary Air Commodore Winston Churchill; and the Oxford University Air Squadron was equally glamorous. Typically, one of No. 601 Squadron's pilots was W. M. L. "Billy" Fiske, a wealthy and social young American sportsman, who won a gold medal on the U.S. bobsled team at the 1932 Winter Olympics in Lake Placid, married the former countess of Warwick, had an international reputation as a skier and golfer, drove a British Racing Green 4.5-liter supercharged Bentley, and on August 16, 1940, became the first American in the Royal Air Force to be killed in combat in World War II.[1] The Auxiliary squadrons brought to RAF Fighter Command an additional element of dash and high spirits, symbolized by such customs as officers leaving the top button of the tunic open and wearing a brightly patterned silk scarf loosely knotted around the neck, habits of dress that were not always appreciated by RAF Station Commanders, and that soon spread to non-Auxiliary pilots, even to a few sergeant-pilots. The third element, the RAF Voluntary Reserve, was less elitist and less flamboyant, being a more ambitious nation-wide training scheme for aircraftmen. At the beginning of the war, members of the Royal Auxiliary Air Force wore a small brass A on the lapels of their tunic, whereas the members of RAF Volunteer Reserve who were commissioned wore a small brass V, but by the end of 1940 these distinctions were no longer encouraged, or widely observed.

Thus, the Royal Air Force, as it formed for war, was a typically British combination of professionals and amateurs, with an equally typical British concern for class differences—certainly a little less stuffy, at least among the pilots and aircrew, than the more elite infantry and cavalry regiments of the British Army, and a lot less sure of its place than the Royal Navy, but still a recognizably British institution.

The enemy it would face was organized along very different lines, and on the surface, at least, seemed more powerful and more "modern." Forbidden to maintain a military aviation industry under the Treaty of Versailles, Germany had begun systematically evading that restriction early in the 1920s, long before the Nazi Party came to power. General Hans von Seeckt, the austere commander of the *Reichswehr*, was a strong believer in an independent air force; he encouraged the widespread formation of "glider clubs" for German youth; funneled subsidies to the German aircraft industry to design "civil" aircraft that could be adapted or rapidly converted into military ones; made the new German airline, Lufthansa, a clandestine means for teaching young men destined for military aviation to fly; and arranged for those who succeeded to receive advanced training secretly in Soviet Russia. When Hitler became chancellor in January

1933, the foundations had already been laid not only for a modern aviation industry but also for a nationwide scheme for training young people as pilots. All that was necessary was to put a Nazi gloss on what already existed, and pour money secretly into building up-to-date military aircraft. Although Göring's outsize faults were even then clear enough, nobody could deny his energy, his flair for publicity, or his lack of scruples in achieving his ambitions on the largest possible scale; as Hitler's air minister (among his many other offices) he worked hard and cut through every bureaucratic difficulty to make Germany a formidable air power overnight. One consequence was that propaganda about Germany's air power created widespread alarm long before it was in fact a realistic threat; but by 1935, when the existence of the *Luftwaffe* was officially acknowledged by Hitler—Göring was himself the first to display its new uniform, which, despite his bulk, he modeled proudly for his pilots, who were themselves then still dressed in the modest uniform of civilian airline pilots—the infrastructure of a major air force was already complete.

It was, as it would necessarily have been, an air force that satisfied the Führer, who at this stage was more interested in bluff than in war. Hitler remained throughout his life an ex-soldier—airplanes (and warships) did not interest him as intensely as artillery and tanks. About guns and tanks he could never have too much detailed information, and his opinions, though those of a layman, were often perfectly sensible, despite his taste for the outsize and even the gigantic. On the subject of airplanes he seldom interfered, and when he did he was often wrong. Certainly in the 1930s he was willing to leave it all in the hands of Göring. What Hitler wanted was an air force that would overawe and frighten other nations. Bombers interested him more than fighters—he saw no likelihood that Germany would need to be defended from air attacks—and the more bombers, the better.

"Strategic" bombing, as it later came to be known, did not much interest him, either. The *Luftwaffe* was primarily intended from the beginning to intimidate Germany's neighbors, and if intimidation failed, to serve as a major weapon, airborne artillery, for supporting the German army in the event that Hitler's aims could not be won by diplomacy and threats.

It was not just aircraft that were mass-produced on a huge scale—*Luftwaffe* bases sprang up all over Germany, built with a lavish attention to detail and designed in the most ambitious Third Reich style. At a time when most RAF stations had wooden huts for housing, with outside "ablutions" and a cast-iron coke stove for heating, the buildings Göring put up were brick and stone, centrally heated, with comfortable rooms for the airmen, even better accommodations for the officers, and mess halls that were well lit, clean, and comfortable. Officers' messes had chrome and marble bathroom fittings, big fireplaces, and leather furniture. Instead of looking as if they had been plunked down by a careless hand in the middle of nowhere on godforsaken heaths and soggy meadows, the bases of the *Luftwaffe* were handsomely landscaped and set among winding paths and forests of pine trees—at first glance they looked like plush health resorts rather than military bases.* Göring, who stinted himself of nothing, did not stint his airmen either; they were the envy of the other two services.

Without wishing to make the *Luftwaffe* sound more attractive than it was—it was, after all, a Nazi organization, with all that that implies—it was by far the least class-conscious of the German services, and offered the best chance of promotion for lower-class and

---

* Even in 1952, when the author served in the Royal Air Force in Germany, we were awed by our quarters at a former *Luftwaffe* base near Hamburg, which not only had indoor baths and showers but featured a mysterious-looking porcelain basin set in the wall which was too small, too high up, and too elaborately decorated to be a urinal, and which turned out to be a flushing *vomitorium* for those who had drunk too much beer.

middle-class young men, provided of course that they were Aryan and had joined the Hitler Youth. Just as in the RAF, enthusiasm for sports mattered a lot, and just as in the RAF pilots were not necessarily commissioned. At least half the *Luftwaffe* pilots, bombardiers, and navigators (and of course all the air gunners, flight engineers, and wireless operators) were "other ranks." In one significant way *Luftwaffe* practice differed from that of the RAF—in British aircrews, the pilot was always "captain" of the airplane whatever his rank, in absolute command from the moment the engines started up, even if he was a sergeant and his navigator and bombardier were both officers; but in the German aircrews, the senior officer on board was "captain" of the aircraft, even if he was not the pilot. In another respect, German practice differed from ours—German bombers, like German tanks, were deliberately designed to place the members of the crew as close together as possible, both to raise their confidence and morale and to enable them to help a comrade who was wounded, or take his place when necessary. The advantages of this were obvious, but there were also disadvantages—a single good burst from a fighter could disable the whole crew, and the gunners lacked elbow room to use their machine guns effectively, and did not have isolated power turrets giving them a full field of fire. That said, German and British aircrews were equally well trained and German and British fighter pilots about equally matched.

German and British fighter pilots were about equally "mounted" too. Like the Hurricane and the Spitfire, the Bf 109, with various updates, would remain in production until the end of the war, and would be continually modified to carry more powerful weapons than it had originally been designed for. Like them too, both the aircraft and the designer achieved celebrity status.

.   .   .

Willy Messerschmitt, like Reginald Mitchell, was a visionary genius of airplane design, and like Sydney Camm he could turn his hand to anything with wings (his versatility was such that before the end of the war he would be responsible for the design of the world's largest transport plane, the six-engine Me 323; the world's first operational jet fighter, the Me 262; and the world's only operational rocket-propelled fighter, the Me 163). Messerschmitt was unlike Camm and Mitchell, however, in that his fighter did not at once win the confidence and enthusiasm of the air force it was designed for, and from the first it was inextricably mixed up in the politics—or the vicious personal rivalries that passed for politics—of the Third Reich.

In the early 1920s, Messerschmitt had founded his own aircraft firm in Bavaria, and received a subsidy from the Bavarian state government (as well as clandestine funding from the defense ministry in Berlin). [2] His rival was another Bavarian aircraft manufacturer, Bayerische Flugzeugwerke, but in 1927, in the bad economic times and under severe financial pressure, the Bavarian government, unable to subsidize both firms, forced them to merge—a shotgun marriage that pleased nobody.

Unlike Camm and Mitchell, Messerschmitt was not just a gifted airplane designer; he was a businessman-entrepreneur with large ambitions, who had no desire to simply sit at his drawing board designing airplanes for other people to build and profit from. From the very beginning of the unwelcome merger, he dominated the new company, which got its first windfall in the shape of an order for a small, ultrafast modern monoplane airliner, designed to carry ten passengers. The order came from the new national airline Lufthansa, whose managing director and director of procurement was Erhard Milch. Half Jewish or not (the question was not yet of critical importance in 1927), Milch was, then as later, overbearing, an intriguer, opinionated, and a bad man to have as an enemy. Messerschmitt promptly proceeded to make an enemy of him. The airplane he had designed crashed during its development testing in 1928, and Milch canceled Lufthansa's order. Messerschmitt quickly produced an improved prototype, and the order was reinstated, but after further delays Milch once more canceled it—the relationship between the two men was already touchy—and demanded the return of Lufthansa's down payment. Bayerische Flugzeugwerke was unable to return the money, having spent it to produce the two prototypes, and as a result was forced into bankruptcy in 1931. During this disagreeable period dislike between the two men ripened into outright loathing, so it was not good news for Messerschmitt when Hitler came to power in 1933 and Milch emerged as the second most powerful figure after Göring in the German aviation world.

Like Mitchell, Messerschmitt was a man who always sought simple, elegant solutions to technical problems. He was not as successful in his business dealings, however. Milch had made it very clear that Messerschmitt's reconstituted company would get orders only to build other companies' aircraft as a subcontractor, but Messerschmitt went ahead and designed several innovative training and small transport aircraft, which, since it was clear that Milch would never buy them for the *Luftwaffe*, he proceeded to sell abroad, securing contracts for the trainer from Romania. Milch chose to treat this as something like an act of treason, precipitating a Gestapo investigation—after all, who could predict on which side Romania might be, if it came to war?—which caused another crisis, requiring the intervention of Göring himself to smooth things over.

A series of misfortunes continued to plague Messerschmitt. He designed a plane to compete in an air speed race, the Challenge du Tourisme Internationale, only to have two of the prototypes crash in succession. Then, changing plans, he turned the Romanian trainer into a high-speed, all-metal tourer, with a flush-riveted, stressed skin of exceptional strength and smoothness. The Bf 108A, as the aircraft came to be known, was full of technical innovations, elegant, fast, and easy to fly. It was admired by everyone who saw it, and looked, in fact, exactly like a scale model of the Bf 109 to come. Enthusiasm for the Bf 108A was in fact so great that it survived despite a crash in which one member of Milch's own staff was killed while flying the airplane, and even the fact that it was beaten in the 1934 Challenge du Tourisme Internationale by a Polish airplane. It did, however, record the fastest speed reached in the race, and won the praise of experienced pilots like Theo Osterkampf, who had initially been a fierce critic of the aircraft (and who would later go on to become one of the most beloved *Luftwaffe* commanders in the Battle of Britain—he was known as "Uncle Theo" to his pilots).

In 1934, when the *Reichsluftministerium* (RLM), the German air ministry, sent out a request to manufacturers for a single-seat, all-metal monoplane fighter, with retractable undercarriage and a minimum of two machine guns, to be powered by a V-12 liquid-cooled aero engine—essentially similar, except for the number of guns, to British Air Ministry Specification F37/34, which produced the Hurricane and the Spitfire—Milch deliberately excluded Bayerische Flugzeugwerke from the list of firms invited to submit a design. Messerschmitt's admirers, of whom Göring was one, finally persuaded Milch to relent, but even then the most Milch would do was to offer Bayerische Flugzeugwerke a chance to submit a fighter design at its own expense, as a "developmental project"—that is to say, if the design was accepted, it would be manufactured by another company. Messerschmitt was tempted to give up designing aircraft altogether and take a teaching job instead, but he finally swallowed his pride and sat down to design a fighter, which would have to be so good that it would surpass every other aircraft company's entry by a clear margin, and which, even then, he knew Milch would probably try to sabotage.

There are people who work best under life-or-death pressure, and Messerschmitt was apparently one of them. In record time he sketched out a new fighter design, the smallest and lightest aircraft he could build around the proposed new twelve-cylinder engine, all metal, and designed so that it could be mass-produced in sections by relatively unskilled labor (a feature it shared with Dr. Porsche's Volkswagen, which dated from the same period), with a pair of thin rectangular wings tapering to squared-off wingtips, an enclosed cockpit, two machine guns in the engine nacelle and—a daring novelty—a twenty-millimeter cannon firing through the propeller hub. The Bf 109 benefited from the same innovations as the Bf 108A: a sleek, flush-riveted metal skin; leading and trailing edge slats that would open automatically to increase the aircraft's maneuverability and lift; and, above all, the thinnest possible wing, supported by a single spar, as revolutionary as Mitchell's elliptical wing for the Spitfire, but much easier to manufacture.

The wing was both the curse and the blessing of Messerschmitt's design. Its perfection was the central feature of the design, but to achieve that narrow, knife-edge thinness required putting everything that would add weight or bulk to it into the fuselage—hence the armament was all placed ahead of the pilot, and the landing gear and its operating mechanism were fixed to the fuselage, only the strut and wheel retracting outward into the wing. The wings themselves would have to bear the weight of the aircraft only when it was actually in the air. This gave the Messerschmitt fighter its characteristic narrow track and pigeon-toed look on the ground, and contributed to the very high accident rate during taxiing that plagued it throughout its long service life (and was, to a lesser degree, a problem with the Spitfire as well). Ironically, power in the prototype was to be provided by an imported Rolls-Royce Kestrel twelve-cylinder engine, the precursor of the PV XII Merlin, since neither the Junkers nor the Daimler-Benz engine intended for the new generation of *Luftwaffe* fighter had as yet completed its trials.

The aircraft that emerged caused considerable controversy. Pilots disliked the thin wings and delicate tail structure,* both of which they predicted would break off in violent maneuvers; the hinged cockpit canopy, heavy and shaped like a greenhouse, which opened to the starboard side so that there was no way of sliding it back in flight; and the wing slots, over which the pilot had no control. The plane was startlingly small, too, as if Messerschmitt had carved away every unnecessary square inch of metal. In any event, the general assumption was that this particular horse race was fixed—Milch would never allow Messerschmitt to win it, and that was all right anyway, since most pilots preferred the robust Heinkel (He) 112, which, with its reassuringly thick wings and its superwide track undercarriage, was visibly the better (and sturdier) aircraft.

Messerschmitt continued to produce modified prototypes, the third one at last giving up the Rolls-Royce engine for the Junkers Jumo engine; and as test followed test, the plane that couldn't win became the one to beat. Two of the three contenders (from Arado and Focke-Wulf) dropped out, leaving only the He 112 as the competition, and,

---

* Messerschmitt strengthened the horizontal stabilizers with external struts, which were criticized by British and American airmen as either cautious or old-fashioned, but in fact Sydney Camm also used two struts to support the horizontal stablizers of his Hurricane prototype. They were removed only because, in Camm's absence during a brief hospitalization, one of his staff decided they weren't needed and had them taken off. Camm was livid when he returned, but since the tailplane seemed just as strong without them, he eventually came around to the idea himself.

embarrassingly for Milch, Messerschmitt's fighter consistently out-classed the Heinkel in every possible way—speed, maneuverability, climbing ability, ceiling, high-speed diving ability. There was simply no comparison.[3]

Ernst Udet, Göring's old war comrade from the Richthofen Squadron in World War I, now promoted to colonel and technical director of the *Luftwaffe*, and converted into a fervent supporter of Messerschmitt's fighter, put on a surprise demonstration of it in front of Göring at Rechlin, the *Luftwaffe* test center. Udet managed to "shoot down" in mock combat not only a flight of bombers, but all the fighters accompanying them. Göring was not much interested in technical details, but as a former fighter pilot himself, he could recognize superior performance when he saw it with his own eyes, and from that moment on the He 112 was a dead duck.* Udet was a brilliant pilot, and in a way his brilliance was his misfortune, since he tended to judge aircraft designs by the seat of his pants, in the air—unlike the patient Dowding, who left that side of things to the test pilots. Another misfortune for Udet was that he was a rival of Milch's for Göring's attention. There was bad blood between Udet and Milch, which was made worse by Udet's fame and glamour. Udet had barnstormed in the early days of German aviation after the war; had flown in numerous German movies about mountains and airplanes, a popular genre in the 1920s, when he had collaborated with Leni Riefenstahl (and, some said, been her lover); and was both a bon vivant (as mentioned earlier) and a brilliant cartoonist, with a gift for mordant caricatures of his fellow senior *Luftwaffe* officers—a talent which often pricked their vanity. It did not

---

* In order to give the impression that the *Luftwaffe* had two fighters, not just one, development of the He 112 continued, and prototypes of what came to be called the He 113 were later shown off at frequent intervals, disguised with varying paint schemes and fake squadron identification markings. As a result, several British pilots claimed to have shot one down in the Battle of Britain, although in fact the He 113 never saw combat.

help either that although Udet and Göring had both won the Pour le Mérite, imperial Germany's highest decoration for bravery, Udet's score of kills was almost three times the size of Göring's. Göring's envy of his old friend was as dangerous as Milch's enmity, and would cost Udet his life in 1941 when he committed suicide.

Despite the political and personal quarrels that surrounded the *Luftwaffe*'s new fighter, it went through its protracted trials with no more than the usual problems of any innovative high-speed design. The Daimler-Benz engine having been selected over the Junkers engine, it was at last introduced into the early production models, and would power the Bf 109 for the next eight years. Messerschmitt had placed a prominent "chin" radiator under the engine nacelle, but like all fighter plane designers, he was obsessed with reducing drag, and eventually was obliged to place a smaller, aerodynamic radiator under each wing—with great reluctance, since it was the first step back from the perfectly "clean" wing he had in mind.* A more serious problem was his inability to make the twenty-millimeter cannon firing through the propeller hub work—the cannon tended to overheat quickly and jam; and when it did work, the recoil tended to create dangerous vibration (Messerschmitt would eventually get all this right in 1941, with the Me 109G).† This left the Bf 109 with only the two fuselage machine guns—not enough firepower, especially in view of the RAF's decision to ask for an eight-gun fighter. The only solution was to put a machine gun in each wing, eventually to be replaced

---

* Mitchell was afflicted with the same problem. He had originally designed the Spitfire with a retractable radiator that would be lowered only as needed during takeoff, climbing, and landing, but the Merlin engine produced far too much heat for that, and he was eventually obliged, with much reluctance, to put a coolant radiator under the starboard wing and an oil radiator under the port wing, spoiling the smooth airflow below his perfect elliptical wing.

† By then Messerschmitt's name was considered a propaganda asset, and his aircraft began to be named after him (Me), instead of after the Bayerische Flugzeugwerke (Bf).

in time for the Battle of Britain by a twenty-millimeter cannon in each wing. Once again, Messerschmitt's perfect wing was degraded—the gun added weight to the wing, and required a streamlined raised blister to house the ammunition drum. (Aircraft designers fight a constant battle against increases in drag because of operational requirements—additional weaponry, radio antennae, cooling vents, and worst of all, exterior bomb racks, all of which inevitably add to drag and reduce speed.)

Messerschmitt had one great advantage over Mitchell and Camm. In late 1936 and early 1937 several of the preproduction Bf 109s were shipped secretly to Spain, to be tested by *Luftwaffe* pilots of the Condor Legion in combat, in the Spanish Civil War. Valuable lessons were learned—among them the absolute need for the additional two wing machine guns, and a rush program was undertaken to replace them as soon as possible with cannon*—and many modifications were made to correct the kind of flaws that only real combat can reveal. Like the Hurricane and the Spitfire, the Bf 109 progressed from a fixed-pitch wooden propeller to a metal constant-pitch propeller to a three-bladed variable-pitch propeller, changes that progressively increased its performance.

That said, the Bf 109E, with which the *Luftwaffe* would fight the Battle of Britain, was a formidable and well-designed weapon, and in some respects better equipped for combat (largely as a result of the Germans' experience in Spain) than its British equivalents. Dowding

---

* The RAF was also experimenting with twenty-millimeter cannon. It was obvious that the greater weight of the shell, and the fact that the shell was explosive, would make bringing down an all-metal aircraft easier than it was with rifle-caliber bullets, but the trade-off was that most of the cannon suitable for installation in an aircraft had a fairly low velocity and a slow rate of fire. The twenty-millimeter cartridge was certainly a killer, but in the two seconds a fighter pilot had in which to hold an enemy aircraft in his sight and "kill" it, only an expert could achieve enough "hits" with slow-firing cannon to do the job. At least one RAF squadron given cannon-equipped fighters in 1940 demanded to have its older, machine-gun-equipped fighters returned to it.

had been concerned with preserving the integrity of the fuel tanks in the event of a crash, and as a result did not pay enough attention to the new technology of self-sealing fuel tanks, which might have prevented many of the fires that killed or disfigured his pilots. Nor were RAF fighter aircraft fitted with a rubberized one-man life raft that automatically inflated and bobbed to the surface in case of a crash at sea, with the result that many RAF pilots found themselves dog-paddling in the frigid water of the English Channel in their Mae West life jacket, hoping against hope to be seen and picked up by an RAF launch, instead of sitting in a life raft with a vastly better chance of surviving.

The fact that the Daimler-Benz engine had fuel injection instead of carburetors was a plus for the Bf 109—Rolls-Royce engineers, with their taste for the tried-and-true, had preferred to stick with carburetors, which, in sudden, violent dives, sometimes starved the Merlin of fuel. Experienced British fighter pilots learned to perform a quick "flick" of the aircraft before diving to fill the float of each carburetor, but it was an unpleasant experience for less proficient pilots when the engine suddenly cut out in the middle of a dogfight.[4] On the other hand, Dowding, with his usual dogged persistence, had browbeaten the Air Council and Rolls-Royce into using 100-octane aviation fuel in the Merlin, whereas the Germans stuck to lower-grade eighty-seven-octane aviation fuel. This was a big and risky decision, since there was at the time no refinery in the United Kingdom producing 100-octane fuel. The fuel had to be imported from the United States, making Fighter Command in 1939 and 1940 dependent, among other things, on the Treasury's supply of dollars, on the prowess of the German U-boat commanders, and above all on the willingness of merchant sailors to man tankers filled with thousands of gallons of high-octane fuel that one torpedo would turn into a white-hot explosion incinerating in a second both ship and crew.* The gain in perfor-mance by the decision to use American 100-octane fuel in British fighters to some degree offset the advantage of German fuel injec-tion, but it was another one of those things that only a man as objec-tive, determined, and sure of himself as Dowding could have brought off in the face of a skeptical Air Council and Treasury. As in the *Luft-waffe*, early combat experience also led to the addition of armor plate behind the pilot's seat, and many a pilot would owe his life to this plating.[5]

The "glamour boys" of the *Luftwaffe* from September 1939 through May 1940 were not, as it happened, the fighter pilots, who had very little to do—much of the Polish air force was destroyed on the ground—but the Stuka pilots. The ungainly Junkers Ju 87 Stuka, in-stantly recognizable by its gull-shaped wings and fixed undercar-riage, was Udet's brainchild, inspired by the experiments the United States Navy had been making with shipborne Curtis dive-bombers. Overnight, the Stuka became, along with the German tanks, the trademark of the blitzkrieg and the darling of the filmmakers produc-ing war documentaries at the ministry of propaganda, devastating enemy formations far behind the front lines and sowing panic among soldiers and civilian refugees along the roads (a siren fitted to its wing created a piercing screech as it dived, increasing the fear of those on the ground). With regard to the Stuka, Udet got it right—it was cheap to manufacture, simple to fly, and a very effective weapon. Above all, it solved one of the German army's problems in mobile warfare: the heavy artillery was still mostly horse-drawn and moved

---

* The merchant seamen tanker crews are among the many unsung heroes of the Battle of Britain, as are the young women of the WAAF who continued to call in radar fixes to Fighter Command HQ from wooden huts aboveground at the radar sites while under di-rect attack from German dive-bombers.

forward at much slower pace than the tanks and motorized infantry of the panzer divisions. The Stukas could, when necessary, play the role of heavy artillery—indeed, the reason why the French high command thought that the German army could not come through the Ardennes in May 1940 was that it saw no way the Germans could bring their heavy artillery over the narrow mountain roads, not realizing that the Germans would rely on the Stuka squadrons instead to replace their big guns as they emerged toward the Meuse.

In the skies over Poland, Norway, the Netherlands, Belgium, and France, the fighter pilots had very little to do, except to escort the Stukas and the heavier twin-engine bombers, against minimal opposition. They had learned to treat the Hurricanes with respect, but the Hurricanes were few and far between in France; and, operating off hastily prepared grass airfields with no radar or fighter control to support them, they did not give the German pilots a realistic foretaste of what it might be like to fight them over southern England. Thus, the opening stages of the Battle of Britain took place before either side had a realistic view of the other.

Despite all the preparation on both sides of the Channel, Clausewitz's famous comment about the "fog of war" still held true, even in the air.

CHAPTER 5

The First Act:
Dunkirk and the Dowding Letter

Nobody, least of all the Führer, had predicted the rapid collapse of the French army in May 1940. The effect on the *Luftwaffe* was to bring it forward within easy reach of Britain in one unexpected swoop, as the Germans took over the airfields of the Dutch and the Belgians, and quickly afterward those of northern France. This put an immense logistic burden on the *Luftwaffe,* at the very moment when the air battle, far from being won as the land battle was being won, was only just beginning. The first serious skirmish in the Battle of Britain in fact took place in the cloudy, smoke-filled sky over Dunkirk—dark columns of greasy black smoke rose from burning ships, vehicles, and oil storage tanks—as the British Army sought to hold the town and the beaches long enough for the Royal Navy (and the famous "little ships," ranging in size from lifeboats and motor yachts to holiday paddle steamers) struggled to bring the troops home to Britain.

For whatever reason, Hitler had been reluctant to attack the British perimeter with his panzer divisions, much to the indignation of the generals, and he accepted Göring's promise that the *Luftwaffe* could do the job instead. Without knowing what was in Hitler's mind—never an easy task—we can still say that the fate of the British Army did not, at this point, seem to interest him much. His eye was on Paris, and the growing likelihood of France's imminent surrender. Once that had been taken care of, it no doubt seemed to him likely that Churchill's government would fall and be replaced by a government of "reasonable" men willing to negotiate a peace. The United Kingdom, he thought, to quote from Gracie Fields's famous music hall song of the period, was "dead but he won't lie down." That, at any rate, was what Ribbentrop, Hitler's vain, arrogant foreign minister and former ambassador to the Court of St. James's, believed. "Ribbentrop knows the British," Hitler said to Göring, who had expressed doubts. "Yes, *mein Führer*," Göring replied glumly; "but the problem is, *they* know Ribbentrop."

In any event, Hitler's basic demand of the British was that they stay out of European affairs altogether from now on, and the departure of the British Expeditionary Force (BEF), leaving behind all its guns and heavy equipment, was certainly a step in that direction. It is possible too that Hitler wanted to show the British he could be reasonable, even merciful, rather than presenting them with a massacre on the beaches of Dunkirk. If so, he failed to achieve that effect.

The fact that the air battle above Dunkirk was invisible was to lead to great bitterness between British troops of the BEF and RAF personnel when the former returned home. There were numerous fistfights and pub brawls—from the point of view of the men on the beaches or the moles of Dunkirk, the only aircraft they actually saw were the Stukas bombing and strafing them. In fact, high above the smoke on the ground, the first real clash on something like equal terms between the RAF and the *Luftwaffe* was taking place, and since it was just beyond the useful range of RAF fighter control and radar, it was something of a free-for-all, with swarms of aircraft attacking each other. Churchill himself accurately described the desperate fighting over Dunkirk as "a kind of no-man's-land," in which British fighters, heavily outnumbered and mostly from Air Vice-Marshal K. R. Park's No. 11 Group in the southeast of England, flew nearly 3,000 sorties in the course of nine days.

The fight above Dunkirk also led, on both sides, to some immediate and painful reassessments. The British had invested a good deal of time and effort in the idea of a modern all-metal monoplane mounting a four-gun power-operated turret, an idea that was based on the two-seat fighter of World War I (the Sopwith "one-and-a-half strutter" and the RE-8 had been examples). Mitchell had actually been asked to design one, but very luckily for him, the Air Ministry chose the Boulton Paul company's design instead. The Defiant, as it was eventually named, looked like a modern fighter but carried no forward-firing guns—behind the pilot was a bulky, heavy four-gun power turret and its gunner. The pilot's job was to fly the plane as a steady gun platform, and the gunner's job was to shoot the enemy down. As one might have expected, the drag and weight of the heavy turret slowed the Defiant and decreased its maneuverability in dogfights to the point where it was a sitting duck for a Bf 109, a problem made worse by the fact that the only way for the gunner to get out if the plane was hit was to crank his turret around until the guns were in line with the fuselage, since otherwise the streamlined fairing prevented him from opening his escape hatch. Not many Defiant gunners whose planes were hit lived to tell the tale, and this fact did little to increase the Defiant's popularity with its crews; it was almost immediately withdrawn from combat. Dowding had always been pessimistic about the Defiant, which was slow, was overweight, and had four guns instead of the eight in his Hurricanes and Spitfires; and as usual, he was right.

On the German side, a good deal more time and effort had been invested in producing Messerschmitt's Bf 110, a particular object of Göring's enthusiasm. It was designed to be a *Zerstörer* ("destroyer"). A large, sleek, powerfully armed, long-range, twin-engine escort fighter with a crew of two, the Bf 110 carried four machine guns and two twenty-millimeter cannon in its nose, as well as a gunner with two machine guns facing aft. But the Bf 110 was underpowered for its weight, and also lacked the maneuverability of a single-engine fighter, so despite the undeniably formidable Sunday punch in its nose, it was difficult for the pilot to get his sight fixed on a British fighter long enough to fire. Far from destroying enemy fighters, the Bf 110 turned out to be an easy victim for them. That was unfortunate for Göring, since it represented a substantial part of the *Luftwaffe*'s strength.

The Junkers Ju 87 Stuka, which had created such havoc in Poland, the Low Countries, and eastern France, where it had been unopposed, was still an effective (and terrifying) weapon against troops spread out on the roads and beaches, but it was also slow, ungainly, armed only with a single gun facing aft and two forward-firing fixed MGs, and totally helpless when attacked by a modern eight-gun fighter. This too came as an unpleasant shock to the *Luftwaffe* high command, and particularly to Udet—the Stuka had been built in great quantity and represented a critical part of the *Luftwaffe*'s strategic thinking. There was now some question as to whether it could stay in the air long enough to do any damage in the presence of enemy fighters. On the other hand, considering the number of Stukas in the three *Luftflotten* preparing for the air attack against Britain, not using them was hardly an option.

The air battle over Dunkirk was basically a draw, although given the *Luftwaffe*'s superiority in numbers, it ought not to have been. The British fighter pilots learned quickly that the Bf 109 outperformed the Hurricane at altitudes above 18,000 feet; that the Spitfire and the Bf 109 were fairly equal in performance at all altitudes; and that both British fighters could turn more tightly than the Bf 109, a vital factor in a dogfight, whereas the Bf 109 could often break off a fight by suddenly plunging into a steep, powered dive, since fuel injection prevented its Daimler-Benz engine from cutting out.[1]

German fighter pilots learned that although both British fighters were more maneuverable than their own, the RAF still stuck to outdated, rigid formation flying in combat. The basic unit of RAF fighters doctrine was still three aircraft flying in a V-shape formation known as a "vic"—a full squadron of twelve aircraft would consist of four vics, usually flying line astern of the leader, the whole squadron divided into two "flights" of six aircraft. Given that formation, the leader, usually the squadron commander, would call out "Tally-ho!"* once he saw the enemy, then call out for a specific form of attack from "the book." Each vic would then attack in turn as prescribed, and after these attacks the squadron would re-form as soon as it could.

Combat experience in Spain had led the Germans to adopt a different, looser formation, based on what was called a *Schwarm* of four fighters. This can best be visualized by holding the right hand out with the fingers stretched as far from each other as possible. The longest finger represents the leader, the index finger represents his wingman flying slightly behind and below him to watch his back,

---

* The traditional English foxhunter's cry on seeing a fox. The German fighter pilots too used old hunting cries.

and the two remaining fingers represent another fighter and his wing-man in the same position (each pair was called a *Rotte*). Instead of flying as close to each other as possible—the "nice, neat, wingtip to wingtip formation," beloved of RAF senior officers—the German fighters flew about 200 meters apart, and at different altitudes. They could see each other, and at the same time stay out of each other's view to the rear, for it was a given that danger would almost always come from above and out of the sun. There was no need for them to cling to rigid formation flying; indeed, most *Schwarm* leaders dis-couraged it. As in a dog pack, all the fighters but the leaders moved about on the edge of the pack, looking for trouble or opportunity, drawing closer when they saw a chance to attack, and spreading themselves wider at the first sign of an enemy attack. A *Schwarm* remained "loose and maneuverable," each pilot searching his own segment of the sky instead of trying to keep his eyes on the wingtip of the fighter next to him, as British pilots were expected to do. The RAF fighter pilots referred to the German *Schwarm*, with some envy once they had encountered it, as a "finger four" formation, and toward the end of the Battle of Britain they began to adopt it them-selves.[2]

Of course, in practice, once an air battle started it was more like a catfight than a dogfight—the neat, numbered diagrams that RAF pi-lots had memorized and practiced in formation flying tended to de-generate instantly into a wild, swirling, three-dimensional, high-speed tangle of sudden surprise attacks and quick, violent attempts to es-cape, with the whole thing over in minutes or seconds. (This kind of flying had been discouraged in the RAF before the war, not only be-cause it was dangerous but also because the early Merlin engines, with their notoriously leaky seals, tended to spill hot oil during tight, high-speed maneuvers, leaving long, ugly black oil streaks to mar the regulation Duck Egg Blue paint on the lower surfaces of British fighters—an eyesore to neatness-minded senior officers, as well as to ground crews, who were judged as much on the appearance of the aircraft they were responsible for as on the planes' performance.) Inexperienced pilots quickly learned not to waste their ammunition by firing long bursts, and to fire their guns for a maximum of only two seconds at the precise moment when the enemy was in the center of their sight. Conventional prewar wisdom had at first led the RAF to "harmonize" the eight guns of the Spitfire and the Hurricane so that the bullet streams from them (usually referred to as the "cone of fire") converged at a distance of 650 yards. Dowding was well aware that the standard of marksmanship among his fighter pilots was low, and that there was little opportunity to improve it, so he deliberately chose to give them a widespread pattern, rather like that of a garden hose turned to full spray, on the assumption that at least some of their bullets would hit home. Experience in combat over France had led to realigning the guns to converge at 400 yards, but by the beginning of the Battle of Britain experienced pilots were defying official policy and getting the ground crew to readjust the alignment of the guns so that they converged at 200 yards, or even less.

The Germans made the same discovery, in their case made necessary by the low muzzle velocity and slow rate of fire of their twenty-millimeter cannon.* In both air forces, fighter pilots learned that "the book" was wrong, and the closer they were to their target before they opened fire, the better. "Don't fire until you see the

---

* The two MG FF (Oerlikon) cannon in the wings of the Bf 109E (each with sixty rounds) fired on an "open bolt," as opposed to a closed bolt—that is, the breech opened as they fired, like that of a submachine gun. This made them lighter (they also had a short barrel, to save weight) by eliminating a complex and heavy breech-locking mechanism, but also substantially reduced the muzzle velocity (submachine guns are designed this way so that they don't overheat). Consequently, in 1940 the Bf 109E's wing guns, though they packed a deadly punch, operated at a very low rate of fire and with insufficient muzzle velocity.

whites of their eyes," was just as good advice at 25,000 feet in a fighter as it had been to infantrymen on the ground during the American Revolutionary War. At 350 miles per hour, however, a distance of 200 yards (let alone 150 or 100 yards) is terrifyingly close, and the risk of a collision increases dramatically as the distance between the two aircraft dwindles. It needed nerves of steel, acute eyesight, and a steady hand for a pilot to get so close to his prey that he could be sure of bringing it down with a perfectly aimed two-second burst of gunfire, then brutally shove the stick forward to dive out of the way.

Pilots in training all over the world are instructed to handle the controls of an aircraft gently—"like a woman," a cliché with which flying instructors have been admonishing their students since before 1914—but in combat, a pilot had to yank on his control stick with all his strength if he wanted to survive, and stamp his heavy, thick-soled flying boots mercilessly on the rudder pedals with his full weight as if he were kicking somebody on the floor in a life-or-death barroom brawl. In any case, hands and feet were too cold and cramped for gentle movement. The temperature at 25,000 feet was thirty degrees below zero, and the cockpits of the fighters weren't heated—Dowding had persuaded a reluctant Air Council to specify ducting from the engine exhausts to the wings of the Hurricane and Spitfire as a last-minute modification to prevent the gun breeches from freezing,* but hadn't thought it necessary to provide heat for the pilot. Even so,

---

* In order to prevent moisture (rain or fog) from entering through the open gun ports in the wing and freezing on the gun breeches as the plane took off and climbed rapidly into colder air, Dowding had the ground crews cover the gun ports with "sticky tape," very much like what is now called duct tape. That used by the RAF was bright red, hence the bright red square patches on the leading edge of the wings of British fighters. The first bullet simply cut a hole in the tape. Armorers usually left taping over the gun ports to the last, after they had cleaned and reloaded the guns, so the intact red patches were a sign that the fighter was ready for action again.

THE ANTAGONISTS

Air Chief Marshal Sir Hugh Dowding.

*"To him the people of Britain
and of the free world owe
largely the way of life and the
liberties that they enjoy today."*

Hitler greets a heavily bemedaled
Reichsmarschall Hermann Göring.

Stanley Baldwin.

Neville Chamberlain.

Sydney Camm, designer
of the Hawker Hurricane.

R. J. Mitchell, designer of
the Supermarine Spitfire.

Mitchell's record-breaking seaplane, the Supermarine S.6B, in 1931.
The sleek lines would be repeated in his later design for the Spitfire.

The Spitfire Mark I, with Mitchell's famous, instantly recognizable elliptical wings.

General Erhard Milch.

Willy Messerschmitt.

A "finger four" formation of Messerschmitt's Bf 110E fighters,
in the usual camouflage at the time of the Battle of Britain.

"The Beauty Chorus" at the plotting table at RAF Fighter Command Headquarters (above) and at No. 11 Group Sector Fighter Control, RAF Uxbridge (below).

Hitler and his air staff. Hugo Sperrle, the Führer,
Hermann Göring, Albert Kesselring.

Ernst Udet, the daredevil, seat-of-the-
pants pilot, in a typical dashing pose.

Hugo Sperrle, "The elephant
with a monocle."

THE RIVAL AIR MARSHALS (GERMAN)

Cartoons by Udet

Sperrle and Kesselring.

The ubiquitous and fast-paced Milch.

Keith Park (typically,
in flying helmet), in the
cockpit of his personal
Hurricane.

Trafford Leigh-Mallory.

The king and queen pay an informal visit to Fighter Command Headquarters at the height of the battle, September 6, 1940. Dowding is on their left.

Right: A German fighter squadron, looking very much like a British one, prepares to take off.

Below: A German Dornier bomber approaches the English coast.

British pilots in their dispersal hut wait to be "scrambled."

British fighter pilots stretched out on the grass, waiting to be "scrambled." These are the classic photographs of the Battle of Britain, and the images by which it is always remembered.

British fighter pilots in an improvised dispersal hut, a camouflaged holiday "caravan," or trailer, at a forward airfield in Kent.

"Scramble!"

A British sergeant pilot ready for takeoff.

The American pilots Red
Tobin, "Shorty" Keough,
and Andy Mamedoff.

Douglas Bader, the legless
British ace, on the wing of
his Hurricane.

Billy Fiske before the war,
holding his Olympic
bobsledding trophy.

Werner Mölders.

Adolf Galland, in conversation with the Führer.

A German He 111 bomber photographed above London, with the Thames clearly seen below it.

Winston Churchill views the ruins of his beloved House of Commons, Brendan Bracken in the foreground.

The king and queen, while inspecting the damage to Buckingham Palace, pause to chat with workmen.

Captured German aircrew under the guard of the Royal Military
Police. Note their youth—true of aircrew on both sides.

One of "the few."

pilots sweated heavily as they manhandled their machines through violent maneuvers in the cold, bright sky five miles above the ground at 300 or 400 miles an hour, instruments and the horizon spinning crazily as they rolled, twisted, and dived; the sudden changes in g force making their limbs feel as light as a feather for one fraction of a second, and heavy as lead the next; the muscles of their neck aching fiercely from the need to keep looking behind for an enemy who might be transformed from a tiny, almost invisible dot in the sky— hardly more than a speck of dust on the transparent plastic of the cockpit canopy—at one moment to the blunt front profile of a Bf 109 appearing suddenly and brutally at close range in the rearview mirror, gun flashes bright from its fuselage and wings and tracers arcing straight at you.

The controls were not "power assisted" in any way—you moved them at high speed by sheer physical force, greater in the Messerschmitt than in the British fighters, but still considerable in all the fighters of the time, as the pilot dived, turned, looped, and rolled, pushing the stick and the rudder pedals against the combined force of gravity and of air compressing itself against the control surfaces. Combat was physically exhausting for even the strongest of fighter pilots, requiring enormous effort from limbs that were stiff with cold, as well as constant, almost superhuman alertness, split-second reaction to danger, and complete physical indifference to rapidly building g forces and stomach-churning changes of direction that no fairground ride in the world could have imitated—with your mouth dry from breathing oxygen; your eyes smarting from the fumes of gasoline, oil, and exhaust seeping into the cockpit and from staring into the sun; and the radio pouring into your ears a constant tumult of static, orders, warnings, and awful cries of pain and despair. All this in the knowledge that you were sitting behind (or in the Messerschmitt in front of and above) many gallons of high-octane fuel that could turn you into a blazing torch in seconds, not to speak of hundreds of rounds of ammunition, while somewhere from above and behind you another nineteen- to twenty-year-old might already be swooping down on you from out of the sun to change your role in an instant from hunter to prey and end your life in a burst of fire lasting less than a second. If the fellow knew what he was doing, the sudden surprise of your own death would be the first sign you had of his presence.

Much has been made of the "chivalry" of air combat, but in World War II, as in World War I, your object as a fighter pilot was primarily to sneak up on your opponent from behind and above and kill him before he was even aware you were there, while your opponent's objective, if he was lucky enough to catch a fleeting glimpse of you approaching from behind in his tiny rearview mirror, was to escape by means of violent evasive action, then turn tightly, close in behind you, and kill you. Fighter pilots who survived were cold-blooded killers, but this is not to say that many of them actually *liked* killing—it was simply their job, the sole and only purpose of their long and expensive training, and of the even more expensive machine it had taken so many man-hours to create and build.

Instant death was a commonplace. There was a brutal "learning curve" (to use a phrase from a later age) in air combat. A pilot coming to a fighter squadron fresh out of an Operational Training Unit had almost no chance at all of surviving his first five "sorties" in combat. If he did survive them, by sheer luck or superhuman natural skill, then his chance of surviving the next fifteen sorties increased on a rising curve as he gained experience and confidence. After twenty sorties, however, the law of numbers took over, and his chance of surviving began to decline rapidly toward zero again. The survivability of a newcomer to a fighter squadron with no combat experience was not improved by the fact that he would naturally be assigned the oldest, slowest, most often patched and repaired, and most "clapped out" fighter in the squadron, serviced by the least efficient and least motivated ground crew, or that he would very likely end up in the position of "tail-end Charlie," the last aircraft in the formation, bringing up the rear, and therefore the natural target for any enemy fighter pilot looking for an easy kill. There would be cases during August and September 1940, when the battle was at its peak, of a young RAF pilot arriving at the squadron to which he had been posted and being rushed straight into a fighter before he had even unpacked his suitcases, and killed before anybody knew his name. Opening the suitcases he had left in the entrance to the mess was the only way for the Adjutant or the Station Warrant Officer to learn who he had been.

Nor was death in the air necessarily quick and clean—the risk of being burned alive was considerable, and many WAAFs who served in ground control remember to this day hearing through their earphones the screams of young men trapped in a flaming cockpit, unable to slide back the canopy because their hands were too badly burned. The machine itself, for all the thought that had gone into it, was inherently dangerous—a missing cotter pin, a filler cap insufficiently tightened, or a moment's carelessness on the part of an exhausted aircraftman in your ground crew could kill you as surely as an enemy air ace. A nick in your oxygen tube could put you into hypoxia and send you plummeting to the ground from 30,000 feet to your death, unconscious and helpless. A bad landing, particularly in a Spitfire or Bf 109, with its narrow tracks, could easily turn into a ground loop and trap you upside down in your aircraft as it burst into flames on the runway. A stray seagull crashing into your plane's radiator intake on takeoff could bring your plane down with an impact that scattered it and its pilot in a fiery circle fifty yards wide. A parachute jump from a crippled fighter might send you drifting into the sea, where, particularly for British pilots, the chances of being found and picked up by an RAF rescue launch were remote.*

All three fighters—the Spitfire, the Hurricane, and the Bf 109— were a tight fit, even for a pilot of modest height and girth. The Bf 109 was the worst in this respect—it not only had an incredibly narrow, cramped cockpit but was claustrophobic, since the heavy, metal-framed cockpit canopy opened sideways, like the lid of a coffin, and pressed down against the leather helmet of a taller pilot when it was closed.† In all of them, the cockpit canopy was narrower than the width of an average person's shoulders, so it was easy to feel trapped by the inward-curving sides of the fuselage. Getting into any one of these aircraft was difficult enough, but getting out of one quickly in midair was harder. The Bf 109 had an advantage over British fighters in this respect—by pulling a red handle on the port side of the cockpit, the pilot could jettison the entire canopy structure (which looked something like a sturdy miniature greenhouse), whereas the pilot of a Hurricane or Spitfire had to push back the canopy with both hands to get out. On the other hand, Mitchell had wisely designed the Spitfire's cockpit with a hinged, downward-opening panel on the port side, and the larger Hurricane had a metal panel on the starboard side that could be jettisoned; both devices gave the pilot a little more

---

* Oddly enough for a seafaring nation like Britain, the *Luftwaffe* was better organized and equipped for picking their pilots up from "the drink." German aircraft had self-inflating life rafts, and their airmen were provided with a bag of bright lime-green dye attached to their life vests to mark their position in the water and help the rescue seaplanes spot them.

† The canopy of the Bf 109 had been made even heavier and more coffin-like by the addition of a piece of armor plate attached to it behind the pilot's head, which also restricted the pilot's ability to see what was behind him.

legroom to push himself out of the cockpit in an emergency. All the same, pilots of all three aircraft usually tried to take advantage of gravity by doing a quick half roll to bring their plane upside down so they could unfasten the seat harness and drop out—not an easy thing to do if the controls were damaged, or if you were wounded, or on fire. The half roll also reduced the chance of being stunned or decapitated by the tailplane as you left the cockpit and were carried down by gravity and back by the slipstream.

Of course all this has to be seen in context. No doubt plenty of nice old ladies sitting in front of a cozy fireplace with a cup of tea in their hand and a cat dozing in their lap were vaporized when a German 250-kilogram bomb fell on their house—you didn't have to wear a uniform or go looking for trouble at 20,000 feet to die suddenly and violently during World War II. Still, the fact, though much resented by frontline soldiers and naval personnel on ships, that fighter pilots, if they lived, came back at the end of the day to have a drink and dinner in the mess and spend the night in their own bed, does not diminish the courage it took to go back up in the air the next morning and fight three or four times a day.

Despite the danger, to most fighter pilots it was an exhilarating, adrenaline-producing, incredibly intense experience, very often over—one way or the other—before there was even time to be frightened by it, and repeated day after day until the inexorable law of numbers caught up with you. But even for the young, fit, and self-confident—and by definition all fighter pilots were supremely young, fit, and self-confident—it was a grueling experience; and exhaustion, mental weariness, and, in some men, the slow draining of their stock of courage, took its toll as the weeks and months of the Battle of Britain went by. High in the air, in the dizzying rush of combat, it was easy for a pilot to suddenly find himself alone in the sky, perhaps with his ammunition exhausted, his fuel running low, and a cloud cover below him that prevented him from seeing the ground, and at such times a fighter pilot experienced extreme loneliness and a sense of helpless exposure to danger that could unnerve even the bravest of men.

A not untypical example of what it was like to be a fledgling fighter pilot was Geoffrey Wellum, who at three months short of nineteen years old was plucked from Flying Training School before he had completed his course, or had even seen a fighter, and posted straight to an operational squadron, where, after a few hours of flying a Spitfire, he met his "baptism of fire." "Will I have the courage needed?" he asked himself, as he watched his fellow pilots take off, and precisely because he wrote about a young man's first experience of air combat, his account, in *First Light*, a classic of its kind, still seems fresh and believable. He notes the pertinent small details, such as taking off his tie and loosening his shirt collar before getting into his aircraft so as not to chafe his neck as he constantly turns his head to look behind him, and as he listens to the ground crews starting up the engines at first light he wonders for the first time, "Which one of us is going to be killed today?"

Going into combat for the first time, he carefully checks his oxygen as he reaches 10,000 feet—he's very good on the small rituals with which pilots steady their nerves—and suddenly hears his squadron commander shout to the ground controller, "Tally-ho! Tally-ho! I can see them. They are at least angels one five* and what's more there are hundreds of the sods!" Wellum "looks up into the far distance, the vast panorama of the sky," and sees the enemy, like "a swarm of gnats on a warm summer evening," Dornier bombers, Bf 109s (referred to as "snappers" by the RAF) above them. Wellum has never seen so

---

* "Angels one five," means 15,000 feet.

many aircraft in one place in his life, but he wills himself to follow the drill he has been taught—turn the reflector sight on, set the gun button on the control stick handle to "fire," adjust the airscrew pitch to higher revs, lower his seat as far as it will go, and tighten his Sutton harness. He holds tight to his leader's Spitfire, its wingtip less than thirty feet away, and follows him into "a mix-up of aeroplanes, in fact bloody chaos," keeping his eye on the Dornier he has selected despite streams of tracer bullets arcing toward him as his squadron attacks the Germans head-on from below, at a closing speed of about 500 miles per hour:

Sight on, still on, steady . . . Fire NOW! I press the gun button and all hell is let loose; my guns make a noise like tearing calico . . . I get the fleeting impression of hits and explosions on the glass nose of the Dornier, and of Brian's Spitfire breaking away, its oil-streaked belly visible for a fraction of a second. . . . For Christ's sake break off or you'll hit him. . . . I stop firing, stick hard over, I even hear his engines as he flashes by inches overhead. . . . In less time than it takes to think about it, I am at 3,000 feet . . . Stick back and I pull up, feeling the g loading and using full throttle, regain the level of a real old mix-up, everybody split up, each man for himself . . . Keep turning, Geoff, don't fly straight for a second. The R/T is alive with shouts, warnings and odd noises . . . The effort required is enormous . . . A 109 crosses my front. I fire a quick burst and I manage to fasten on to him but a Hurricane gets in my way and I have to break off . . . There's tracer behind me and very close indeed. I break down hard and a 109 I hadn't seen pulls up flying at terrific speed . . . I see . . . a Heinkel 111 going like a bat out of hell between me and the coast . . . Ease the stick forward, throttle open and I drop out of the sky after him . . . Sights on, never mind the return fire, steady, fire again, a long burst this time . . . Certainly I hit him . . . The rear gunner has stopped firing and the nose of the Heinkel has dropped . . . My guns fire a few rounds and then stop . . . Sod it, out of ammo . . . I break away. A flash, bright like magnesium and a sharp, very loud explosion . . . I've been hit. So this is how a fighter pilot dies . . . Looking back over my shoulder an ME 109 is sitting on my tail not thirty yards away . . . I hold on to the turn for all I'm worth and even tighten it . . . A quick glance at the gauges. How seriously has he clobbered me? I start to black out. Must be pulling six g. Lean forward, raise my feet on to the rudder pedal extensions. God, they're heavy . . . The physical effort is tremendous and the perspiration starts to pour off me . . . The German pilot is trying to tighten his turn still more to keep up with me and I'm sure I see the 109 flick. You won't do it, mate, we're on the limit as it is . . . He stops his turn . . . This is it, now get the hell out of it! Stick over and roll on to my back; let her go. Stick centre, take off the bank and pull through hard into a half roll . . . Throttle still open and hold the vertical dive . . . Speed is building up at a tremendous rate . . . Ailerons getting heavy as hell; hold it, hold the stick over, desperate straits need desperate remedies. Blimey, we're shifting . . . I take the Spitfire down to ground level, flying very, very fast . . . The sky is clear, except for a few dispersing smoke trails . . . Not another aeroplane in sight . . . I can't really explain it but I realize how lonely I felt up there . . .

Wellum's description of his first fight is about as good as words get in describing the indescribable. He went on to fight through the Battle of Britain, win a DFC, do more than 100 sorties over France, and fly a Hurricane off a carrier deck to land on the besieged island of Malta and fight there. Summing up what he had learned about air combat, he wrote, "No amount of training can prepare you for mortal combat . . . You must remember a simple, straightforward golden rule: Never, never fly straight and level for more than twenty seconds. If you do, you'll die."

A lot of young men on both sides learned that lesson in the sky above Dunkirk from May 26 to June 4, 1940, and for some of them the lesson was fatal. Whatever the troops on the ground thought, Fighter Command had played a significant role in making their evacuation* from Dunkirk possible and had put up an extraordinary fight against overwhelming odds, for the 200-odd fighters of Park's No. 11 Group were facing two entire German *Luftflotten* above Dunkirk. In the twenty-four days since the German attack on France and the Low Countries, the *Luftwaffe* had lost more than 1,200 aircraft, and the RAF 959, but for the British the most significant number was that 477 of these were Dowding's precious fighters, which he had never wanted sent to France in the first place, and which he dispatched to Dunkirk with infinite reluctance and foreboding.

Others, including the prime minister, still retained hope that France would survive the initial disaster of the war, as it had survived the Battle of the Marne by a hairbreadth in 1914, when the Parisian taxis had shuttled General Joseph-Simon Gallieni's troops from the Gare des Invalides to the front in time to save France. Churchill, however poorly he spoke French, was a devoted, passionate Francophile, and although the writing was, all too clearly, on the wall, his generous nature and his romantic impulses prevented him from seeing, at first, the full and shameful extent of the French military and political

---

* Some 338,000 troops, more than two-thirds of them British, were brought off the beaches of Dunkirk.

collapse. Throughout most of his lifetime, France had been Britain's only European ally; he himself had commanded an infantry battalion in the trenches in France in what was still called the Great War; many of the senior French generals and not a few of the politicians were his friends. Accordingly, Churchill was profoundly and sincerely reluctant to leave France in the lurch. Dowding, however, shared none of these emotions, nor the illusions that they kindled in the prime minister's breast. He had never had much confidence in the idea that the Maginot Line or the French army would stop the Germans, still less any confidence in the French air force, which he knew was poorly equipped and trained, and possessed neither modern fighters, nor radar, nor an efficiently organized fighter control organization. Dowding took it for granted that the Germans would attack Britain as soon as they gained possession of the French, Dutch, and Belgian airfields; that Britain's survival would depend on his fighters; and that every fighter and every fighter pilot sent to France directly weakened his strength. He did not believe that his Hurricanes—his few Spitfires were too valuable to even consider sending to France—could stop or even slow down the German advance, or that their presence would restore the morale of the French army. The British fighters in France were flying from makeshift, primitive airfields, without radar and fighter control to guide them; the French had no modern antiaircraft guns to protect the fields; and a long, tenuous supply line went all the way back to the Channel ports (which were now being taken one by one by the Germans) and was dependent on the French railways and road system, both prime targets for German bombers. Fuel, equipment, ammunition, and spares seldom reached the places where they were most needed through the chaos of the French retreat, which led to the rapid wastage of British aircraft and pilots for no gain whatsoever.

. . .

The French, not surprisingly, saw the matter from a different point of view. Lord Gort's British Expeditionary Force had been too small to make a difference in the major land battle, and had in any case returned to Britain via Dunkirk, leaving the French army to fight on alone, with lessening cohesion and rapidly sinking morale. Nobody in France seriously expected the British to summon up an army of many divisions overnight and ship them to France, but the one thing they did have, apart from the Royal Navy, was a powerful modern air force. Now, in the view of the French government, at the supreme moment of crisis, was the time to send it into battle, to give the French army a breathing space in which to establish a viable line of defense.

What the French wanted most was fighters, despite the fact that an eight-gun Hurricane was powerless against a tank, and the reason for this has to be explored, for it was to become the major issue between the British and French governments, and between Churchill and Dowding. The military alliance between Britain and France was a relatively recent historical development, an unusual happy interlude in a 900-year history of mutual warfare, rivalry, and contempt—a history that still made many Britons and most of the French uneasy. Old prejudices die hard and slowly, and the fact that the French and the British had fought on the same side in the Crimean War and in World War I had done nothing to erase the French people's memory of Crécy, Agincourt, Trafalgar, and Waterloo or their suspicion of "perfidious Albion," or to reduce British contempt for the "frogs." Nowhere were these feelings stronger than among the senior officers of the armed forces of both nations—indeed, after World War I the air defenses of Great Britain had been built up with France in mind as the potential aggressor, until Germany revived sufficiently to resume that role.

One effect of this long-standing hostility between the two allies was that the parties behaved toward each other, as in a bad marriage, with exaggerated politeness and a total lack of frankness. Thus, although it was clear enough that French generalship had failed spectacularly and that the French army had, with a few signal exceptions,* fought very badly indeed, where it had fought at all, the British were deeply reluctant to say so, and since their own small army had distinguished itself so far only by conducting a well-disciplined retreat and a providential evacuation, they were in any case in no position to criticize France. As for the French, a proud nation with a rich tradition of military *gloire* second to none, and fresh memories of victory in World War I, they themselves naturally did not jump to the conclusion that their troops had fought badly or that their generals had bungled. They looked for another reason, and found it in the fact that the Germans controlled the air.

The French government and generals agreed that this was the problem. Although the Germans had not in fact launched a serious bomber campaign against French cities, they had used their Stukas as airborne artillery, as well as for strafing the roads. Retreating soldiers and civilian refugees alike, jamming France's road system, had been terrified by the sudden appearance of German dive-bombers—one of Udet's shrewdest moves had been to fit the Ju 87 with a siren that gave out a banshee howl as it dived, sowing panic among all who heard it. Though the actual number of deaths caused by the *Luftwaffe* in France was low, particularly compared with the casualties that France had suffered in World War I, the psychological effect was enormous, spread mostly in the form of horrifying rumors, which

---

* One exception occurred when General Charles de Gaulle, newly promoted to command the French Fourth Armored Division near Laon, on May 28, 1940, carried out a bold, sustained, and successful counterattack against much larger German forces, demonstrating what might have been done had the French used their own armored forces aggressively. The success was unusual enough that he was shortly afterward made undersecretary of state for national defense by Paul Reynaud.

paralyzed the government, eroded the already doubtful morale of the army, and terrified the civilian population. It also served as a simple, all-purpose explanation for France's defeat—not only had the British not done their share of the fighting; they had also failed to provide enough fighters to protect the French army.

This subject had already come up during a dramatic early-morning telephone call between the two prime ministers, Paul Reynaud and Winston Churchill, on May 15, only five days after the king had asked Churchill to form a government. "We have been defeated," Reynaud said, in English, when Churchill picked up the telephone by his bedside. "The front is broken near Sedan."[3] The way to Paris, Reynaud warned, was open.

The next day, following the grim news of the surrender of the Netherlands, Churchill flew to Paris to meet with Reynaud and the French war cabinet at the Quai d'Orsay. The meeting was not made any more cheerful by the sight, through the window, of "venerable officials pushing wheel-barrows of archives" of state documents into the garden and dumping them into "large bonfires,"[4] from which the smoke rose high above the French ministry of foreign affairs. The glum admission of the French commander in chief, General Gamelin, that he possessed no strategic reserve with which to stage a counterattack, and his obvious belief that the war was lost, was followed by a vigorous demand from him, and from all the French present, for more squadrons of fighters from Britain. General Gamelin pointed out that only the fighters could stop the German tanks—a belief which was to be repeated at every Anglo-French meeting until the end, and stubbornly contradicted by Churchill. It is difficult to see how Gamelin imagined that fighters could stop tanks. The Mark I Hurricane had no provision for bomb racks; nor had the pilots any training in attacking targets on the ground.

Also, the .303-caliber bullets of the British fighters' eight guns would have bounced harmlessly off a tank's armor. What the French needed to do was to dig in their own field artillery, the famous *soixante-quinze*, which had served them so well in World War I and which, with its rapid rate of fire, high velocity, and flat trajectory, was still capable of disabling a *Panzerkampfwagen* II or III, the type of tank that then constituted the bulk of the German armor. Fighter planes, even if the British had them in abundance, would not have stopped the advance of the German panzer divisions, although they might of course have helped with the Stukas. However, whatever differences existed between General Gamelin, Prime Minister Reynaud, and Monsieur Daladier, who was the minister of national defense and war (and the differences were considerable), on this subject they were as one—*now* was the moment to send every fighter to France. Churchill, during the telephone conversation from his bed with a distraught Reynaud the pervious day, had agreed to send four more squadrons of Hurricanes to France. Now, faced with the signs of collapse all around him, both in the room and outside in the garden, and moved by the plight of the French, he agreed to seek the British War Cabinet's consent to send another six squadrons as well. "It would not be good historically if their requests were denied and their ruin resulted,"[5] Churchill cabled from the British embassy, and late that same night he was driven to Reynaud's apartment to tell him that all ten squadrons would be sent the following day. Reynaud had already retired to bed and emerged in his dressing gown, leaving his mistress, the formidable Hélène de Portes (whom one wit described as "the only man in the government"), in the bedroom to listen behind the door.

It was a moment of high emotion, perhaps the most dramatic and positive in a succession of increasingly difficult and depressing meetings between the French and the British prime ministers; but on the other side of the Channel, when he heard the news, it alarmed an already apprehensive Air Chief Marshal Dowding, and set off an equally difficult disagreement between the British prime minister and the Commander-in-Chief of Fighter Command.

Probably no subject in history has been written about in such detail as the relationship between the British and French governments from May 10, when the Germans attacked, to June 22, when the French government, by then headed by the aged, defeatist Marshal Pétain, signed an armistice with Germany. In the English-speaking world, the account of those calamitous events that has fixed our view of what happened is Winston Churchill's. His was, after all, the central role in the drama; he himself drafted (with considerable care and thought for the opinion of posterity) most of the important documents and cables on the British side; he alone survived the war victorious to tell the story. Nearly half of *Their Finest Hour*, Volume II of Churchill's *The Second World War*, is devoted to the fall of France, and they are perhaps the most dramatic and compelling pages in the entire six volumes, as full of light, shadow, emotion, and human detail as history can be, a Shakespearean tragedy rendered in the Gibbonesque prose style of which the prime minister was the undisputed master.* On the British side, almost everybody else who was involved has written about it, in memoirs, published diaries and letters, but it is Churchill who still dominates the scene now, as he did then—after all, it was not only "their" finest hour, it was *his*.

A whole book—indeed a sizable and distinguished one†—has been written about the way Churchill subtly and sometimes not so

---

* It is instructive, of course, to read French accounts of these events for balance, particularly the memoirs of De Gaulle and Reynaud.

† *In Command of History*, by David Reynolds, Allen Lane/Penguin, London, 2004.

subtly shaped his description of events and artfully edited the documents at his disposal when it came time to write "his" history of the war. Nowhere in the six volumes and nearly 2 million words of *The Second World War* does he go to more trouble to build a case for himself than on the subject of the fighter squadrons he wanted to send to France, and Dowding's objections to doing so. Indeed, it is perhaps the only place in the whole massive structure—which won him the Nobel Prize for Literature—where one can hear the stage machinery creaking and clanking as Churchill tries to escape blame and diminish the strength of Dowding's opposition, one of the very few episodes about which Churchill appears to feel, if not shame, then at least a certain embarrassment.

To understand why, it is necessary to consider the size, scope, and purpose of the RAF presence in France, to which, from the very beginning, Dowding had forcefully presented his objections regarding his fighters. It had always been the government's intention to send a British Expeditionary Force (BEF) to France in the event of war with Germany, and it was also a firm commitment made, with whatever reluctance, to the French. The BEF, which would eventually include nine divisions, was to take its place in the "line of battle" on the French frontier, centered on Lille, with the French Seventh Army on its left and the French Ninth Army on its right, and in the event of a German breach of Dutch and Belgian neutrality, was to advance to the Dyle River and hold a line from Louvain to Wavre.* It was understood that the BEF would need its own air support, and to supply that the RAF had created what became known as the Royal Air Force

---

* Indeed the whole French plan of attack was named *le Plan D*, after the Dyle River, though French officers often joked that the name stood for *le plan Débrouillard*, best translated as "trying to sort out a hopeless mess," as in *débrouillez-vous*, "sort it out yourself."

Component of the British Expeditionary Force (a bit of a mouthful, sometimes shortened to "the Component"), to consist of five squadrons of Lysanders for reconnaissance and communications work, four squadrons of Blenheim twin-engine light bombers, and four squadrons of Hurricanes, to be increased by six more "if necessity arose." All these were based at airfields in northern France, behind the BEF. As it became apparent just how weak the French *Armée de l'Air* was, a further British force, known as the Advanced Air Striking Force (AASF), was dispatched to France, with ten squadrons of Battle single-engine bombers and twin-engine Blenheims, and two further squadrons of Hurricanes, all to be stationed farther south, behind the Ardennes and the Maginot Line, and to serve as a bombing force to support the French and British armies. Together, these made up a considerable though ill-assorted force of aircraft, spread out over dozens of widely separated airfields in northeastern France. Both the Component and the AASF came under the overall command of Air Marshal A. S. Barratt, who in theory could, if he thought it necessary, "request" assistance from Bomber Command in Britain.[6]

Bomber Command, as it happened, was as reluctant to commit its medium and heavy bombers to supporting the Allied Forces in France against German attack as Dowding was to release his Hurricanes—it took the view that the best way for its bombers to support the Allied armies in France was to bomb the vital points of German industry.* This was the theme song of "strategic bombing," which

---

* In fact, at this point in the war, Bomber Command had neither the equipment nor the expertise to do much serious damage to the German war effort; and prior to May 10, 1940, it had in any case been more or less restricted to dropping bundles of propaganda leaflets over Germany, since the French government feared reprisals by the *Luftwaffe* if Germany was bombed, and the British government was equally determined not to provoke Hitler. When the RAF suggested bombing ammunition dumps in the Black Forest the then Secretary of State of State for Air, Sir Kingsley Wood, remarked indignantly, "Are you aware that is private property? Why, you will be asking me to bomb Essen next!" (Essen was the home of the Krupp steel works.)

would be replayed again and again from 1940 to 1945. (Though the air marshals were loath to admit it, the big bombers had in any case very little chance of hitting small targets near the front line, like bridges or road junctions, by day, and none at all at night, and were unlikely to survive against sustained flak and fighter attack.)

The reluctance of Bomber Command to come to the rescue of Air Marshal Barratt if requested to do so was nothing compared with Dowding's feelings about letting even a single one of his Hurricanes get out of his hands. At the very beginning of the war, Dowding had been indignant to learn that four squadrons of his fighters were to go to France as part of the Component Force, and even more upset when he discovered in "the small print" that six more might be taken from him "if necessity arose." He was astute enough to know that necessity would almost certainly arise, and protested vehemently, in person and in writing, to the Air Council, the Secretary of State for Air, and the Chief of the Air Staff, but got nowhere except to confirm in everybody else's mind the notion that he was difficult, unreasonable, and the victim of an idée fixe. Dowding was doubly indignant because he had always made it clear that the absolute minimum number of fighter squadrons he required for the successful defense of Great Britain was fifty (this number was later raised to sixty), and he had been given to understand that the four squadrons for the BEF would not leave Britain until he had his fifty squadrons in place. Instead, they had been removed while he did not yet have even half that number, and as an experienced military bureaucrat he knew that once they were out of his hands, he would never get them back.

Also, as he constantly tried to explain, the fighters and their pilots were only a part, admittedly the most glamorous part, of an intricate and well thought-out system, in which numerous participants played

vital roles: the young women drawing up the plots at the radar stations; the "beauty chorus" moving the markers on the big board at
Fighter Command Headquarters; the GPO telephone engineers installing and keeping in good repair the hundreds of buried telephone
lines from Bentley Priory to and from the Group commanders and the
radar stations; the "boffins" constantly perfecting and improving the
radar network; the civilian ground observers, with their helmets and
their binoculars; the fighter controllers; and even the men driving the
big Scammell trucks (known as Queen Marys after the giant ocean
liner), who transported damaged Hurricanes and Spitfires to civilian-
staffed regional repair centers where they could be repaired and sent
back to fighting units quickly. The fighters on their own, without this
organization in place, could not save Britain even if Dowding had his
fifty (or sixty) squadrons, and could certainly not save France.

Sending Hurricanes to France was, in Dowding's view, turning on
a tap which the politicians and the Air Council would never have the
courage to turn off, and through which Britain's lifeblood would
pour. Removed from the structure of Fighter Command, spread out
on makeshift airfields with inadequate maintenance facilities, and
sent into battle without radar or ground control to guide them, the
Hurricanes and their pilots would simply be wasted. On the subject
of this vital point, nobody wanted to listen, and no matter how hard
Dowding tried, Churchill never grasped it, or perhaps, to do the
prime minister justice, he never *wanted* to grasp it—a fact it might be,
but it was an inconvenient fact, and if he wanted to keep France in the
war he could not afford to accept it.

As early as October 1939, Dowding had clashed sharply with the
Chief of the Air Staff, Sir Cyril Newall, who had wanted him to make
advance preparations so that fighters could be sent to France quickly,

if necessary. Dowding smelled a rat, and replied, crushingly and with no hint that he was willing to compromise, that "the French difficulties are largely due to the pathetic inefficiency of their Interception System. I have not been told what steps they are taking to set their house in order, even at this late date."[7] Far from sharing Newall's belief that Britain could lose the war in France from a lack of fighters there, Dowding believed that France was a lost cause anyway, and that Britain could survive the French defeat if—and only if—he had enough fighters to protect British ports and aircraft factories from the enemy, and to maintain air control over the Channel.

Events in France between May 10 and the evacuation of Dunkirk just over two weeks later served to confirm Dowding's opinion. The French air force was incapable of making any impact on the enemy, and indeed hardly even tried; and the RAF forces were rapidly destroyed. On the very first day, of the thirty-two Fairey Battles sent to bomb the advancing German columns (over the vehement objections of General Gamelin, who wanted to avoid "a bombing war" for fear of German reprisals against French cities), thirteen were shot down and all the rest severely damaged. A force of Battles sent to attack the bridges over the Albert Canal at the urgent request of the Belgians was completely destroyed—the raid accomplished nothing but the subsequent award of two (posthumous) Victoria Crosses. By May 14 General Gamelin, now reacting with something approaching panic to the speed and unexpected direction of the German advance, had changed his mind and was begging the RAF to bomb the bridges over the Meuse River. Although it was well known that a bridge is almost impossible to hit from the air, and that the only reliable way of destroying one is to mine it and blow it up before the enemy reaches it, the French had neglected to destroy the vital Meuse bridges. Air Marshal Barratt nevertheless obliged General Gamelin with a raid in which forty out of seventy-one bombers sent were shot down—the highest "rate of loss"[8] that the RAF had ever experienced in an operation of this size. The operation did almost no damage to the bridges, and slowed the German advance down by at best a few hours. The Hurricanes sent to protect the slow, vulnerable Battles and the poorly armed Blenheims performed prodigies, but, inevitably, Dowding's darkest predictions had come true—the forces of the RAF in France were being destroyed piecemeal for no possible gain. The tap had been turned on, and nobody wanted to face the political consequences of turning it off.

Four squadrons of Hurricanes had been sent to France at the start of the German attack, in addition to the six that were already there. By May 13, as anguished demands for fighters poured in from the French, as well as from the foundering Dutch and Belgian governments, the question of sending more Hurricanes to France had become the hottest of political hot potatoes. It was discussed at a meeting of the War Cabinet, where the new Secretary of State for Air, Sir Archibald Sinclair, who had been Churchill's second in command during the brief period when the prime minister had commanded the Sixth Battalion of the Royal Scots Fusiliers in Flanders in 1916, reminded the War Cabinet of the Air Staff's estimate that sixty squadrons were required to defend the country against German attack, and that only thirty-nine were available.

When it came time to write his own version of these events, in 1948, Churchill naturally chose to portray himself in a concerned and judicious role, balancing the demands of the French against the requirements of the Air Staff, but in fact most of those who were there that day remember him as a glowering, overbearing presence, at his most obstinate and difficult. Against this, it must be said in describing

Churchill at the time that the phrase "bearing the weight of the world on his shoulders" comes to mind. The Dutch were being overrun and would surrender in two days, the Belgians would surrender not long afterward, and the first signs of incompetence and defeatism in the French army were already clear enough to see, much as the prime minister did not want to see them. Perhaps hoping to gain time, or to postpone the decision to send more fighters to France, the Chief of the Air Staff cannily suggested that before a decision was made to reduce the number of fighter squadrons in this country by sending further squadrons to France, the Commander-in-Chief, Fighter Command, should be given the opportunity of expressing his views, and pointed out that Dowding would almost certainly not want to release more Hurricane squadrons unless he was overruled by the War Cabinet. In short, Newall, who already knew very well what Dowding's position was—he had heard it many times before—was passing the buck to Dowding, and at the same time warning everyone that Dowding not only would oppose sending more Hurricanes to France, but would certainly also go on the record as having opposed it.

Newall was present at the War Cabinet above all because the prime minister wanted the RAF to begin bombing Germany at once—something the French government opposed vehemently, and would continue to oppose to the very end out of fear of German retaliation. Despite the objections of the French, turning Bomber Command loose against the Ruhr was the chief subject on Churchill's mind at the cabinet meeting of May 13 so far as the RAF was concerned, rather than the French demand for more British fighters, or Dowding's reluctance to send them.

The idea that Bomber Command could strike a crippling blow against the Ruhr, the heart of German heavy industry and war production, was an illusion still shared by Churchill and many others,

even Newall, who should have known better. The scenes of mass
destruction predicted by H. G. Wells (and by Churchill too in his
speeches in the late 1930s) were still affecting everybody where the
subject of bombing was concerned. The idea terrified the French, and
of course made Churchill all the more anxious to turn the bombers
loose on the Ruhr for what he imagined as a decisive blow. He was
not much concerned by the possibility of German retaliation against
Britain—on the contrary, he expected it, and indeed hoped it would
draw German air strength away from the battlefield, thus allowing
the French army to form and hold a line, and to counterattack in
force from the south and cut off the German "bulge."

What had not yet occurred to anybody (except perhaps Dowding)
is that bombing the Ruhr would produce merely a damp squib, as
opposed to a dramatic shock that would bring Hitler to his senses, or
to his knees. In fact, Bomber Command had as yet neither the aircraft
nor the navigational skills nor the scientific and technical expertise to
seriously damage German industry. By day, its aircraft were too slow
and too poorly armed to survive in the skies over Germany, and by
night they had, even in clear weather, no reliable way of locating their
targets. What seemed to the prime minister, and to those around him
in the Cabinet Room at 10 Downing Street, a grave, difficult decision, with far-reaching consequences, we can now see, with the benefit of time and hindsight, to have been of no importance at all
compared with the threat to reduce the number of Dowding's fighter
squadrons in the United Kingdom.

In the event, Dowding did not get his chance to make his case before
the Chiefs of Staff Committee of the War Cabinet until two days
later, on May 15—an indication of his comparatively low position on
the scale of Churchill's priorities. By that time a flood of bad news

from the continent had increased Dowding's anxiety about further reducing the number of his fighter squadrons in the United Kingdom. On the 14th the Germans, anxious to prevent any delay in the time-table of Army Group B's attack across the neutral Netherlands toward the Dyle River by continued Dutch resistance, however slight, decided to teach the Dutch a lesson in *Schrecklicheit* by bombing Rotterdam. The city's historic center "was devastated, 20,000 buildings destroyed, 78,000 people rendered homeless and nearly 1,000 of the inhabitants killed." There was no resistance—the Dutch air force had been destroyed on the ground the day before, and Rotterdam had no antiaircraft guns. The *Luftwaffe* pilots took their time, methodically bombing from an altitude of only a few hundred feet at their leisure, and set off "a raging inferno" in the heart of the city. The next day, the Netherlands surrendered. Here was exactly the scenario that the French feared most, and not surprisingly they dug in their heels even more firmly at the idea of bombing Germany. But to the British it demonstrated, on the contrary, the power of bombing, and erased whatever doubts and scruples remained in the War Cabinet about bombing the Ruhr for fear of inflicting civilian casualties there.

In fact, the tragedy at Rotterdam was not one the Germans could repeat over Paris or London, even had they wished to. Rotterdam was a small city, easily visible against a flat landscape, completely undefended, easy to find in clear weather (all you needed was a good road or railway map), less than 100 miles from the German border, and within easy range of numerous *Luftwaffe* bases—like Guernica, it was the air war equivalent of stealing candy from a baby.

If the bombing of Rotterdam shook the French government, it set off a full-scale political crisis in Belgium, the next neutral country in the path of Army Group B. Belgium would surrender less than two weeks later, and the attitude of King Leopold III was already raising serious concern among British representatives in Brussels, including Admiral of the Fleet Sir Roger Keyes, a member of Parliament. Churchill's pugnacious old friend Keyes had been sent to serve as the prime minister's personal emissary to the king of the Belgians.

The meeting of the Chiefs of Staff in the Cabinet War Room at ten in the morning on the 15th, a meeting at which Dowding was to make his case in person, was not, as is sometimes imagined, small, select, serene, and orderly. People came in and out with news or information, and the prime minister, who was in any case late to arrive, was visibly distracted despite his formidable powers of concentration. He had had, as the saying goes, a lot on his plate during the past twenty-four hours. The day before, he had left 10 Downing Street briefly to greet Queen Wilhemina of the Netherlands and the Dutch royal family,* who had fled to London to avoid becoming prisoners of the Germans; in the early morning of the 15th he had been awakened by Reynaud's panicky call from Paris about the German breakthrough at Sedan; Admiral Keyes was already reporting rumors that the Belgian government was considering leaving Brussels; in the afternoon, Churchill would be drafting the first of his numerous long letters as prime minister to President Roosevelt, among other things requesting fifty destroyers from the United States.† The dominant issue on everybody's mind was of course the unexpected speed of the

---

* It was the right and patriotic decision—Wilhemina's fellow sovereign Leopold III would be widely criticized, and forced to abdicate after the war, for remaining in Belgium under German occupation, together with his mistress Lillian Baels, later the princess de Réthy. Among the other sovereigns who fled to London to keep their freedom of action were the kings of Norway, Yugoslavia, and Greece; among the other governments in exile in London were those of Poland, Belgium, Czechoslovakia, and France (in the shape of Charles De Gaulle's Free France).

† President Roosevelt had initiated what Churchill called this "intimate, private" correspondence in September 1939, when Churchill was still First Lord of the Admiralty in Chamberlain's War Cabinet. The letters between them fill three very substantial volumes—*Churchill and Roosevelt: The Complete Correspondence*, edited by Warren F. Kimball, Princeton University Press, 1984.

German advance, and the increasingly apparent chaos, dislocation, and defeatism of the French army.

The meeting began with Air Chief Marshal Newall in the chair, and those present included the First Sea Lord, the Chief of the Imperial General Staff (i.e., the three service chiefs), General Hastings Ismay as Churchill's chief of staff in the latter's novel dual capacity as prime minister and minister of defense, as well as a good number of their deputies and staff officers. At ten-thirty the meeting was briefly adjourned, and almost immediately resumed with Churchill himself in the chair. He reported on his telephone conversation earlier that morning with Reynaud, and added that the French prime minister had requested ten more fighter squadrons, to be sent to France immediately. At this point, Dowding, who had been waiting outside, was brought into the meeting, along with the Vice-Chief of the Air Staff, Sir Richard Peirse.

Dowding was not a complete stranger to Churchill—for one thing, he had commanded four squadrons of RAF bombers sent to Iraq in 1920, shortly after Churchill, T. E. Lawrence, and Gertrude Bell had created that country by drawing a line on a map of the former Ottoman Empire in a hotel suite in Cairo, to demonstrate that the warring Iraqi clans, sects, and tribes (united only in their dislike of British rule and of the Hashemite, Sunni king the British were about to impose on them) could be more cheaply and effectively subdued by bombing them than by maintaining a large and expensive garrison of British and Indian troops there. Since then, Dowding had clashed from time to time before the war with Churchill's prickly, imperious scientific adviser Frederick Lindemann (later Lord Cherwell), stubbornly rejecting some of his (and Churchill's) pet ideas on air defense. (For example, Dowding had defended radar in its infancy against Lindemann's mistaken belief that infrared rays were a better way of detecting aircraft.)

Stubborn, stiff, argumentative, unyielding, and of course as "stuffy" as his nickname promised, Dowding would not normally have been the kind of man who appealed to Churchill. Churchill's admirers always claim that he was a good listener, and there was some truth to that, but having listened, he expected to win the other person over to his side of the argument. Warmth of personality usually went a long way to win Churchill's respect for a man—that and a robust sense of humor—but nobody has ever claimed either of those qualities for Dowding. It was just as well that Churchill did not know that Dowding was a firm believer in the spirit world and thought he received guidance from his dead pilots as well as his late wife.

Churchill may also not have known that Dowding was a man with a grievance—actually several grievances. First, Dowding believed that he had been promised the post of Chief of the Air Staff, which his rival Newall now held; second, he had been fighting what he called the "inertia of the Air Staff" for years, and threatening to document in writing their neglect of Fighter Command's needs; third, the Air Staff had already retaliated by making it clear that no mercy would be shown to him when his appointment as Commander-in-Chief of Fighter Command ran out on July 14, 1940, and that he could almost certainly expect to be retired. (Although it was by far the youngest of the three fighting services—at the time only twenty-two years old—the RAF had more than its share of rivalry, mutual contempt, intrigue, and backstabbing among senior officers, and there were hardly any of his fellow air marshals whom Dowding had not at one time or another offended.) Churchill would have been made aware by Sinclair and Newall that Dowding was stubborn and difficult, if he did not already know it, but this cannot have been in the forefront of his mind that morning, when so much else was going on. Finally, apart from the grievances, and the long-standing hostility with the Air Staff, Dowding was also a man with a mission: to prevent the prime minister from doing what he wanted to do.[9]

Under any circumstances this would have been difficult for a mere Air Chief Marshal* to accomplish, but when the prime minister was Winston Churchill, as formidable a figure as British politics has ever produced, it was almost unthinkable. Churchill had clashed with senior military and naval officers from the very beginning of his career, starting with no less imposing a figure than Field Marshal the Earl Kitchener of Khartoum, and including along the way Admiral of the Fleet Lord Fisher, by far the most feared and respected First Sea Lord of his time, and Field Marshal Sir Douglas Haig. At no time, whether in or out of office or uniform, had Churchill ever hesitated to reject military advice or to confront even the most distinguished brass hats with his criticism and opinions. He was not, in the best of circumstances, a man who took opposition to his own plans, or even criticism of them, lightly or easily, and circumstances could hardly have been more difficult than they were on the morning of May 15. In short, Dowding was about to step on a hornet's nest, and knew it.

Neither this knowledge, nor the scowling presence of the prime minister seated in his wooden armchair at the table, apparently prevented Dowding from making a clear statement of his case. This moment in British history has been much embellished over the years with such stories as that of Dowding getting up, putting his charts of fighter strength in front of the prime minister, and forcing Churchill to look at them while leaning over his shoulder, drawing Churchill's attention to the important numbers by tapping at them impatiently with his pencil. But that seems unlikely, and those who were present

---

* The equivalent in the United States would have been a full (or four-star) general.

do not mention it; nor does there seem to be any credible founda-
tion for the story that Dowding threw his pencil down on the table
"in exasperation," though he may very well have felt like doing so.
Dowding was courageous, but not foolhardy or rude, and by nature
he was not a man for flamboyant displays of temperament. All we
know for sure is that Dowding, with his usual common sense, inter-
jected into the discussion of the first item on the agenda that he
"welcomed the proposal to attack the Ruhr," and sensibly deprecated
fears of German retaliation, since this was "bound to come sooner
or later"; and on the second item, the vital question of dispatching
more fighters to France, he "solemnly warned"* the prime minister
and the members of the War Cabinet against the danger of sending
any more fighters.

The matter of how many squadrons Dowding needed had been
brought up by Newall at the previous day's War Cabinet meeting—
Dowding thought that fifty was the absolute minimum, wanted (and
had been promised) sixty, and now had forty-six, of which the prime
minister was proposing to strip ten—but it was not discussed at this
meeting. Less than one-fifth of the meeting, in fact, was spent on the
subject of the fighters—the main subject of discussion was the decision to start bombing the Ruhr.†

However, Dowding's warning was "solemn" enough to impress
on the War Cabinet the need for caution on the subject of fighters.
That is hardly surprising, since Dowding's manner was deeply solemn to begin with, even over trifles. Newall, asked by Churchill to
give his opinion, replied, for once agreeing with Dowding, that he

---

* These are the words used by General Ismay in his *Memoirs*.

† A mixed force of about 100 twin-engine RAF bombers attacked the Ruhr on the night of
May 15–16; sixteen were unable to locate their target, and the remainder inflicted little
serious damage.

would not advise the dispatch of any additional fighters to France, and to Dowding's great relief the War Cabinet decided then and there that the prime minister should so inform Reynaud—another disagreeable conversation to which Churchill can hardly have been looking forward.

Perhaps because Churchill's mind was fixed on bombing, and because Dowding was telling him only what Newall had predicted, the prime minister seems to have come away from the meeting firmly (or conveniently) convinced that Dowding required only twenty-five squadrons with which to defend Britain. At any rate, this number stuck in Churchill's mind. In fact, when he wrote about it after the war, he went so far as to claim that Dowding had personally assured him that "twenty-five squadrons was the final limit."[10] This number is not reflected in the minutes of the War Cabinet meeting, and Dowding not only denied it vehemently to the end of his life but contradicted any such assumption in writing the next day.

Of course the significance of the number twenty-five in Churchill's mind was that if Dowding had forty-six squadrons and ten were sent to France he would still have more than the minimum number he needed to defend Britain. This would seem to indicate that while Churchill had heard Dowding (and Newall) out patiently, and subscribed to the decision of the War Cabinet, he retained "mental reservations" on the subject, and did not feel obligated to stop sending fighter squadrons to France, whatever Dowding might think about it.

Perhaps too, with all that was on his mind, he was neither listening nor doing sums in his head as carefully as he might have been. That being the case, it is easy enough to see how the prime minister may have mistaken the twenty-five *additional* squadrons that Dowding wanted for the total number he needed. In any event, Churchill was as likely as the rest of us to hear what he wanted to hear, and he was in a position to carefully rewrite history after the battle was won to show that his decision to send the fighters to France was in accord with Dowding's requirements.

Churchill devoted a lot of space, ingenuity, and thought to this subject in *Their Finest Hour*, Volume II of *The Second World War*, but for once he fails to be altogether convincing, since the only way he can show that he was doing everything he could do keep France in the war and defend Britain against attack is to claim that Dowding had promised him he could do so with twenty-five squadrons of fighters. Given Churchill's skill as a stylist—repetition is not one of his faults as a writer—the number of times he repeats this as a fact is a fair indication that it wasn't true, and that he knew it wasn't true.

As events proved, Dowding's "victory" was short-lived. The next day, further bad news from France (it was rumored, mistakenly, that German armored forces were within a day's march of Paris), together with the agonized calls for help from the French—and urgent signals from Air Marshal Barratt, the RAF Air Officer Commanding in France, to report that his fighter squadrons were being destroyed piecemeal rapidly, since they "had to deal every day with waves of 40 bombers every hour, heavily escorted by fighters," and that exhausted pilots were carrying out "4 to 5 sorties a day," despite "great numerical inferiority"—persuaded Churchill to overrule the War Cabinet's decision and send six more fighter squadrons at once to France. Newall, pointing out that this directly contradicted what Dowding had been told the day before, eventually managed to persuade him to reduce the number to four. Later in the day, however, the prime minister flew to Paris to meet with the French war cabinet, where the climate of pessimism and defeat was now so strong that when he went back to the British embassy late that night, "impressed by the moral gravity of the hour" and deeply concerned by the fact that the French were united in blaming the failure of their army on the lack of sufficient British fighter planes, he cabled the War Cabinet to increase the number of squadrons to be sent to France from four to ten.[11]

Either Dowding lost confidence in what the War Cabinet had promised him as soon as he was back at his desk at Fighter Command headquarters, or something that was said during the War Cabinet meeting triggered his doubts. Dowding was tactless; he never hesitated to tread brutally on the toes of his fellow air marshals and politicians; and he sometimes seemed inhumanly remote—but he was nevertheless a shrewd enough judge of men to tell when he was being led down the garden path (or "fed a line," in RAF slang). He did not trust Newall, and apparently he was not entirely convinced by Churchill's promise not to take away any more of his precious fighter squadrons. He therefore sat down to write surely the most important letter of his career, and put on the record exactly what he required to defend Britain:

> I have the honour to refer to the very serious calls which have recently been made upon the Home Defense Fighter Units in an attempt to stem the German invasion on the Continent.
>
> . . .
>
> 2. I hope and believe that our Armies may yet be victorious in France and Belgium, but we have to face the possibility that they may be defeated.
>
> 3. In this case I presume that there is no one who will deny that England should fight on, even though the remainder of the Continent of Europe is dominated by the Germans.
>
> 4. For this purpose it is necessary to retain some minimum fighter

strength in this country and I must request that the Air Council will inform me what they consider this minimum strength to be, in order that I may make my dispositions accordingly.

5. I would remind the Air Council that the last estimate which they made as to the force necessary to defend this country was fifty-two squadrons, and my strength has now been reduced to the equivalent of thirty-six squadrons.

   . . .

9. I must therefore, request that as a matter of paramount urgency the Air Ministry will consider and decide what level of strength is to be left to the Fighter Command for the defence of this country, and will assure me that when this level has been reached, not one fighter will be sent across the Channel however urgent and insistent the appeals for help may be.

10. I believe that if an adequate fighter force is kept in this country, if the Fleet remains in being, and if Home Forces are suitably organized to resist invasion, we should be able to carry on the war single-handed for some time, if not indefinitely. But, if the Home Defence Force is drained away in desperate attempts to remedy the situation in France, defeat in France will involve the final, complete and irremediable defeat of this country.[12]

Nobody could have put the situation in simpler or more brutal terms, and there is no doubt to whom Dowding was referring when he wrote, "not one fighter will be sent across the Channel however urgent and insistent the appeals for help may be." His letter made an instant convert of Newall—no mean feat, considering the degree of enmity between the two men—but it is hard to judge what effect it had on Churchill, who does not even mention it in *Their Finest Hour*, since it would have contradicted his statements that Dowding told him he needed only twenty-five squadrons. In the end, Churchill continued to press for more Hurricanes to be sent to France at the request of the French, but with increasing reluctance and alarm, while Dowding came up with the idea of basing the Hurricanes in southern England and flying them over to makeshift airfields in France for the day as a kind of sop to the French. Neither was satisfied, and the drain on Dowding's stock of Hurricanes continued until France surrendered.

In *Their Finest Hour*, Churchill is lavish with praise for Dowding—even, perhaps, suspiciously overlavish—but given what was to come on the subject of Dowding's future in the RAF one senses a carefully orchestrated attempt on Churchill's part to disguise a certain degree of dislike and resentment toward a man who not only had contradicted him but had turned out to be right. For Dowding's estimate of the number of squadrons he needed was exactly right, and even then he won the battle by only the very narrowest of margins. He had, as he surely guessed when he asked to present his case to the War Cabinet—again, Churchill confounds matters by suggesting that he invited Dowding to attend, whereas, in fact, it was Dowding who had insisted on being there—forfeited his future in the Royal Air Force. He would never become a Marshal of the Royal Air Force, the ultimate "five-star" rank, despite the personal intervention of the king; nor would he hold another active command. His enemies would be promoted over his head, and even his strategy for winning the Battle of Britain would be questioned officially, as if he had lost the battle rather than winning what was perhaps the most important victory of the war. Yet despite all this, it is Dowding who is rightly remembered as the man who won Britain's first victory in World War II, and who saved Britain from invasion. On a bronze plaque honoring him at Bentley Priory, his headquarters, the last paragraph reads,

TO HIM THE PEOPLE OF BRITAIN AND OF THE FREE
WORLD OWE LARGELY THE WAY OF LIFE AND THE
LIBERTIES THAT THEY ENJOY TODAY.13

In that sense, at any rate, it is "Stuffy" Dowding who had the last word.

CHAPTER 6

Round One:
"Der Kanalkampf"

With the return of more than 250,000 British soldiers from Dunkirk, there was a short interlude in the war. That is not to say, of course, that people were not dying—at sea, the Royal Navy and the German submarine fleet sparred; in France the fighting would continue until the French surrendered; in the air German and British aircraft fought when they saw each other; in Poland forced labor camps for Jews and frequent shootings and pogroms marked the first stages of the as yet unnamed "final solution." But both the Germans and the British were frantically (or systematically) preparing for what each knew was the next act of the war: the Battle of Britain.

The Germans first had to organize the military occupation and political control of Belgium, the Netherlands, Luxembourg, and most of northern France; and the *Luftwaffe* had to begin moving two entire

Luftflotten—General Albert Kesselring's *Luftflotte* 2 and General Hugo Sperrle's *Luftflotte* 3, a total of nearly 3,000 aircraft and all the personnel, equipment, and supplies needed to maintain them— forward to new airfields, a mammoth task. (*Luftflotte* 5, commanded by Colonel General H.-J. Stumpff, was installed in Norway and was intended to bomb the north of England.) On the British side, the fighters and fighter pilots returning from France had to be refitted as squadrons, and the aircraft lost between May 10 and the completion of the Dunkirk evacuation had to be replaced—a total of 453 of Dowding's precious fighters had been destroyed in combat, in accidents, or on the ground.

This was the period in which the British prepared themselves for invasion—the period of the Local Defence Volunteers (as noted earlier, Churchill would shortly produce for them the more inspiring name Home Guard) training with antiquated weapons on the village greens of southern England and harassing motorists at improvised roadblocks; the period in which the troops who had returned from Dunkirk were rearmed, reintegrated into their regiments, and transformed back into "real soldiers" with shiny boots and gleaming brass by drill sergeants and sergeant-majors at regimental depot parade grounds all over the country; the period in which children by the thousands were evacuated to the countryside, or, in some cases, across the Atlantic,* in anticipation of the battle to come. Rumors spread fast and wide—that German parachute troops had descended in Belgium disguised as nuns to seize or blow up vital points (this

---

* The author was evacuated to Canada (in the early autumn of 1940) at the age of seven, as were his friends the distinguished historians Sir Alistair Horne and Sir Martin Gilbert. Churchill deplored this vast upheaval of children, which was a relic of the Baldwin/Chamberlain era, when it was believed that major urban areas would be destroyed overnight by bombers. He finally managed to put a stop to the evacuations after the *City of Benares*, carrying hundreds of evacuees, was torpedoed by a German U-boat hundreds of miles from shore.

rumor prompted policemen and busybodies to harass puzzled and indignant nuns all over southern England); that the bodies of thousands of German soldiers had floated ashore onto the Channel beaches after a failed invasion attempt; that German spies had placed numbered metal markers on the telephone poles leading inland from the beaches to guide the German invading forces toward London (these were of course the GPO's standard tin tags identifying the poles as post office property). Road signs were hastily removed, to the great inconvenience of travelers, and a brash and newly promoted lieutenant-general, Bernard Montgomery, first came to the attention of the prime minister by suggesting that his corps should be held as a mobile reserve and transported to where it was needed in confiscated tour buses when the invasion came.

President Roosevelt had responded politely with a discouraging message about the fifty destroyers Churchill had requested—the fact was, and Churchill sensed it better than anyone, that although the "miracle of Dunkirk" had won guarded admiration in America, it was nevertheless a defeat. Backing Britain was still a bet against the odds. From London, the United States' ambassador, Joseph Kennedy, sent home to Washington deeply pessimistic messages about Britain's chances of survival,* and despite Churchill's rhetoric there was widespread doubt throughout the neutral world that the British could or would resist Hitler when the crunch came. Britain needed not only American destroyers, but rifles, ammunition, steel, oil, aviation gas, aircraft of all kinds, beef from Argentina, wheat from the Midwest, and above all unlimited credit with which to purchase all these things

---

* Kennedy's dislike of the British was deeply reciprocated by them. He made no secret of his belief that they were beaten, or of his lack of confidence in the RAF. His fear of being bombed made him leave London every night he could, prompting one Foreign Office wit, according to the historian Andrew Roberts, to remark, "I thought my daffodils were yellow until I met Joe Kennedy."

and more. The only way to secure that credit was with a victory—an evacuation, however heroic and successful, would not persuade hard-headed bankers, businessmen, politicians, and treasury officials to loosen their purse strings. The British Army was clearly in no position to provide one, and the world at large was apt to take for granted any victory at sea by the Royal Navy. The only people in a position to provide a convincing display of the British will to fight—and, more important, to deliver a victory—were Dowding's young fighter pilots, his "chicks," as he liked to call them, of whom he had at this time just over 1,000.

To put this in perspective, in the early days of June 1940, when the attention of the entire world was turned toward Britain, its survival depended primarily on four things: (1) Dowding's 1,000 "chicks," (2) the daily output from the factories of enough new Hurricanes and Spitfires (and the Rolls-Royce Merlin engine which powered them) to make up Fighter Command's losses, (3) the efficiency of Dowding's "system," and (4) the validity of his strategy.

This fourth point was to become a fiercely controversial issue between Dowding and his critics, no doubt in part as a result of his reluctance to communicate or share with others what he had in mind. He took it for granted that the Germans would outnumber the forces at his disposal (in this he was perfectly correct), and therefore did not want to fight big air battles, which might give the enemy a chance to calculate the real strength of Fighter Command. His approach was that of a skilled poker player—he intended to bluff the Germans by never revealing what he had in his hand. In order to achieve this, Fighter Command would attack them in squadron strength, an endless series of lethal pinpricks that would inflict on the German bomber force a rate of loss it could not afford to sustain in the long run, while at the same time allowing the Germans to believe that Fighter Command was much weaker than it was. He did not want a big battle, a kind of aerial Trafalgar or Waterloo; he wanted to wage a war of attrition that would keep the Germans guessing. Göring's inflated overconfidence was an asset Dowding counted on: he wanted the Germans to think that Fighter Command was at the end of its resources, so they would keep on coming—and continue to take heavier losses than they could replace. He also wanted his pilots to concentrate on the German bombers, not the fighters, because the bombers were more expensive to produce and carried a highly trained crew of four, much harder to replace than a single fighter pilot. In short, Dowding's strategy was to surprise and baffle the Germans—it was his answer to the unavoidable fact that the Germans, when they came, would outnumber him in men and machines. Above all, he wanted to hide from the Germans the fact that radar and ground control were Fighter Command's most important assets.

Unfortunately for Dowding, whose tactics (and character) in some respects resembled those of General Mikhail Kutuzov, the heroic historical figure who appears in Tolstoy's *War and Peace*, neither his colleagues at the Air Ministry nor some of his senior commanders nor many of his pilots understood what he had in mind. His intention was to bleed the *Luftwaffe* to death, not to prevent it from bombing England, which he had not the strength to do—and not to encourage fighter-to-fighter combat, which was a waste of men and machines.

The difference between Dowding's strategy and what the War Cabinet and the Air Staff wanted became apparent as soon as the *Luftwaffe* took over airfields in northern France and launched a series of initially small-scale attacks against British coastal convoys sailing through the Channel. The Germans had moved their Stukas to the new airfields first—with its fixed landing gear and robust construction the Ju 87 was easy to maintain and to fly off relatively primitive grass airfields, and of course was ideal for providing the equivalent of aerial artillery for the German army. It was also, at least in theory, the perfect weapon for sinking British coastal steamers and Royal Navy destroyers as they plodded through the English Channel in small convoys on their way from Belfast, Liverpool, Cardiff, or Bristol to London. Dowding would have preferred to eliminate the convoys altogether, which in his opinion would merely have put a somewhat greater strain on the British railway system, rather than to waste precious fighters and fighter pilots defending them, but here he confronted a firmly entrenched element of British pride going all the way back to the days of the Spanish Armada and beyond—neither the prime minister nor the Royal Navy could contemplate conceding control of the Channel to the Germans. Whatever value the convoys had—the bulk of what they carried was coal—there could be no question of allowing the Germans to stop them. Attempts to equip the convoys of small, slow steamships with barrage balloons trailing long wires did not discourage the German attacks on them, and Churchill complained that the precautions taken for the safety of the convoys were "utterly ineffectual"—indeed when one of them lost thirteen ships out of twenty-one, he described it, with pardonable exaggeration, as "one of the most lamentable episodes of the naval war as it has so far developed."[1]

As the two German *Luftflotten* settled into their new airfields, the *Kanalkampf* heated up. For the *Luftwaffe*, it was both a trial of strength and a good way of training crews for what was coming. The single-engine Ju 87s were soon joined by larger twin-engine bombers like the Ju 88s, and covered by an escort of Messerschmitt fighters, and by early summer a considerable air battle was taking place every day over the English Channel.

This was a source of concern to Dowding—the German airfields were so close to the Channel that there was not enough time for his radar operators to give the fighter squadrons of No. 11 Group sufficient advance warning to be useful, and the German bombers often flew too low for the radar beams to pick them up, and also took the opportunity of carrying out hit-and-run rooftop raids on English coastal towns. This meant that Dowding's fighters had to fly patrols over the Channel, and that the fights inevitably degenerated into disorganized aerial brawls at low altitude, wild "mix-ups," as British pilots described them, just the kind of uncontrolled chaos Dowding most wanted to avoid. The Stukas had at first been easy prey—they were slow, and when they pulled out of a dive they were completely vulnerable to fighters attacking from above—but as the Messerschmitts began to protect them from above, British losses started to mount up. During June and July Fighter Command lost ninety-six aircraft, and the Germans 227.* The Germans were actually losing more than twice as many aircraft attacking the coastal convoys as Fighter Command was losing defending them, but that was no consolation to Dowding, who wanted to build up his strength, not to dissipate it protecting coal.

Some hard lessons were learned on both sides. One was that the Germans were far better provided with emergency equipment in case they came down in the sea. German aircrews not only had rubber dinghies that rose to the surface and inflated automatically but also had bright yellow flying helmets that, along with fluorescent dye, made

---

* Throughout this book I have tried to use the actual number of aircraft shot down on both sides, as confirmed in German and British postwar records. Very few of Fighter Command's aircraft were then equipped with a "ciné camera" to record "kills" during the Battle of Britain, and in the confusion of an air fight many pilots naturally claimed the same plane. The Germans also exaggerated the number of British aircraft they shot down. In both countries confusion was abetted by propaganda.

their airmen more visible in the water to the crews of German rescue seaplanes. Many British pilots, by contrast, would die of hypothermia, bobbing in the sea in their Mae West jackets within sight of the bathing beaches of southern England. Air Vice-Marshal Park finally managed to secure a few Lysander reconnaissance aircraft to operate with the eighteen motor launches that should have been in service long before, but the rescue of airmen from the sea remained one area in which the *Luftwaffe* continued to act with more efficiency and apply greater resources than the RAF.

As for the Germans, they could hear the calm, steady voices of the fighter controllers on the ground talking to the British fighter pilots, and they concluded that each squadron of British fighters was directly controlled. In short, they assumed that the organization of British squadrons was both local and too rigid for squadron commanders in the air to make tactical decisions on their own, exactly the opposite of what was true—and above all they failed to guess the degree to which the whole system depended on radar and was centralized at Bentley Priory under Dowding's constant supervision. Since Dowding deliberately kept his attacks small, the Germans also jumped to the conclusion, early on, that the British had far fewer fighters than was really the case, and that these would soon be worn down to an insignificant number.

The air battles over the Channel gave Dowding a chance to rethink his strategy. Clearly, the situation that had faced Fighter Command in 1938 and 1939 was radically altered, because the Germans now held the French side of the Channel. The short distance from the German airfields there to London meant that German bombers could carry their maximum capacity of bombs, vastly increasing their "weight of bombing," to which would have to be added the bomb loads of Stumpff's 129 bombers in *Luftflotte* 5, in Norway, although they would have to attack without fighter cover, since the distance was too great for the Bf 109s to accompany them across the North Sea.

Dowding therefore faced a number of serious new problems, with very little time to correct them. First of all, the prewar assumption that the thrust of the German attacks would come from northern Germany over the Netherlands in a westerly direction was no longer true. The bulk of the attacks would now be coming almost directly north from Belgium and France instead, and at a much closer range. This necessitated an expansion and a quick reconfiguration of Dowding's radar coverage, which would also have to be extended to the north of England and Scotland to cover attacks from Norway, particularly those aimed at the Home Fleet's vital anchorages in the north. It also required the refinement of his plan for dividing the United Kingdom into independent but mutually supportive Fighter Groups. There were now four Groups: No. 13 Group in the north, with its headquarters near Newcastle; No. 12 Group in the Midlands, with its headquarters near Nottingham; No. 11 Group to cover the southeast of England (including London) from a line drawn from Southampton to Bury Saint Edmunds, with its headquarters at Uxbridge; and No. 10 Group to cover the southwest of England and Wales, with its headquarters near Bristol. Since Dowding anticipated that the major German attack would be made around the greater London area, Group No. 11—under the command of Air Vice-Marshal Keith R. Park, DSO, DFC, a New Zealander—was the strongest of the groups in numbers of squadrons, aircraft, and airfields. To Park's north, No. 12 Group was commanded by Air Vice-Marshal Trafford Leigh-Mallory, CB, DSO (a brother of the ill-fated British mountain climber who had become a national hero when he died attempting to climb Everest). Leigh-Mallory, a pugnacious and independent-minded commander, was no friend of Park's, nor, when the time came, particularly loyal or even obedient to Dowding.

The boundaries of each group were drawn with great care, and had been carefully thought out by Dowding. They might be invisible from the air, and at 300 miles per hour it was easy enough for pilots to overlook them, but they served a purpose in his plan and he did not intend them to be ignored when the serious fighting began. In this he was optimistic, or perhaps naive—certainly, throughout his career Dowding expected (and deserved) more loyalty than he got.

The most significant exception was, of all people, the dynamic and widely distrusted press tycoon Lord Beaverbrook, millionaire owner of the *Daily Express* and the *Evening Standard*, whom Churchill had made Minister of Aircraft Production over the strong objections of the king (and the queen). "The Beaver," as he was known to those close to him (Evelyn Waugh caricatured him triumphantly as "Lord Copper," owner of "the *Daily Beast*," in his novel *Scoop*), was one of Churchill's most loyal friends, and one of the very few people on whose advice Churchill counted in both his political and his private life. (Another was Brendan Bracken, against whom the king and queen had raised even stronger and more outraged objections when Churchill eventually made him Minister of Information.*) Beaverbrook was mischievous, temperamental, shrewd, demanding,

---

* The author met Lord Beaverbrook several times—he was a friend of Alexander Korda's, and like Korda he enjoyed spending time on the Côte d'Azur, where he had a luxurious villa. Brendan Bracken (later the Viscount Bracken, PC) was another family friend, and also a self-appointed adviser and godfather figure to the author as a young person. Both Beaverbrook and Bracken were larger-than-life personalities, brash, acerbic, witty, tough-minded, and self-confident, whose only allegiance, apart from self-interest, was to Churchill.

mercurial, capable of great charm when it suited him and brutal when it did not, and endowed with a sharp, boisterous sense of humor (though largely at the expense of other people), as well as being a world-class hypochondriac, gossip, and womanizer. He ran his newspaper empire like a dictator. William Maxwell ("Max") Aitken was by birth a Canadian (hence his choice of Beaverbrook for his title). He had been a power behind the scenes in British politics since before World War I, and had made and unmade prime ministers, amassing a huge fortune and many enemies along the way. Beaverbrook and Bracken, both adventurers from humble (and in Bracken's case, somewhat mysterious) backgrounds who had risen to wealth and power in England, were generally described by more conventional Conservatives, whose instinctive loyalty was still owed to Neville Chamberlain, as "gangsters." (Anthony Eden and the circle around him were known derisively by the same kind of people as Churchill's "glamour boys.")

Churchill, overruling the Beaver's pleas of ill health, chose him for the job of increasing aircraft production, which had fallen badly behind schedule, counting on Beaverbrook's energy and ruthlessness to get the job done, even though Beaverbrook knew little or nothing about manufacturing airplanes. This turned out to be an advantage—what Beaverbrook did know how to produce was results, and of course how to motivate and when necessary bully men; and he did in fact quickly succeed in increasing aircraft production significantly, despite the fury of the Air Council and the aviation industry at having control over the production of all types of aircraft taken out of their hands by a brash, rude, hard-driving ex-colonial Fleet Street newspaper proprietor. If Beaverbrook did not quite perform the miracles he later claimed—good public relations for himself was one of the things the Beaver understood best—he nevertheless kept the flow of aircraft coming out of the factories in sufficient quantity to meet Fighter Command's needs, and devised ingenious ways to make new aircraft out of damaged ones, and even out of the Air Ministry's jealously hoarded stock of spare parts. His most curious accomplishment was that although they were, on the face of it, complete opposites, he and Dowding got along like a house on fire from the very first.

This was only in part because they both had an only son serving as a fighter pilot (the Honorable Max Aitken would go on to become a Wing Commander and win the DSO and the DFC) each of whom called his father every evening to report that he was still alive; Beaverbrook also appreciated the fact that Dowding, like himself, did not hesitate to challenge accepted wisdom, hated meetings and committees, and treated anybody who got in the way of what he wanted as an enemy or an idiot. Dowding's peculiar (but profound) religious beliefs, his shyness with strangers, and his down-to-earth common sense, earnestness, and distrust of higher authority struck Beaverbrook, a Canadian, as more natural and familiar than these qualities seemed to most native-born Englishmen. Dowding, though he sometimes appeared unworldly, had made a career of shocking people and defying authority (although in his own more quiet way) just as Beaverbrook had, and the two men slipped almost immediately into a comfortable working relationship. Neither Dowding nor Beaverbrook bothered to go through channels, deal with paperwork, or inform the Air Ministry—the most important priority of the war at the time was dealt with by a single telephone call between two busy men every night. Every evening Beaverbrook would pick up the telephone and call Dowding (or Air Vice-Marshal Park, the only one of his commanders for whom Dowding seemed to feel affection, whose No. 11 Group would take the brunt of the losses), and ask how many fighters were needed for the next day; and in the morning the fighters would arrive without fail or fuss, often delivered by young civilian women pilots of the Air Transport Auxiliary (ATA).

A flight mechanic's reaction to that remarkable innovation, on his first sight of an ATA pilot, is quoted in Richard Hough and Denis Richards's book: "A Hurricane landed and taxied up to the watch office. The pilot switched off the engine and got down from the cockpit, and while walking to the watch office took off the flying helmet and patted up her hair—a 'flapper'—couldn't have been more than nineteen—delivering a Hurricane to replace one of our losses. I couldn't believe it!"

Just like Dowding, Beaverbrook ignored hierarchies. He gave the most important posts in the Ministry of Aircraft Production to successful businessmen, not to RAF officers or to presumed experts from the aviation industry; it was his idea to have women ATA pilots take fighters straight from the factories to the airfields;* he rode roughshod over anyone, of any rank, who got in the way; he kept important people waiting while he talked to technicians or craftsmen who could tell him how to produce more Hurricanes, Spitfires, and Merlin engines faster; he made what he thought the RAF should have, not what the Air Ministry said it needed, and delivered it where he (and Dowding) thought it ought to go—the two men might have been made for each other.

Beaverbrook succeeded in part by ruthlessly concentrating on fighter production at the expense of other kinds of aircraft, and in part by refusing to allow for the modifications and improvements in the existing designs continually demanded by the Air Ministry, but

---

*The Air Transport Auxiliary was formed in 1940 and included 166 women pilots, who delivered everything from Spitfires to bombers.

he somehow managed to raise the number of fighters produced each month from 261 to nearly 500. It was not a miracle, but it was enough. Like "Stuffy" Dowding, the Beaver was not one to pause and seek anybody's permission—when thwarted, he went straight to Churchill, or, via his friend Harry Hopkins, to Franklin Roosevelt if the matter involved the United States. Indeed, he made one of the most important decisions of the war, when, fed up with negotiating with a reluctant Henry Ford to mass-produce Rolls-Royce Merlin engines in America, he swiftly changed horses and made a deal with Packard to manufacture them instead. This would lead to putting the British aircraft engine into an American airframe, that of the P-51 Mustang, hitherto powered by the somewhat anemic Allison engine, thus creating the P-51 D, the first successful long-range escort fighter of the war, which would make possible the American daylight bombing campaign against Germany from 1943 on.

From the other side of the Channel there was still, despite British expectations of an invasion or an aerial onslaught at any moment, a certain amount of hesitation. Stepping out of character, the usually cautious General Milch had advised Göring to attack Britain before the British troops had even been evacuated from Dunkirk. Milch's rival generals in the *Luftwaffe* might make fun of him as an airline official dressed up in a general's uniform—not to speak of the fact that he was either half Jewish or illegitimate, depending on which story you chose to believe—but his suggestion to Göring was bold and brilliant and might just have succeeded. He saw at once that dive-bombing the British Army at Dunkirk was not going to prevent most of the troops from getting off the beach, and advised an astonished Göring to forget about Dunkirk altogether and attack Britain at once, before the British had a chance to sort themselves out. Use the Stukas to destroy Fighter Command's forward airfields in southeastern England and to disrupt road and rail communication, drop the elite *Luftwaffe* paratroop division to seize and hold several carefully selected airfields, then fly in as many troops as the Ju 52 transports could carry—undertake, in short, a daring and unprecedented aerial coup de main to gain a beachhead in England, and do it *at once*, while the British were still reeling from defeat in France and Belgium; then follow it up with whatever the German army and the navy could get across the Channel.

Göring was dismayed by Milch's idea and the vehemence with which Milch urged it on him, and it has since been dismissed by most historians as foolish, but it might in fact have made more sense than sitting around for the next ten weeks or so while the *Luftwaffe* and Fighter Command fought in the skies over the Channel and southern England. True, most of the big airborne operations undertaken in World War II would prove to be disasters, with the exception of the British and American air drops the night before the D-day landings,* but who knows what a bold, imaginative move might have accomplished? Certainly, the War Cabinet of May 26, during which Halifax announced that he had been talking to the Italian ambassador about asking Mussolini to inquire of the Führer what terms he would offer Britain for peace, might have taken a very different course if the Germans had been in Kent, rather than on the other side of the Channel.

---

* The German parachute attack on Crete in 1941 was a success, but also a classic Pyrrhic victory—losses were so high that henceforth the German parachutists fought as an elite light infantry division. The American parachute landing in Sicily in 1943 was disastrous, and the full-scale attack on Arnhem in the autumn of 1944 by British parachute forces was a heroic and bloody defeat, brilliantly described in the book and the film *A Bridge Too Far*.

In any event, Göring turned Milch down, arguing rather weakly that he had only one parachute division, and that the army would not divert any of its forces while fighting was still going on in France. Though few people were closer to Göring than Milch, or more realistic about most things, it was Milch's misfortune to have retained his illusions about his boss. Göring enjoyed a reputation for boldness, but he remained hopelessly subservient to Hitler, and he knew better than anyone else that Hitler had not yet made up his mind what to do about Britain. Not until mid-July would Hitler finally give the order to proceed with the planning for Operation Sea Lion, as it would be called. And the tone of the eventual order is not the usual crisp "Off with his head!" style of Hitler's directives to initiate major military campaigns, like the one for the invasion of Czechoslovakia ("It is my unalterable decision to smash Czechoslovakia by military action in the near future"). Rather, it reads: "Since England, despite her hopeless military situation, still shows no sign of readiness to come to an understanding, I have decided to prepare a landing operation against England and if necessary carry it out."

This is not exactly a stern rallying cry; indeed, it seems to suggest that Hitler was still waiting hopefully for good news from London in the form of a peace offer or a change of government, almost six weeks after Churchill had put an end to Halifax's cautious feeler. This pause was all the time Dowding (and Beaverbrook) needed to prepare Fighter Command, so long as the fight over the Channel was not allowed to get out of hand and Churchill was restrained from sending any more Hurricanes to France. Very fortunately the downward spiral of the French government, once it had abandoned Paris and set out on a series of moves to shabby hotels and town halls in provincial France, was swift enough to persuade even so passionate a Francophile as the prime minister to "turn off the tap"

of Hurricanes to France, in Dowding's phrase, though not a minute
too soon.

Dowding's own personal situation had not improved, despite the
crisis—his command was still scheduled to end on July 14, and even
this date had been reached only after a lamentable number of slights,
which Dowding strongly resented. In 1937, he had been promised
that he would be employed until he reached age sixty (in 1942), only
to be told in 1938 that he must relinquish Fighter Command immediately and retire; then, after his replacement was injured in an air
crash, he was given a rather grudging reprieve for one year, and at
the same time informed that he must leave the RAF by June 1939—a
decision made more painful for Dowding by the fact that somebody
in the Air Ministry leaked to the press the false news that he had
retired long before he was due to. His retirement date was then
pushed back until the end of the year, and then extended orally to
the end of March 1940. At the last moment, however, his old rival
Newall called him "one day before his scheduled retirement and
asked him to stay on until July 14th." One day! This was a deliberate
act of rudeness, but Dowding swallowed his pride and did not resign, much as he was tempted to—he was not a vain man, but he
knew that nobody else in the RAF could do the job, or understand
the system he had built, as well as he could. He carried on a punc-
tilious but increasingly prickly, one-sided, and resentful correspondence with Newall and the Air Staff on the subject of his retirement,
and asked—not unreasonably in the circumstances—whether he
had the full confidence of the Secretary of State for Air and the Chief
of the Air Staff. It is clear enough that he was being treated with remarkable discourtesy, and that many of his fellow air marshals were
intriguing against him. Dowding's own confidence in his political
and military masters was not increased by the fact that so much of

this was done at the last minute and by telephone in an undignified spirit of hugger-mugger, leaving ample scope for deniability and last-minute changes of mind.

Dowding seems to have behaved throughout all this with quiet dignity—certainly with more dignity than his enemies—and he did not let it affect his job. Nor did he voice any complaints to those around him—he was in any case the polar opposite of the kind of "matey" commanding officer who chats with his subordinates over a drink—or go public on the subject of his ill-treatment by leaking it to the press, and his fighter pilots and the people around him at Fighter Command headquarters therefore remained unaware of the hostility toward their commander.

As for himself, Dowding was a supreme realist, and so was entirely conscious of the fact that the prime minister was unlikely to have enjoyed being told, at the War Cabinet of May 15, that he was wrong about sending more fighters to France. He had been very conscious that he was putting the remainder of his career at risk when he insisted on appearing at the War Cabinet to make his case. Dowding later said of Churchill and himself that after this meeting, "there was no chance of our ever becoming friendly," which was putting it mildly. Many historians have argued that Churchill admired Dowding for having stood up to him, but Dowding's view was surely closer to the mark. Though Churchill covered himself very adroitly in his memoirs, in fact he neither forgot the incident nor forgave Dowding, who could not—and did not—count on the prime minister's support in any dispute between himself and the Air Ministry.

Dowding was still scheduled to give up his command on July 14, and so, as he surely must have been aware, he would be leaving Fighter Command (and very likely the RAF) just as the force that he had largely created went into action to save the country from invasion.

Ironically, the date when Dowding was to leave Fighter Command would be only two days after Hitler finally signed his long-awaited directive to the German armed forces putting the planning for Sea Lion into high gear, and was only extended at the very last minute to October, with considerable fuss and bad feeling, after the prime minister himself learned of it and personally intervened.

There can have been very few other instances in warfare when a commander was required to give up his post on the eve of a decisive battle.

CHAPTER 7

Round Two:
Sparring

To those who still remember it, the summer of 1940 was idyllic—warm, halcyon days; blue skies; perfect weather—or at least as perfect as it gets in and around the United Kingdom. All over southern England, people near the seacoast were being evacuated in anticipation of the invasion—100,000 sheep were also evacuated, to safer pastures farther north—while soldiers dug trenches, built pillboxes, and sited what little they had in the way of artillery and machine guns in anticipation of a German landing. The argument about what should be done with Fighter Command's forward airfields in the event of an invasion was succinctly settled as usual by Dowding, who sensibly ordered that they were to be "defended at all costs and for as long as possible." Once the aircraft had been removed, remaining RAF ground personnel were to join the soldiers to defend the airfields with whatever weapons they had, and demolition of the runways, equipment, and buildings should take place only at the last possible moment.

Among Dowding's many concerns was the continued unreliability of radar in indicating the height of an enemy attack. This was a known defect of the radar system—the vital third dimension of height was a problem the boffins (scientists) had been working on for months, with only spotty success. One of the main reasons for backing the radar chain up with the Observer Corps was that in good weather an observer on the ground with a pair of binoculars and an elementary knowledge of trigonometry could calculate the height of an enemy raid the moment it came into view, but of course there was no way to do so when German raids formed up over the sea or approached their target from above the clouds. Dowding relied in part on the reasonable assumption that the Germans would probably bomb from about the same height as RAF Bomber Command, which was then seldom much more than 12,000 feet, since at the time not all RAF bombers were provided with reliable oxygen or heating equipment. This was a reasonable assumption— most of the German bombing force was not much better equipped in these respects than the British, except for the more modern Ju 88, which had its own problems. Dowding estimated that 15,000 feet would be about the maximum height for German bombers, but of course the escorting fighters would be coming in much higher, well above them, so as to have the advantage of speed when they dived to engage the British fighters that were climbing to attack the bombers.

Throughout the battle to come, Fighter Command would operate with an excellent picture of the course and speed of German raids, a fair estimate of the number of aircraft in each raid, and a somewhat unreliable estimate of their height, unless it had been confirmed from the ground. The system was not perfect—there had not been enough time to make it so—but it would be good enough.

Dowding was more concerned with the need for his group commanders to prevent their pilots from concentrating on the German fighters flying at high altitude and ignoring the bombers below them. He recognized that fighter-to-fighter combat in the tradition of "Von Richthofen and his Flying Circus" during World War I would be an almost irresistible temptation; but the bombers were the more valuable prey, and the objective was to stop them from bombing. In short, he wanted discipline and control maintained over the battle, not a free-for-all in the skies, and achieving this, as it turned out, would give him almost as many problems as the Germans did.

Dowding's forces included approximately 700 Hurricanes and Spitfires;* 1,400 balloons (or "gas bags"), which, with their trailing wires, would present low-flying German aircraft, particularly the dive-bombing Ju 87s, with serious problems; and Lieutenant-General Sir Frederick Pile's antiaircraft guns and 4,000 searchlights. Many of Pile's heavy guns were superannuated; he was well below strength in more modern rapid-fire guns like forty-millimeter cannon; and there were never enough to go around to defend every city, port, factory, and airfield in the United Kingdom—before the war the chiefs of staff had estimated that he would need 4,000 guns, their latest estimate was 8,000, and the reality was that he had about 2,000. However, the mere presence (and sound) of Pile's antiaircraft guns would be a source of comfort to everyone close to them, and volunteers to man them (and the searchlights) would soon include HRH Princess Elizabeth, the elder daughter of King George VI and heir to the throne, as

---

* Although about two-thirds of Dowding's fighters were Hurricanes during the Battle of Britain, the glamour of the Spitfire was such that German aircrews invariably claimed to have been shot down by *Spitfeuren* even when the fighters in question were Hurricanes.

well as a curious assortment of the nobility, writers, poets, artists, and intellectuals.

Once again, just as he had before Dunkirk, Hitler hesitated, with the result that Dowding had a welcome, though unexpected, breathing space to review and consolidate his forces. His fighters were divided into four principal groups, the two weakest being No. 13 Group, covering the north of England and Scotland; and No. 10 Group, covering the west of England. Of the two strongest Groups, No. 12 Group covered the largest area, basically the industrial Midlands; and No. 11 the most likely target area, the south of England and London, as well as the beaches where the invasion would land when it came. No. 11 Group, commanded by Air Vice-Marshal Park, was the strongest, containing twenty-five squadrons (including one Canadian and one Polish squadron); No. 12 Group, commanded by Park's ambitious and energetic rival Air Vice-Marshal Leigh-Mallory, consisted of nineteen squadrons (including four Polish and two Czech squadrons).

By the end of June, Dowding had just over 1,300 fighter pilots. Most of them were British, and few of them had had any combat experience. During the course of the battle Fighter Command would also draw on fifty-six carrier pilots from the Royal Navy's Fleet Air Arm, as well as a mixed bag of twenty-one Australians, 102 New Zealanders, ninety Canadians,* twenty-one South Africans, two (white) Rhodesians, one (white) Jamaican, nine Irish volunteers, seven Americans, 141 Poles, eighty-six Czechs (one of whom, Sergeant Joseph František, would become the RAF's second-highest-scoring ace in the Battle of Britain), twenty-nine Belgians, thirteen Free French aviators, and one Palestinian Jew.[1]

---

* A few of the Canadians were, in fact, Americans who had crossed the border and joined the RCAF to get in the war, to the consternation of U.S. ambassador Joseph Kennedy in the UK, who was anxious to keep American citizens from joining the RAF.

Three of the more colorful Americans served together in No. 609 Squadron—they had volunteered to fly with the Finnish air force against the Soviet invaders; journeyed, with numerous adventures, from Helsinki to France when Finland surrendered to Stalin; and from there caught the last Channel crossing to England. They were spending the last of their money in a pub near the Air Ministry at lunchtime and told their story to a sympathetic RAF Air Commodore over a drink who told them "to get in touch with him tomorrow." The next day they were given commissions in the RAF, and sent out with money to buy their uniforms. Pilot Officer "Red" Tobin from California had worked as a studio messenger at MGM to pay for his flying lessons. Pilot Officer "Shorty" Keough, was, at four feet ten inches, the shortest pilot in the RAF, and needed a couple of inflatable pillows under his parachute to see over the cowling of his Hurricane. Pilot Officer "Andy" Mamedoff, a stunt flier from Miami, had barnstormed his own plane all over America. None of them survived the war.[2]

By the official end of the battle just over one-third of Dowding's pilots would be casualties—killed, seriously wounded, or missing. There is a tendency in modern fiction about the Battle of Britain to present Fighter Command as a kind of happy-go-lucky multinational force, full of foreign volunteers and soldiers of fortune, but except for the Polish and Czech squadrons and the one Canadian squadron, foreigners were relatively few and predominantly English-speaking; the vast majority of the pilots were British, middle-class, and very young. That they were high-spirited almost goes without saying—for many it was the great adventure of their life, and a large number of them went straight from school to the cockpit of a Spitfire or a Hurricane.

The Germans' primary goal during the battle was to destroy Fighter Command, but thanks to Dowding's cautious tactics—although he was not a card player, he had a deft poker player's instinctive skill at concealing what was in his hand—they would never come nearly as close to doing so as they fondly believed. Although Dowding always complained that he was short of pilots, his strength actually grew during the four crucial months of the battle, from 1,456 to 1,727; and the number of fighter aircraft available for operations on a daily basis remained constant at about 700, with an average delivery of about 1,000 new fighter aircraft a month to the operational squadrons. At the height of the battle, in August and September, the number of new aircraft in storage units being prepared to operational readiness would certainly dip alarmingly (to the consternation of the prime minister), but at no point would the *Luftwaffe* come anywhere near to crippling Fighter Command, let alone, despite Göring's boasts, to clearing the skies above the Channel and southern England for long enough to make a German invasion possible, or even plausible.

Although it is usual to portray the Battle of Britain as a kind of modern, aerial contest between David and Goliath, with the *Luftwaffe* playing Goliath, the reality is that although the German bomber force in the three air fleets facing the British was very substantial—nearly 1,000 serviceable bombers on August 10, 1940—the number of single-engine fighters meant to protect them was not all that much greater than those available to Dowding: 805 serviceable Bf 109s versus Dowding's 749 Hurricanes and Spitfires. In the category of fighter aircraft, the additional 224 Bf 110 twin-engine "heavy fighters," far from being an asset, would themselves require the protection of the single-engine Bf 109s to survive in air combat.* (The 261 Ju 87 Stuka dive-bombers would also prove almost useless.[3])

---

* The official numbers of aircraft in both air forces were separated into three distinct categories—"establishment," meaning the number of aircraft a unit was supposed to have, on paper; "strength," meaning the number of aircraft it actually had on a given date; and "serviceability," meaning the number of aircraft in full repair and ready for operational service on a given date. These numbers are frequently mixed up, carelessly, by historians,

In pilot strength, the Germans had certain advantages. *Luftwaffe* major generals did not pick up foreign pilots in bars—first, because the vast, covert Nazi training schemes from 1933 on had created large numbers of pilots; and second, because the *Völkische* nature of Nazi Germany meant that service in the air force was limited to those young men of pure German (or Austrian-German) birth, who could satisfy the authorities that they were of Aryan descent. Ultimately, the British were willing (though not necessarily eager) to take anyone who was white (i.e., "European," American, or from the dominions and colonies) and could fly an airplane, whereas in Germany, aircrew status was limited to those with "pure German blood."*

The actual number of German fighter pilots available was roughly similar to that of Fighter Command, but mere numbers do not of course tell the whole story. Since the battle would be fought largely over England (or the English Channel), in most cases when a German aircraft was shot down it—and more important, its pilot—would be gone for good, whereas British pilots, if they were lucky, could parachute or crash-land their aircraft on British soil, and might be back with their squadrons and in action again on the same day. (As for the aircraft, Lord Beaverbrook had made elaborate and very efficient arrangements for the immediate repair or salvage of downed Spitfires and Hurricanes, at Civilian Repair Depots, and for salvaging downed

---

as if they meant the same thing, but it is only the last category that matters. Aircraft being serviced or repaired, or standing idle because a part is missing, do not fly on operations. Thus, to take an example at random, on August 10, the three German *Luftflotten* assigned to attack Britain were supposed to have 1,011 Bf 109s, but in fact had 934, of which 805 were serviceable.

* Under German racial laws, those of "mixed" blood, i.e., *Mischlinge* of the first degree, with one or two Jewish grandparents, were on the one hand obligated to serve in the armed forces, but on the other could not rise above the rank of sergeant or serve in such elite units as aircrew or submarine crews. They were also constantly threatened by the Gestapo's determination to treat the *Mischlinge* as if they were full Jews, which the German army resisted, not out of an interest in racial justice, needless to say, but because such a policy would reduce its manpower pool.

German aircraft to produce aluminum for building more British fighters.) The Germans could certainly replace pilots who were killed or captured, but in most cases they were obliged to replace an experienced fighter pilot with one just out of flying school—not the same thing at all.

Thus, German losses of men and machines were final, whereas those of the RAF were not necessarily so. This was a factor that neither Göring nor anyone else in the *Luftwaffe* seems to have considered seriously when contemplating a full-scale aerial attack against Great Britain. Dowding, on the other hand, had given it a good deal of thought, in his typically logical and precise way. It explains his lack of enthusiasm for letting Park's No. 11 Group loose to tangle with the *Luftwaffe* over Dunkirk, and his reluctance to use Park's fighters to protect coal convoys in the English Channel from German air attack—in Dowding's view, such protection was largely an exercise to prove to the Germans that the Channel was still English. Aircraft shot down over the Channel were gone for good, and pilots who parachuted or crash-landed in the Channel were difficult to recover, especially since they didn't have the inflatable life rafts, fluorescent water markers, and bright yellow flying helmets with which the *Luftwaffe* equipped its aircrews.

Dowding's stubborn, logical mind often brought him to conclusions that surprised other people, whose judgment was more easily swayed by emotion. It was Dowding's decision that the slow, cumbersome German He 59 air-sea rescue floatplanes, although painted white and marked with conspicuous red crosses, were not entitled to any protection under the Geneva Conventions. They were picking up from the Channel downed German aircrews who would be used again against Britain as soon as they were back with their units, and were also suspected of radioing back the course and position of British convoys. He ordered Fighter Command to shoot them down, or to machine-gun them if they were on the sea performing a rescue (a position in which they were truly sitting ducks), an unsporting order that surprised his pilots and outraged the Germans. This gave the Germans a short-lived propaganda victory, until they gave up the red crosses, camouflaged the He 59s, marked them with a swastika and black *Luftwaffe* crosses, and armed them with a machine gun.

Who but Dowding could have worked out in his mind, following the same line of reasoning, that under the Geneva Conventions the Germans were entitled to machine-gun British pilots in the air over England as they descended to safety by parachute, because they would return to their units to fight again; but British pilots were not entitled to machine-gun Germans parachuting from their damaged aircraft, since they would be made prisoners of war on landing? This decision struck many of Dowding's colleagues as either inhumane or ridiculous, but that was because, unlike Dowding, they had not read the Geneva Conventions attentively or unemotionally and had not drawn the correct conclusion. As it turned out, in practice very few fighter pilots on either side were likely to deliberately machine-gun a man parachuting to the ground, or at 300 miles per hour had any way to determine if he was British or German. Dowding himself did not think it was likely; he merely wanted a neat, tidy resolution to the question. It was the kind of mental exercise, however, that did not win him friends among politicians or his fellow air marshals—indeed even the prime minister questioned his judgment, comparing a parachuting airman to "a drowning sailor"[4]—and made even a few of Dowding's pilots wonder if their Commander-in-Chief might be cracked.

By July 3, the underlying tension between Air Chief Marshal Dowding and Air Vice-Marshal Leigh-Mallory, the commander of No. 12 Group, had become apparent, at a conference about tactics held at

Fighter Command Headquarters. Dowding and Leigh-Mallory disagreed about the length of time the Germans would spend attacking Fighter Command's airfields before an invasion, and Dowding then proceeded to make it clear that he expected his group commanders to keep "a pretty good control" over their squadrons, and to ensure that each squadron received precise orders as to whether to attack the enemy bombers or enemy fighters. He was determined that fighter pilots should not become "obsessed" with the German fighter escort above instead of attacking the bomber force itself, which could be expected to be flying at a lower altitude. In short, Dowding wanted the Group Commanders to prevent "a free-for-all" battle in the sky over England—they were to use their squadrons judiciously, keep an ample number in reserve, support each other, and follow his orders. Since Dowding already knew that Air Vice-Marshal Park would do just that without being told, and since No. 10 Group and No. 13 Group would be on the fringes of the battle, it is hard not to guess that his remarks were aimed at Leigh-Mallory.[5]

Leigh-Mallory was not Dowding's only problem air marshal. Dowding had already clashed with the ambitious, hard-thrusting Air Vice-Marshal Sholto Douglas, Assistant Chief of Air Staff in charge of training and the purchase of new equipment at the Air Ministry, on the subject of the Boulton Paul Defiant and on the usefulness of twenty-millimeter cannon instead of .303-caliber machine guns in his fighters, among other things. Douglas was the polar opposite of Dowding, a burly, pugnacious, aggressive former fighter pilot and a member of the numerous Douglas family, which included Lord Alfred Douglas, Oscar Wilde's beloved Bosie, as well as his father, the ninth marquess of Queensberry, who was the popularizer of the famous rules for boxing matches and who brought about Wilde's ruin.

About the Defiant, Dowding had been proved right, an outcome that won him no friends at the Air Ministry; and on the subject of twenty-millimeter cannon he was not impressed by either of the two types that had so far been tested, or convinced that four cannon would necessarily give better results than eight machine guns. Dowding was all in favor of arming fighter aircraft with cannon in the long run, but first he wanted to make sure they were reliable, and in his opinion this was not yet the case. In the short run, he did not want to disrupt the production of Spitfires and Hurricanes by changing their armament. In the corridors of the Air Ministry, it was easy to portray Dowding's caution on such subjects as a lack of enthusiasm for new ideas, and attribute this to his age, his stubbornness, and his own crank notions, as well as to the fact that it had been very long since he had flown himself.

It is hard to know if Dowding was aware at this stage of the degree of hostility that already existed between himself and the two men who would be most instrumental in bringing about his downfall (and would benefit most from it), but it would have been out of character for him to have shown any concern or interest, still less to try to patch things up. After all, his enemies already included the Chief of the Air Staff and, in the aftermath of his blunt talk on May 13 about the danger of sending more Hurricanes to France, very likely the prime minister, even if Churchill's enmity was at an unconscious level. A different kind of Commander-in-Chief might have made a man-to-man effort to win Leigh-Mallory over, or at least to keep him in line (Eisenhower would later do so quite effectively for a time), and to sweet-talk Sholto Douglas, a man with a considerable ego even for an air marshal, who was at once vain, prickly, and well-connected. Dowding had no gift for this kind of thing, however, and no taste for it. It was not in him to flatter, persuade, charm, inspire, or trade gossip with his fellow air marshals, still less to involve himself in their interminable intrigues.

He understood how to win the battle, and that was that—he had been thinking about nothing else since 1936.

Across the Channel, as the *Luftwaffe* moved into the French airfields of Normandy and Brittany and made itself at home, German strategy was still unclear, awaiting Hitler's decision about the invasion. The navy was beginning to assemble a growing invasion fleet of tugboats, river barges, and sea barges, whose effectiveness has been depreciated by most historians, though it is worth remembering that an even less promising and much more hastily assembled fleet of Channel steamers, motor yachts, lifeboats, Thames River day cruisers, tugs, and fishing vessels had brought more than 250,000 British soldiers off the beaches of Dunkirk and home to England, despite the best efforts of the *Luftwaffe* to stop them. Compared with the "small ships" of the Dunkirk evacuation, the German navy's fleet of tugs and barges seems quite impressive, especially considering that it was being improvised at high speed and with no advance preparation, since until Dunkirk, the prospect of invading Britain had never come up. The British and the Americans would labor for more than four years to create a fleet for the Normandy invasion, whereas the Germans were attempting to do it in less than three months.

What hampered the Germans was a combination of sloth and wishful thinking at the top. Hitler was still stunned by the magnitude and completeness of his victory over France, and no doubt still expected to receive a call from England any day, from Lord Halifax or Lloyd George, to ask for peace terms; and Göring was enjoying himself in Paris and savoring the endless congratulations and promotions for himself and his favored commanders. Lower down on the totem pole, overburdened staff officers struggled to solve the problems of an improvised invasion and to produce a coherent strategy for victory once the troops were on shore in Britain, but the timetable was still unclear, and there was no single, energetic commander-in-chief—no equivalent of Eisenhower—to pull the three German services together in a single, united effort.

Hitler's patience came to an end abruptly and unexpectedly on July 3, when a British battle squadron, commanded by Vice-Admiral Sir James Somerville, appeared off the French naval base of Mers el-Kébir, near Oran in French Morocco, and demanded that the French fleet anchored there, commanded by Admiral Gensoul and including two battleships and the two powerful modern battle cruisers *Dunkerque* and *Strasbourg*, sail either to a British port or to a French port in the Caribbean, or that Gensoul should sink his own ships within six hours. Failing this, Somerville reported regretfully, he had orders from His Majesty's Government "to use whatever force may be necessary to prevent your ships from falling into German or Italian hands."[6] Negotiations continued throughout the day, but Admiral Gensoul finally rejected the British demands. A few minutes later, at five-fifty-three that evening, Admiral Somerville opened fire, crippling the French fleet and killing more than 1,200 French sailors.

French warships in Alexandria, Egypt, as well as Portsmouth and Plymouth, were boarded by British sailors and seized, and a modern French battleship in Dakar was fired on. Announcing this tremendous show of naval force (albeit against a former ally) to the House of Commons, Churchill concluded, with tears in his eyes, "A large proportion of the French Fleet has, therefore, passed into our hands or has been put out of action or otherwise withheld from Germany. . . . I leave the judgment of our action, with confidence, to Parliament. I leave it to the nation, and I leave it to the United States. I leave it to the world and history. . . . The action we have already taken should be, in itself, sufficient to dispose once and for all of the lies and rumors . . . that we have the slightest intention of entering into negotiations in any form and through any channel with the German and Italian Governments. We shall, on the contrary, prosecute the war with the utmost vigor." [7]

Here was the long-awaited answer to Hitler's "peace offer" speech, and, by the way, also to Halifax and Lloyd George. In a highly dramatic way, Churchill had demonstrated both Britain's sea power and his own resolve to keep on fighting. For the first time as prime minister he received the loud, unstinting applause and cheers of his own party—for while the conservatives had accepted, with whatever reluctance, the inevitability of Churchill as prime minister on May 10, their hearts had until now remained with Neville Chamberlain, who had hitherto received warmer applause from his own side of the House than Churchill had even for some of his greatest and most memorable war speeches. But this time the lion had not only roared, he had struck, and struck hard, and all over the world (particularly in the White House) people took notice at last that whatever had happened to France, Great Britain remained an undefeated imperial power, with a measure of its old ruthlessness and defiance, and that the voice of Britain was not a plea for peace at any price, but the thunder of fifteen-inch naval cannon. Nowhere was this message heard more clearly than in Berlin.

On July 13 Hitler at last signed off on the army's plan for Operation Sea Lion, setting a target date of August 15 for the invasion and turning the *Luftwaffe* loose to destroy RAF Fighter Command before that date. He was still not fully committed to the invasion: that is, he had mental reservations about whether he should do it or not. But it was no longer theoretical; it was a plump military plan, with fixed dates and elaborate maps, and it was now up to Göring to strike the first blow.

Still not in a hurry, the newly created *Reichsmarschall* (a unique rank placing Göring one step above a field marshal) did not meet with his *Luftflotte* commanders until July 20, at his baroque country estate, Karinhall, where they were left to their own devices to come up with a strategy. By now, the Führer was becoming impatient for action, though at the same time, giving way to the reality of the army's and navy's slow preparations for the invasion, he delayed the target date for the invasion to September 15, with the *Luftwaffe*'s grand full-scale air attack to begin on August 5. Even so, he retained firm control over the decision to launch the invasion, which he intimated he would make only after the RAF had been destroyed.

There are two observations to be made about this. The first is that any military undertaking of this size and complexity should not have too many "escape clauses" built into it—an army needs to know that on such and such a date an attack will begin, with no ifs, ands, or buts. The second is that May, June, and July are the months when a cross-Channel invasion has the best chance of succeeding, because of the weather and the long hours of daylight. In 1944, Eisenhower was obliged to postpone the invasion of Normandy from early May to early June, and was prepared to delay it if necessary until July, but he regarded September as dangerously late in the year—the days would be too short; the weather would be chancy; the possibility of major storms would be vastly increased. If Milch (now promoted to field marshal) had been able to persuade Göring to persuade Hitler to launch a hastily improvised invasion immediately after Dunkirk, before the British were organized to resist it and while the weather was most propitious, it might have succeeded. But choosing September 15 as the target date was a landlubber's decision, and should have been resisted by the German admirals, who knew better.

In short, Hitler still resembled a man in bathing trunks on a beach, dipping his toe into the sea and unable to decide whether to plunge in or not. As for the *Luftwaffe*, pending the full-scale attack, it set about a series of smaller-scale raids on English coastal towns and seaports to test the British air defenses. On July 15, it bombed Yeovil (hardly a worthwhile military target); from the 16th through the 18th it was (shades of things to come) hampered by bad weather; on the 19th it took advantage of some good weather to bomb Dover; and from the 20th through to the end of July it raided shipping, concentrating on the Dover area. During July it shot down 145 British aircraft but lost 270 of its own—not exactly a triumph.* At the same time, this was hardly a triumph for Fighter Command, either. By attacking the seacoast of England from across the Channel in small numbers and at a low altitude the Germans were, without realizing the fact, depriving the radar operators of enough time to scramble RAF fighter squadrons. By the time the Germans appeared on the radar screens, it was too late. Things would be very different, Dowding realized, once the Germans began to come in force and attack inland. Dowding's critics felt he should be getting his fighters scrambled sooner and in larger numbers, so that he could attack the Germans in force and "give them a bloody nose," but that was exactly what he did *not* want to do. His strategy

* For the day-by-day details of the Battle of Britain, I have relied on two principal sources: *The Royal Air Force Battle of Britain Campaign Diary*, which is very accurate about weather, British fighter losses, and RAF and civilian casualties, as well as the exact damage inflicted by *Luftwaffe* raids, but is not necessarily accurate about German losses; and *The Narrow Margin*, by Derek Wood and Derek Dempster, Pen and Sword Military Classics, Barnsley, U.K., 1961, which is almost equally detailed and gives revised, accurate numbers for German losses, based on an analysis of postwar German records.

was to make the Germans think Fighter Command was weaker than it was, to concentrate on their bombers, and to bleed them to death by a constant rate of attrition. He did not want large losses, and he particularly did not want large losses over water.

As it happened, the Germans believed exactly what Dowding wanted them to believe. The relatively low numbers of British fighters they met convinced them that Fighter Command's strength was small—Göring was informed that the British had left, at most, 300 or 400 fighters—and that, when the time came, a few massive full-scale attacks were all it would take to destroy them. The Germans were also lulled into not thinking seriously about the effect radar and Dowding's system of centralized control would have over the battle once they attacked farther inland in large numbers—indeed, they seem to have paid hardly any attention to it.

The weather in the first days of August was marked by frequent low clouds, drizzle, and thunderstorms. As a result, Göring, who was waiting for four uninterrupted days of clear weather in which to launch the great attack that was intended to cripple Fighter Command—now grandiosely code-named *Adlerangriff*, "Eagle Attack"—kept putting it off, in anticipation of "a belt of high-pressure from the Azores" that stubbornly failed to appear. *Adler Tag*, "Eagle Day," had been scheduled for August 5, but haze prevented it—in the event, a small, inconclusive fight between British and German fighters over the Channel resulted in the loss of six German aircraft to one British. August 6 and August 7 passed with little activity, since the German *Luftflotten* were busy preparing for the great attack. On the 8th, a large attack against Channel convoys by Ju 87 Stuka dive-bombers guarded by Bf 109s gave further proof, if any was needed, that the Stuka was vulnerable in the presence of British fighters—the Germans lost thirty-one aircraft to nineteen British. (The *Luftwaffe* claimed to have shot down forty-nine British fighters, and the RAF claimed sixty German aircraft downed, causing rejoicing at 10 Downing Street, and showing just how far pilots' claims exceeded reality on both sides.) Eagle Day was now moved to the 10th, then canceled once again because of bad weather; and the 11th resulted in a large-scale brawl over the Channel, apparently intended to draw large numbers of British fighters over Dover to be "bounced"* by Bf 109s while the German bomber force attacked Portland, a tactic that would have worked only if the British hadn't had radar. The result was a day of bitter fighting, which ended in almost equal losses, thirty-eight German to thirty-two British. The most important event of the day, unbeknownst to the British, was the first sign of the high-pressure weather from the Azores that Göring had been waiting for. Eagle Day was hastily moved to August 13, with a preliminary "softening up" on the 12th, during which the *Luftwaffe* would knock out the forward British fighter airfields on the coast and the radar stations—ironically, the 12th was an important date on the British upper-class sporting calendar, the "glorious twelfth," the opening of grouse-shooting season.

Though he was not normally an early riser, *Reichsmarschall* Göring himself, clutching his new baton, attended the beginning of operations at seven in the morning on the 12th, accompanied by field marshals Sperrle, the commander of *Luftflotte* 3; and Kesselring, the commander of *Luftflotte* 2, and surrounded by a glittering staff. Expectations were high.

August 12 would be a taste of things to come. The weather was fine; the Germans came in large numbers; and their strategy was well

---

* "Bounce" was RAF slang for a surprise attack. You bounced or got bounced by the enemy. The origin is social-sexual—an overenthusiastic, or unexpected and unwelcome, sudden embrace, as in "She got bounced in the taxi on the way home."

thought out, but largely thwarted by poor intelligence work, severe overoptimism, and faulty interpretation of reconnaissance. German bombers struck at Fighter Command coastal airfields like Manston, Hawkinge, and Lympne and dropped large numbers of bombs, but most of the airfields were back in service again by the next day, although the *Luftwaffe* wrote them off as "destroyed." Certainly, a great deal of damage was done, but for the most part it was nothing that couldn't be put right with shovels and a bulldozer—and of course a great many of the bombs fell in the surrounding fields, where they did no harm except to the crops of nearby farmers. The concentrated attack against the radar stations should have paid off, but the dive-bombers aimed at the tall radar towers, which looked fragile but were almost impossible to hit from the air, instead of concentrating on the more vulnerable underground operation centers and the plotting huts, without which the radar masts were useless. In most cases the radar stations continued to function, and Dowding's decision to use young women from the WAAF as radar plotters was justified—without exception, they showed amazing courage and coolness, and continued to work even when under direct attack. The day proved, even to doubters, that the young airwomen could take it as well as men, and also saw the first casualties among the WAAFs.

Dowding's foresight in burying the connecting telephone lines from the radar stations to the group and command filtering rooms deep underground and shielding them in concrete, a decision about which the members of the Air Council had been so skeptical, also turned out to have been money well spent. At the end of the day the Germans claimed to have destroyed seventy British fighters, whereas in fact the British lost twenty-two aircraft and the Germans thirty-one. Only one radar station was put out of action, and none of the forward fighter airfields was put out of action for long, although the

Germans assumed they had been. The 12th ended on a bizarre note with a German night attack on Stratford-upon-Avon, birthplace of William Shakespeare, and then as now a quaint tourist town, of no strategic importance to Fighter Command. The day that had been intended to maul Dowding's fighters in anticipation of Eagle Day and destroy Fighter Command's "eyes and ears," its radar stations, for tomorrow's big attack, had done nothing of the sort, although the *Luftwaffe* high command was convinced that it had, and that Fighter Command was already on the ropes. One can understand why, of course—if you started with the assumption that RAF Fighter Command might have as few as 300 fighters left, then went on to assume that you had destroyed seventy of them, as well as putting the coastal airfields and two of the radar stations permanently out of action, then the day would seem to have been a promising, perhaps even a triumphant overture to the big attack. But, as it happened, this was not the truth.

Seen from the British side, however, the day seemed worse than it had in fact been. The attacks on the radar stations, although not particularly successful, seemed to demonstrate that the Germans understood the vital importance of knocking them out, and would concentrate on them from now on; and although the attacks on the forward airfields had been ineffective, they had nevertheless done a great deal of damage, and showed that the Germans had the right idea. A sustained and increasingly well directed bombing campaign, concentrated on the radar sites and his airfields, was what Dowding feared most.

Indeed, the day was serious enough that Dowding might have supposed that the 12th was the opening of the big *Luftwaffe* attack he was expecting, if he had not been tipped off by Churchill that it was planned for the next day. Although Dowding was not yet on the se-

lect list of recipients of "Ultra" information,* thanks to the Poles the
code breakers at Betchley had already deciphered the mysteries of the
German armed forces' Enigma ciphering machine, and were able to
read the flow of orders from Berlin to *Luftflotten* 2 and 3, including
Göring's grandiloquent order of the day:

> REICHSMARSCHALL GÖRING TO ALL UNITS:
> ADLERANGRIFF! YOU WILL PROCEED TO SMASH
> THE BRITISH AIR FORCE OUT OF THE SKY.
> HEIL HITLER![8]

*He would be placed on the list October 16th by Churchill personally (Martin Gilbert, *Finest Hour*, page 849).

CHAPTER 8

Adlerangriff, August 1940

I have the heart and stomach of a king, and of a king of England too, and think foul scorn that Parma or Spain, or any prince of Europe should dare to invade the borders of my realm.

—*Elizabeth I, speech at Tilbury, August 18, 1588*

You must consider that no wars may be made without danger.

—*Sir Roger Williams, in a letter to the Earl of Leicester,*
*from the besieged town of Sluys, August 1588**

Despite all the modern technology at the disposal of the *Luftwaffe*—and although it consistently underestimated the importance of British radar, it had, as would shortly become apparent, a few tricks of its own up its sleeve—it was in one respect no better off than the duke of Medina Sidonia was as he led the Spanish Armada, 130 great ships in all, past The Lizard, the first landfall in Cornwall, into the English Channel on July 29, 1588. The weather would still determine the success or failure of the attack, in a part of Europe where bad weather was notoriously common.

Philip II's ambitious plan for the conquest of England had been that Medina Sidonia should sweep through the Channel with his

---

* Sir Roger Williams is thought by many to have been the inspiration for Shakespeare's Captain Fluellen in *Henry V*.

immense fleet, destroying the English fleet on the way, then meet with the duke of Parma—Europe's most formidable soldier—off the ports of the Spanish Netherlands, and help ferry his army across to England in flatboats, to restore the Catholic faith. The Spanish Armada was defeated in part by the smaller and more nimble ships of the English and by the superior seamanship of the English captains in their own familiar waters, but the weather also played a large role. The duke required a good steady wind from the southwest, clear weather, and calm seas for the final stage of his campaign, but none of these was consistently forthcoming. Tacking about in rough seas, with patches of fog, many of his ships became separated from each other in the treacherous waters of the Channel, with its hidden rocks, shoals, currents, and sandbars, and its enormous tides, and fell prey to the English before the "invincible" Armada was anywhere near its goal.

Now, 352 years later, Göring faced a similar problem. He required a protracted period of good weather to bomb southern England on a scale sufficient to destroy Fighter Command's airfields, and the factories in which Hurricanes, Spitfires, and the Rolls-Royce Merlin engine they both used were produced. Every day of fine weather was to the Germans' advantage. On the other hand, every day of rain, fog, or low cloud cover was an advantage to Fighter Command, since it gave Dowding's fighter squadrons a chance to rest, repair damaged facilities, and service their aircraft. We know everything about the weather in 1588—it was such an important factor that on both sides, every captain noted it in his logbook, with every change of wind and course. Likewise, in every detailed, day-by-day account of the Battle of Britain the description of the events of each day begins with the weather for that date. For the airmen, as for the sailors of the sixteenth century, weather was the single most important (and least predictable) element of the battle. Of course meteorology had improved substantially since the duke of Medina Sidonia's time, but it was still by no means an exact science, and failure to get it right could still have serious consequences.

As if to demonstrate this, *Adler Tag*, the opening day of *Adlerangriff*, was a fiasco. Intended as a giant blow with the full strength of *Luftflotten* 2 and 3, it got off to a muddled and disastrous start. The RAF described the weather for the day as "Mainly fair . . . early morning mist and slight drizzle in some places and some cloud in Channel." Perhaps only a British meteorologist would describe mist, drizzle, and cloud as "mainly fair"; in any case, the German meteorologists felt, on the contrary, that the weather forecast was bad enough to call for the delay of *Adler Tag*, and Göring, with whatever impatience, agreed, and ordered the attack postponed until the afternoon, when the weather was supposed to improve. Unfortunately, his signal canceling the morning attack did not arrive in time to stop some of his units, which had already taken off at dawn—a perfect example of the wisdom of Napoleon's famous remark, "*Ordre, contreordre—désordre*," and of Göring's amateurish and self-indulgent behavior as a commander. It is not clear whether the signal failed to reach the German units that went on with the attack or whether they were simply determined to "press on regardless," to use the popular British military phrase for attacking despite an order to stay put or against insurmountable difficulties; but for whatever reason *Kampfgeschwader* (KG) 2,* with seventy-four Dornier 17 bombers under the command of Colonel Johannes Fink, a tough-minded, competent veteran aviator

---

* A *Geschwader* was (very) approximately the equivalent of a British Group, and should contain a strength (on paper) of about 120 aircraft of the same or similar type, though by this time few had anything like that number in fact. A *Kampfgeschwader* consisted of bombers, a *Jagdgeschwader* of Bf 109 fighters, a *Zerstörergeschwader* of twin-engine Bf 110 fighters, and a *Stukageschwader* of Ju 87 dive-bombers.

of World War I, went on even after the signal was relayed to it and many of its fighter escorts had turned back, some of the fighters because they had received the signal, others because they couldn't find the bombers they were supposed to accompany in the clouds. Either way, it was exactly the kind of military muddle Napoleon had warned against.

The plans for *Adler Tag* had been drawn up with exemplary German precision, with exact times and courses for every unit involved— nothing was left to chance, and everything was spelled out in detail. It was a military masterpiece, intended to totally eliminate muddle, but it did not take into account human error (such as Göring's impulsive decision to postpone the attack at the last minute, or the fact that some of the bombing force was equipped with radio crystals of a different frequency from those in the fighters, thus making it impossible for their fighter escorts to communicate with them, and vice versa), or the difficulty of unforeseen weather.

A further problem, which would emerge during the course of the day, was that however sophisticated the plan might be, it was based on poor intelligence. Colonel Josef "Beppo" Schmidt, the *Luftwaffe*'s chief of intelligence, seems to have been better at telling his boss what he wanted to hear than at providing useful targeting information. The purpose, after all, was to deliver a knockout blow to Fighter Command. There was no deliberate intention here of bombing civilian targets, or of sowing terror among civilians, so the situation was unlike the bombing of Warsaw and Rotterdam, or the "Blitz" against major British cities later that autumn, or for that matter the massive "area bombing" of major German cities by RAF Bomber Command from 1942 to the end of the war—and the Germans' targets were carefully calculated with the objective in mind.

Given that objective, it is all the more surprising that the plan called for so many widespread attacks on targets that were unlikely to hurt Fighter Command. It was not as if the British had made any serious attempt to hide or keep secret the location of Fighter Command's airfields, still less the factories in which the fighters were built, or Fighter Command Headquarters, or the vital radar towers, some of which were clearly visible in good weather from across the Channel with binoculars. Much of the information the Germans required was easily available before the war in guidebooks; in the British government's excellent, detailed Ordnance Survey maps, which could be bought at any bookstore; in news stories; or even from the local telephone directory. Had the German air attaché in London cared to spend his holidays before the war driving around southern England with a few Ordnance Survey maps in the glove compartment of his car, and a Shell Motorist's Guide and a pair of binoculars appropriate for bird-watching on the seat beside him he could easily have picked out most of the vital targets of Fighter Command—it did not require the services of a master spy, nor did the Germans have one in Britain. (One of the Japanese military attachés provided Tokyo with a more accurate view of Fighter Command's strength by taking up golf and playing regularly at golf courses close to RAF fighter airfields.) It would be symptomatic of the whole day that although 120 Ju 88 bombers of *Lehrgeschwader*, or LG, 1 (the *Lehrgeschwader* were elite "demonstration" units formed around a nucleus of experienced instructors) spent nearly an hour bombing Southampton in the afternoon, they merely destroyed the Raleigh Bicycle factory, Pickford's furniture storage warehouse, and a refrigerated meat storage depot, leaving untouched the Vickers-Supermarine factory in which Spitfires were produced. (A second, larger "shadow" factory had been completed at Castle Bromwich, near Birmingham, but production difficulties caused largely by the fact that it was under the control of the imperious Lord Nuffield, the automobile manufacturer, who was at odds with Lord Beaverbrook, meant that the Southampton factory was still the primary producer of the aircraft in 1940.)* There was nothing at all secret about the Spitfire factory at Woolston—it was large, easy to find, marked clearly on city maps, and listed in the Southampton telephone directory—and at least in theory one would have thought LG 1 worth sacrificing if necessary to destroy it.

Colonel Fink—whose aircraft had bombed a Coastal Command rather than a Fighter Command airfield, another result of faulty intelligence from Beppo Schmidt's staff—had not been alone in failing to receive the recall message. *Kampfgeschwader* 54 attacked the RAF airfields at Odiham and Farnborough, neither of which was a Fighter Command airfield; and a substantial force of Bf 110 twin-engine fighters that had flown out to support the KG 54 bombers failed to find them in the clouds, made a landfall just west of the seaside resort town of Bournemouth about fifty miles away from KG 54 as the crow flies, and got bounced by British fighters for their pains. By mid-morning those Germans who had failed to receive (or ignored) the recall were back at their bases, having accomplished nothing of value and complaining bitterly— Fink the most loudly of all—about the absence of fighter support and the fact that whatever radio device the British were using to detect German aircraft, it was still working all too well, despite

---

* This was one of the fruits of an immensely ambitious nationwide industrial program going back to the days of Stanley Baldwin and Neville Chamberlain, in which a second "shadow" factory was set up for each of the most critical weapons of the three services, so as to be able to increase production swiftly in the event of war and to ensure an alternative and fully functioning manufacturing site in case the original one was bombed. Once again, the "appeasers" were more foresighted than their critics (or the Germans) guessed.

claims that the whole system had been put out of action the day before. Fink had lost five bombers, and had many more damaged; KG 54 had lost four aircraft; and the Bf 110s of *Zerstörergeschwader* (ZG) 2 had lost one fighter. Despite the iffy weather and poor visibility of the morning, Air Marshal Park's RAF fighter squadrons had apparently experienced no difficulty at all in finding the German raiders—a fact that struck Fink and many others (but apparently not Beppo Schmidt) as deeply disturbing and worthy of further investigation. (It is notable that although Fink was upset by KG 2's losses, they were in fact substantially below 5 percent, which RAF Bomber Command deemed an "acceptable" rate of loss for operations.)

Clearly, Fink, like many in the *Luftwaffe*, assumed that the raids on the 12th had severely damaged Fighter Command's power to resist, and was startled by the number of British fighters that nevertheless appeared, and the apparent ease with which they found him. As it happened, Fink also had the bad luck to be attacked by Flight Lieutenant Adolph "Sailor" Malan of No. 74 Squadron, a burly South African who would prove to be one of the most determined, successful, and intelligent RAF aces of the Battle of Britain. (Malan was the author of "Ten of My Rules for Air Fighting," which was printed as a poster for display at fighter airfield dispersal huts. The first rule was *"Wait until you see the whites of his eyes!"**) Fink had also been attacked by one of the only two Hurricanes in Fighter Command armed with twenty-millimeter cannon instead of machine guns, flown by Flight Lieutenant Roddick Lee Smith of No. 151 Squadron. Smith was a convert to cannon. Despite the fact that the heavier guns and their bulky ammunition drums reduced

---

* Emphasis is Malan's. Rule number ten was "Go in quickly—Punch hard—Get out!" The poster is reprinted on page 170.

the Hurricane's speed and maneuverability, he believed that they "packed a much greater punch and at a longer range," and managed to demonstrate it convincingly.

TEN of MY RULES for AIR FIGHTING

1 <u>Wait until you see the whites of his eyes.</u>
Fire short bursts of 1 to 2 seconds and only when your sights are definitely 'ON'.

2 Whilst shooting think of nothing else; brace the whole of the body, have both hands on the stick; concentrate on your ring sight.

3 Always keep a sharp lookout. "Keep your finger out"!

4 Height gives <u>You</u> the initiative.

5 Always turn and face the attack.

6 Make your decisions promptly. It is better to act quickly even though your tactics are not the best.

7 Never fly straight and level for more than 30 seconds in the combat area.

8 When diving to attack always leave a proportion of your formation above to act as top guard.

9 INITIATIVE, AGGRESSION, AIR DISCIPLINE, and TEAM WORK are words that MEAN something in Air Fighting.

10 Go in quickly – Punch hard – Get out!

The morning, however chaotic, should have been a warning to the Germans that Fighter Command had *not* been seriously inconvenienced by the ambitious operations of the previous day, and should also have given them a clue that Dowding's elaborate, carefully thought out system of radar and centralized fighter control was the key to the battle. German signals intelligence reported that all the radar stations were back in service—the British were sending out a dummy signal to conceal the fact that the Ventnor station on the Isle of Wight was still under repair—but this news does not seem to have interested anyone in the *Luftwaffe* high command, perhaps because Field Marshal Kesselring now had an angry *Reichsmarschall* Göring (and Göring's sumptuous private train, *Asia*) on his hands at his headquarters, as well as an even angrier Fink to deal with.

Kesselring managed to shake off Göring and his entourage long enough to fly to Arras and calm Fink down, and by noon the weather had improved, as promised. The sky cleared, the sun came out, and it was decided to proceed with *Adler Tag* late in the afternoon as if nothing had happened.

If numbers alone could do the trick, the *Luftwaffe* had certainly amassed an impressive force—a combined force of 197 Ju 87s and Ju 88s would attack the Southampton area, with heavy fighter protection, while farther east large numbers of Ju 87s, escorted by fighters, would cross the Channel between Calais and Boulogne to attack the Short aircraft factory at Rochester, in Kent, and the airfield at RAF Detling, near Maidstone. Once again, however, German intelligence seems to have been misinformed. Although the Germans missed the Vickers-Supermarine factory in Southampton, the Short aircraft factory in Rochester took a pasting (the RAF slang of the day for receiving a heavy attack), but it manufactured bombers, not fighters; nor did Fighter Command use RAF Detling, which was yet another

Coastal Command airfield. The airfield at RAF Andover was also attacked in error—the Stuka dive-bombers mistook it for the more important Fighter Command airfield at Middle Wallop. More damage was done to a nearby golf course than to the runway, but the officers' mess was destroyed by a direct hit. A late-night attack by a small number of He 111s on the Nuffield Aero Works, near Birmingham, did "considerable" damage—and ought to have caused somebody in the RAF to ask how the *Luftwaffe* could achieve such accuracy at night—but the damage was nothing that couldn't be quickly put right. In the words of the RAF report for the day, "Enemy aircraft activity over this country has been on a scale far in excess of anything hitherto carried out," but at the end of the day the amount of damage actually inflicted was neither crucial nor impressive. All told, twelve RAF personnel were killed, and twenty-three civilians. The Germans lost thirty-eight aircraft; the British lost thirteen fighters, plus ten bombers destroyed on the ground. Only three British fighter pilots were killed in action.*

It is a measure of the wild overestimates on both sides of the battle that RAF pilots claimed seventy-eight German aircraft "destroyed," thirty-three "probable," and at least forty-nine "damaged" for the day. Even more wildly exaggerated claims of RAF aircraft shot down were made by the Germans, and announced triumphantly over Radio Berlin, preceded by the boastful *Luftwaffe* marching song *Bomben auf England*.

Both sides suffered from the same problem—in the heat of battle, at high speeds, and flying into and out of cloud cover, British

---

* "Only" is, of course, a relative term, and is used here in the full knowledge that every death in war is a tragedy. Still, on a day when the RAF put up "192 patrols involving 916 aircraft," the loss of three fighter pilots in combat was remarkably low, and only one-fourth of the total RAF deaths of the day.

and German fighter pilots and the gunners on German bombers frequently claimed the same "kill" several times over, or counted a plane as "destroyed" when it was merely damaged, or "damaged" when in fact it was still capable of flying home. In fact one German gunner whose aircraft was badly hit, with both engines trailing smoke, took to his parachute only to see, as he descended, the smoke stop and the bomber, together with the rest of his crew, fly on and disappear into a cloud, leaving him to spend the rest of the war as a POW. Excessive and overoptimistic claims on both sides were an inescapable feature of the battle, despite the stringent standards—stricter on the German side than the British—used by intelligence officers (and deeply resented by the fighter pilots) to validate a pilot's claim to a kill, and this would remain so until the universal introduction of the "ciné gun," a small movie camera in the wing of a fighter that filmed the target whenever the guns were fired. Also, on both sides, it was easier to know how many planes your own side had lost than to estimate the number of the enemy that had been shot down—you only had to count the empty places at the dinner table in the mess, or the number of ground crews standing around mournfully on the tarmac waiting in vain for their aircraft to return.

Despite Fink, Göring and his commanders were jubilant. If Beppo Schmidt's estimate that RAF Fighter Command had no more than 300 or 400 fighters left at most was correct, then they had, by their own count, destroyed between one-third and one-fourth of Fighter Command's remaining strength in two days of combat, while rendering a major fighter factory *kaput* and putting out of action several of Fighter Command's airfields. (In fact, Fighter Command actually had 647 serviceable aircraft at the end of the day.[1]) All the flight commanders commented on the relatively small number of British fighters they encountered. However effective the Hurricanes and Spitfires might be—and nobody denied their effectiveness—the actual number engaged seemed comparatively modest. From the German point of view, this suggested once again that Dowding's resources were slender after his losses in France and over Dunkirk. The attack on the 12th against the radar sites was less successful than had been hoped, to be sure, but nobody doubted that these sites would eventually be dealt with by dive-bombers, and in the meantime, a few more days like the 12th and the 13th would no doubt see Fighter Command reduced to its last reserves. It was just a question of continuing to push hard, and of course good weather. Colonel General Halder, the forbiddingly skeptical and competent chief of the army general staff in Berlin, was informed that eight RAF bases were "virtually destroyed," and that "the ratio of German to British aircraft losses was one to three for all types, one to five for fighters." This was tantamount to putting the army on notice that the first condition for Operation Sea Lion might be fulfilled by the *Luftwaffe* at any moment—news which Halder, who was not an enthusiast for the invasion of England, can hardly have welcomed, if he believed it.

Of course, from the viewpoint of Bentley Priory, where Dowding left his office from time to time to watch the progress of the air battles on the big board, with his usual glacial calm, the Germans' jubilation, of which he was in any case unaware, was unfounded. He was not pleased by the loss of thirteen fighters and three pilots, and he was distressed by the damage to the Ventnor radar station, which seemed to indicate that if the Germans tried hard enough (and concentrated on one or two neighboring stations) they could blast a "hole" in Fighter Command's radar coverage for long enough to get a substantial number of raids through without warning. But he had been gratified by the extraordinary courage of the WAAFs at Ventnor, who had gone on working while bombs exploded all around them, eliciting from Dowding a rare personal signal to express his "satisfaction and pride in the behavior of the WAAF in the face of enemy attack." The steady nerves of young women in uniform while being dive-bombed were not the only thing that satisfied him. Park had fed his fighter squadrons into the battle one or two at a time, just as he had been ordered, attacking in squadron strength again and again, drawing blood every time, but never giving the enemy an opportunity to guess what Fighter Command's real strength was. More important still, what we would now call the interface between the radar stations, group operations rooms, the filter room at Fighter Command headquarters, and the individual squadrons in the air had been seamless.

The next day seemed something of an anticlimax. The weather was "Mainly cloudy with bright patches and cloud in the Channel," which in principle was good for the attackers but posed problems for the defenders. The Germans came on and off throughout the day, in small raids spread out all over the southern part of Britain, with no plan that was clearly discernible to the British, although eleven RAF aerodromes were bombed, none of them all that seriously, except for RAF Sealand, where the sergeants' mess was blown up. Railway lines were bombed, apparently at random, but these were quickly and easily repaired; and four RAF personnel and twelve civilians were killed on the ground. Fighter Command lost eight aircraft and had four pilots killed; the Germans lost nineteen aircraft, and the commander of KG 55, Colonel Stoeckl, was killed in action. A disproportionate amount of the German losses on the 14th, as on the preceding days, consisted of Ju 87 Stuka dive-bombers. However effective they were—and in the hands of a good pilot with steady nerves the Stuka could deliver a 500-pound bomb with amazing accuracy—they were so slow as to make them sitting ducks for British fighters. This was doubly so because a Stuka pilot needed to extend the aircraft's dive brakes to slow it down as he dived steeply (almost vertically) toward his target, and lost further speed when he climbed sharply after releasing his bomb. Already, the question was being raised whether it was worth using the four *Stukageschwader* of Air Fleets 2 and 3 over England, though they represented a substantial part of the strength of *Luftflotte* 3.

Although a concentrated attack on the radar stations might have paid dividends, the Germans' effort for the day was largely wasted in "penny packets" (a favorite phrase of General Montgomery), consisting of small raids spread out over many airfields, none of which was seriously damaged. In addition, eight barrage balloons were shot down and the Goodwin Light Vessel was sunk—hardly major targets from Fighter Command's point of view, or challenging ones for the Germans to hit. There was only minimal raiding on the night of the 14th—the RAF described it as "very slight enemy activity"— but one He 111 bomber was shot down by antiaircraft fire near Sealand, perhaps a welcome revenge for the destruction of the sergeants' mess.

The German attacks of the 14th, then, as opposed to those of the two preceding days, were relatively limited, but not from any lack of resolve on the part of the *Luftwaffe*. The perfect weather Göring had been waiting for was predicted for the 15th, and intense preparations were being made throughout all three *Luftflotten* for an attack that would finally deliver the coup de grâce to Fighter Command.

Throughout the battle so far, the Germans had demonstrated a considerable sense of tactics, sending out flights of Bf 109 fighters in strength across the Channel to lure British fighters away from the German bomber formations. This plan had not been successful, largely because it was exactly what Dowding expected the Germans to do, and because Park kept a tight control over the squadrons in No. 11 Group. What was intended for the 15th was something similar, but on a much larger scale. It would, in fact, be the biggest battle in the short history to date of air warfare.

What the Germans had in mind was a vast aerial equivalent of the pincer movement beloved of the German general staff, using, for the first time, the full strength of all three of the *Luftflotten* simultaneously, including General Stumpff's *Luftflotte* 5, which was based in Denmark and Norway. The idea was for *Luftflotte* 5 to attack targets in northern Britain, while the two larger air fleets in France, the Netherlands, and Belgium made an all-out assault on Fighter Command's airfields in the south, thus preventing No. 13 and No. 12 Groups from reinforcing No. 11 Group. There were flaws in this strategy, however, some of which the Germans could hardly be expected to perceive.

Contrary to what was supposed in Berlin, No. 12 Group had *not* so far been supporting No. 11 Group (No. 13 Group was too far north to do so effectively) to any significant degree; in fact, there was already bad blood between Air Vice-Marshal Park and Air Vice-Marshal Leigh-Mallory on that subject. Park, who had always disliked Leigh-Mallory, felt that the latter had been slow and unwilling to respond to calls for support from No. 11 Group—that Leigh-Mallory was, in effect, deliberately ignoring Dowding's orders, given at Fighter Command before the battle at the meeting on July 3. He also felt that when No. 12 Group fighters *did* manage to come to his aid, they ignored the instructions of No. 11 Group's ground controllers and wandered around in the air over Kent, getting in the way and confusing the controllers. In his own quiet way, Park fumed at

Leigh-Mallory's lack of support, while Leigh-Mallory was nothing like as anxious to send his squadrons into No. 11 Group's area as the Germans supposed him to be.

Leigh-Mallory, for his part, resented the fact that the action and most of the glamour and awards were going to No. 11 Group, and he had come to the conclusion that Dowding's tactics (and Park's strict adherence to them) were in any case completely wrong. He had particularly disliked Dowding's suggestion—which would have been better presented to him as a firm, written order—that No. 12 Group should come south to protect No. 11 Group's airfields while No. 11 was engaged in attacking the Germans. This struck him, and his pilots, as a passive, secondary role. He also felt strongly that it would be better to attack the Germans in strength over the Channel with large numbers of aircraft—a "big wing," as it soon became known, consisting of three to five squadrons under a single commander—rather than to chivy them over land in squadron strength. He did not keep his opinion to himself—indeed, it was quickly passed on (and even more quickly embellished) by Dowding's numerous enemies at the Air Ministry.

Leigh-Mallory's theory (which was the exact opposite of what Dowding was so carefully doing) would soon become known throughout Fighter Command as the "big wing controversy," and Leigh-Mallory's part in it was a reflection of the anger felt by his own pilots, who saw themselves as being pushed out of the limelight by No. 11 Group, and deprived of their fair share of the fighting and the glory. Admittedly, Dowding was tired and overburdened with enormous responsibilities, but he was by no means unaware of what was going on between his two most important commanders, and it is hard not to conclude that he should have taken the time to order Park and Leigh-Mallory to appear at his headquarters at once and settle their differences. Dowding's failure to do so was the biggest mistake he made in the battle.*

Although personality (and old, long-held grudges) played a large part in this dispute, Park's objection to the "big wing" was based on straightforward, unemotional reason and experience: it simply took too long for that number of aircraft to form up. Each squadron climbed from its separate airfield and "sauntered" (the RAF word for flying at minimum speed) around at a given altitude and position in the sky looking for the other squadrons; then they all tried to assemble in a coherent formation, with the result that by the time they arrived where they were needed they were often too late to make a difference. The practical limitation was the amount of time it took for the radar operators to detect and track a German raid (and determine its height, its intended target, and the number of "bandits"—enemy aircraft—involved), and there was as yet no way to shorten that process. Park sent his squadrons up one by one to attack as the raid progressed; there was no time to waste forming a "big wing," in his opinion or, more important, in Dowding's.

The leading proponent of the "big wing" theory was Squadron Leader Douglas Bader, commanding officer of No. 242 Squadron at RAF Duxford and part of Leigh-Mallory's No. 12 Group. Bader was perhaps the most flamboyant, determined, tough-minded, difficult, and opinionated personality in all of Fighter Command, despite many competitors, and as much admired by the *Luftwaffe* as he was in the RAF. Bader was and would remain throughout his life a legendary figure—the only pilot on either side of the Battle of Britain to

---

* Although Dowding's eventual dismissal from his post as Air Officer Commanding-in-Chief of Fighter Command is not unrelated to "the big wing controversy," as well as to Churchill's resentment over Dowding's objections to sending more Hurricanes to France, the most important reason, as we shall see, would be his failure to come up with an effective night fighter defense once the *Luftwaffe* took to large-scale bombing by night.

have a hugely successful movie made about him (with Kenneth More playing Bader), based on Paul Brickhill's best-selling biography of Bader, *Reach for the Sky*, which is still in print today and at one time, in an abridged version, was obligatory reading for every British schoolboy. It was as if Bader had been cast by nature for leadership as a fighter pilot in the RAF—he had a solid middle-class English background, with a family that had served for three generations in the Indian military and civil service; was an indifferent scholar; was more than a bit of a bully; and was an accomplished athlete, "full of a breezy, non-stop enthusiasm that infected everyone else . . . dedicated, tireless and fearless." He was also impatient, argumentative, rebellious toward authority, a fierce boxer and a fearsome rugby player, a natural pilot, and a good shot. A cadetship at Royal Air Force College Cranwell, the RAF equivalent of the army's Sandhurst, seemed to everybody the best thing for him, and he was graduated second in his class in 1930, with the note in his report: "Plucky, capable, headstrong." The word that most people used to describe him, then and later, was "cocky."

Assigned to a fighter squadron, he might have become just another boisterous regular fighter pilot. But while showing off in response to a dare by doing aerobatics at ground level in his Bristol Bulldog, he caught a wingtip in the ground and crashed, partially severing both legs. After several excruciating bouts of surgery he lost one leg above the knee, and the other just below it. Bader was slipping quietly into death when he heard one of the nursing sisters outside in the corridor say, "Don't make so much noise. There's a boy dying in there." Bader decided then and there that he would live, and eventually by sheer determination mastered walking on his "tin legs" (being Bader, he refused from the beginning to even consider using a cane). Retired from the RAF because it would no longer let him fly, he married;

learned to play golf to a very high standard, as well as tennis and squash: drove his old MG; and of course turned up at the Air Ministry when war began. The elderly Warrant Officer who presided over medical appointments shook his head when he saw Bader and said, "'Ullo, sir. I thought you'd be along. What's it this time?" "Same again," Bader said. "I think they might pass me this time." Shocked, the Warrant Officer said, "Not A.1.B., sir. Never."* [2]

But in 1939 the RAF needed pilots badly enough that somebody took the trouble to look through *King's Regulations* and found there was nothing in them requiring a pilot to have legs, and except for having no legs Bader was as fit as a man could be. Soon he had gone through Central Flying School with flying colors and the judgment, "Ability as a pilot—excellent." Over Dunkirk, he made his first "kill," a Bf 109. Bader "rammed stick and rudder over. . . . A 109 shot up in front; his thumb jabbed the firing button. . . . A puff of white spurted just behind its cockpit . . . then a spurt of orange flame mushroomed around the cockpit and flared back like a blow-torch." [3] That afternoon he caught one He 111 bomber and killed the rear gunner. Within a few days he was promoted to command No. 242 Squadron, a squadron of recalcitrant, embittered Canadians who felt that they had been buggered about from one end of France to the other. He overcame their instant reaction that being given a new commanding officer with no legs was adding insult to injury by climbing into the nearest Hurricane and doing the same daredevil ground-level aerobatics that had cost him his legs in the first place. By that time he was on his way to becoming one of Fighter Command's most aggressive pilots, and had already made the acquaintance of Air Vice-Marshal Leigh-Mallory, after crashing a Spitfire by trying to take off with the

* A.1.B was the category for those medically fit for flying.

propeller in coarse pitch. Despite the loss of the Spitfire (Leigh-Mallory merely remarked, "That was very silly, wasn't it?"[4]), the two men seem to have struck up a relationship that was unusually friendly and close, given the great disparity in their rank. Certainly, they were both "hard thrusters" and bluff extroverts, not at all like the remote and sometimes otherworldly Dowding, but it seems very likely too that Bader played the role of Iago to Leigh-Mallory's Othello, and managed, whether by design or by accident, to bring out the worst in the character of No. 12 Group's Commander-in-Chief—his ambition; his taste for backstairs intrigue and gossip at the Air Ministry; his desire to be popular with his own pilots; his resentment at having to follow Dowding's orders and play, as he saw it, second fiddle to Air Vice-Marshal Park, a "colonial" from New Zealand. From the first, Bader wanted to form a "big wing" and clobber the Germans in equal numbers, and was impatient with the strict (and from a pilot's point of view, artificial) geographic limits imposed on each of the four fighter groups, as well as the stream of precise orders being radioed to the pilots by the group fighter controller on the ground (or, more often, well below it, since by now the control rooms were deep underground) and by his WAAF subordinates "filtering" information about the enemy raiders. He managed to persuade Leigh-Mallory that the "big wing" would work—an attempt which cannot have been all that difficult, first because Bader could be persuasive as well as forceful, and second because Leigh-Mallory was shrewd enough to see in this dispute over tactics a way of undermining not only Park, but perhaps even Dowding himself. It did not hurt that the idea of massing a large number of fighters to give the enemy a bloody nose, instead of a long-drawn-out battle of attrition, was exactly the kind of aggressive thinking that always appealed strongly to the prime minister. Even though Dowding was winning the battle, it was not difficult, given the number of his enemies at the Air Ministry, to make it seem that his tactics were too cautious, and Air Vice-Marshal Sholto Douglas, with whom Dowding had clashed so many times, was right in his judgment that Dowding was too old and that it had been too long since he had been up in a fighter himself.

Thus, the Germans' assumption that No. 12 Group had been feeding reinforcements to No. 11 Group in the south, and could be prevented from doing so by attacking the Midlands and the north of England with *Luftflotte* 5 from Denmark and Norway, was essentially mistaken, and was compounded by the fact that Stumpff's bombers would have to go without an escort of single-engine fighters to protect them, because the distance was too great for the fuel capacity of the Bf 109.

Indeed, the Germans' expectations for the big attack on August 15, however ambitious in scale, were a curious mixture of optimism and doubt. Göring, far from controlling the battle from Blanc-Nez, watching through powerful military binoculars as his aircraft passed the white cliffs of Dover, as he liked to pretend for propaganda purposes, was in fact at his palatial, grandiose hunting estate, Karinhall (named after his beloved first wife) in conference with the entire *Luftwaffe* high command, including field marshals Kesselring and Sperrle, whom he had summoned to Karinhall but who would have been undoubtedly better placed at that moment in their own headquarters, nearer to their air fleets, and in control of events. (Sperrle lived in almost as luxurious a style as Göring, in Paris. Kesselring's more Spartan headquarters were underground at Blanc-Nez, as close to England as possible, in what was referred to by those who were in awe of him as the "Holy Mountain.") Göring was, in any case in a querulous frame of mind. Bomber losses—particularly among the

Stukas—and losses of his much-vaunted Bf 110 "Destroyers" had caused him to look for a scapegoat, and he had found it among his own fighter pilots, whom he accused of seeking glory in air duels with Fighter Command's Spitfires and Hurricanes, rather than doing their job, which was to protect the bombers. Göring's alarmingly swift mood changes and frequent irritability were not just a reflection of the fact that he had promised the Führer more than he had so far been able to deliver. He was by this time already addicted to para-codeine tablets, which he swallowed in handfuls, scooping them from antique Venetian cut glass bowls scattered all around his house, behavior that was typical of the weaknesses of the most senior Nazi leaders. (It is hard to imagine Dowding, for example, popping pills, or losing his temper at his own air marshals and pilots.)

Göring had already had this argument about the role his fighters should be playing in the battle with his two leading fighter pilots— Adolf Galland and Werner Mölders—while presenting them each with the Gold Pilot Badge at Karinhall. He demanded that they give the bombers "close and rigid protection," and when the two airmen tried to explain that because of the difference in speed and altitude between the Bf 109 and the bombers, this was impossible—that the best way of protecting the bombers was not to slow down to their speed, but to fly well above them, maintaining the critical advantages of height and speed, then dive down to attack the British fighters as they rose to attack the bombers—he was indignant and at his most bullying. He wanted the bomber crews to be able to see their fighter escorts close by. Galland and Mölders attempted to explain that while it might be dismaying and demoralizing to the bomber crews not to see the fighters flying wingtip to wingtip along with them, the fighters could do nothing to help them by making themselves visible, that speed and height were a fighter pilot's best weapons, and giving these up would increase fighter losses without reducing those of the bombers. But the *Reichsmarschall*, irritable, sweating heavily, and raising his voice, was in no mood to listen to reason, even from his best fighter pilots.

Galland was and would remain the most famous German fighter of World War II (his eventual total "score" of "kills" would be 104). A product of Germany's "glider schools," he became a fighter pilot in the new *Luftwaffe*, and after a crash in 1935, his face had been totally rebuilt, giving him a flattened nose and a rakish but rather threatening expression, accentuated by a thick, jet-black moustache and an ever-present strong black cigar (he even had a cigar holder and an ashtray built into the cockpit of his Bf 109, so he could smoke while flying). The crash also cost him most of the sight in his left eye—indeed, the only way he was able to pass the medical examination to resume flying duties again was by getting a friend to copy the letters on the doctor's eye chart so Galland could memorize them overnight. Galland learned his trade fighting with the German Condor Legion in Spain, and by August 1940 he had already made seventeen "kills" and been awarded the Knight's Cross of the Iron Cross, known among German fighter pilots as the "tin tie," since it was worn around the neck, sometimes suspended from a woman's garter. He had every quality a great fighter pilot needed—courage, physical and mental toughness, amazing skill as a marksman despite the fact that he was essentially blind in one eye, and a survivor's instincts as well as a killer's (he had made three kills in one day early in May 1940, and would be fished out of the Channel twice). He was also intelligent, outspoken, and a gifted leader. He was cast from the same mold as Bader—each admired the other and had overcome injuries that would have stopped most men from ever flying again—and it would be one of the typical small ironies of war that when Bader was finally shot down over France and taken prisoner it was Galland who gave him a luncheon party and let Bader sit in the pilot's seat of a Bf 109 before was sent to a POW camp in the Reich.

Mölders was Galland's greatest rival in 1940, but he was more of an intellectual than Galland, more interested in devising new tactics than in simply racking up a high score—the basic German fighter formation, the much-imitated *Schwarm*, was an idea of his. He liked to compare himself to *Hauptmann* Oswald Boelcke, the great German fighter pilot in World War I who invented most of the tactics that became standard for aerial combat and remain so today, while leaving to Galland the swashbuckling role played by *Rittmeister* Manfred Freiherr von Richthofen,* the legendary Red Baron, a born fighter pilot and a killer with ice-cold blood in his veins.

Göring had been infuriated by his two star pilots' argument against sticking close to the bombers—though he himself, as a former fighter pilot, should have known it was the truth—and the two fighter aces had left Karinhall depressed and angry, despite the decorations and the promotions they had received. Even the normally ebullient Galland complained that the entire German war effort was like a huge pyramid "turned upside down, balancing on its apex," that apex being a scant few hundred German fighter pilots flying over the English Channel—a remark that might have been echoed by British fighter pilots, who found themselves in the same situation, as the whole war and indeed the survival of Britain rested briefly on their shoulders. Galland recalled the words of von Richthofen—"Fighter pilots have to rove freely in the area allotted to them, and when they spot an enemy they attack and shoot him down: anything else is rubbish." Even Galland, not normally cautious in expressing his opinion,

---

* In the German army of World War I, a *Rittmeister* was the cavalry equivalent of a *Hauptmann*, i.e., a captain. The distinctive rank eventually vanished along with the horses.

had not dared to quote von Richthofen to the man who had taken command of Richthofen's famous squadron, the "Flying Circus," after his death—Hermann Göring.

The two *Luftwaffe* field marshals and the remainder of the *Luftwaffe* high command were receiving a longer version of this diatribe from Göring, and his anger was enough to subdue even the redoubtable Field Marshal Sperrle, who, immensely tall, impassive, imposing, and weighing almost 300 pounds, was known throughout the *Luftwaffe* as "the elephant with the monocle." Since Kesserling and Sperrle were not fighter pilots, they too did not quote von Richthofen to Göring, but it was ironic that the biggest and most critical day of the Battle of Britain took place with the *Luftwaffe* high command several hundred miles away, arguing about strategy, and dealing with their commander in chief's prickly and swiftly changing moods.

Perhaps even more irritating for Göring was the fact that the day began not with the perfect weather that had been forecast, but with fog over the Channel. The attack was duly canceled while the *Luftwaffe* commanders breakfasted luxuriously at Karinhall, then settled down around the vast gilt-bronze inlaid conference table. By midmorning, however, the weather had improved dramatically (the RAF meteorologists cheerily reported "High pressure giving fine, warm weather"), and in the absence of anybody else with authority the chief of staff of II *Fliegerkorps*, a mere colonel, gave the order to proceed. The *Luftwaffe*'s most critical day of battle would take place, therefore, with the leaders of its air fleets in Berlin, away from their commands and the telephone—another mistake on Göring's part.

By half past ten in the morning, German aircraft began to assemble over the Channel in such quantity that they swamped the British radar operators' ability to estimate their number. This was the beginning of a day that was intended to destroy Fighter Command, and came very close to doing so. More than 100 enemy aircraft crossed the coast at Dover at eleven that morning, followed by seventy-plus at noon, more than 200 at two-thirty in the afternoon, 300 and 400 in the late afternoon, and another seventy or more in the early evening, all of them aiming for Fighter Command's airfields and for the radar stations.

Shortly after noon, nearly 150 planes from *Luftflotte* 5 struck at northeast England—the northern claw of the pincer movement that was intended to prevent No. 12 and No. 13 Groups from reinforcing No. 11 Group. Thus, during the course of the day, almost 1,000 German aircraft would be engaged over southern and northeastern England. To members of the Observer Corps counting them, as well to thousands of spectators on the ground, it was an awesome sight, as seemingly endless processions of enemy aircraft flew overhead in neat formations.

To those who had read H. G. Wells's *The Shape of Things to Come*, or seen the film *Things to Come*, it was exactly the spectacle Wells had described: the skies over Britain darkened by vast fleets of bombers silhouetted against the bright summer sky. But people seem to have been more fascinated than terrified by the sight, and those who knew anything about air warfare could see above the bombers the abstract, swirling zigzag patterns of white contrails* made by the fighter planes as they maneuvered and fought high above the bombers. No photographer was able to capture the sight fully— black-and-white film did not do it justice, and the camera reduced the aircraft to insignificant specks—but a number of painters were inspired to re-create it on canvas and capture something of the scale and awesome beauty of the battle as seen from the ground. The best

---

* A contrail is a white vapor trail usually left by each wingtip of an aircraft flying at high altitudes.

of these paintings is *The Battle of Britain* by the distinguished British modernist Paul Nash (who also produced some of the most original and eerie paintings of the trenches and no-man's-land during World War I); it is now in the collection of the Imperial War Museum in London. Nash managed to put on canvas the bright colors, and the immense sense of distance and space, of a huge and furious battle raging five miles above the ground, and it is as much an icon of patriotism, in its own way, as Lady Elizabeth Butler's famous painting *The Charge of the Royal Scots Greys at Waterloo.*

Those who looked up and saw the battle going on so far above them recall the strange silence—most of the action was too high above them to be heard—and the sunlight catching on the cascades of shiny brass cartridge cases as they tumbled down from the machine guns and cannons in the sky (children were sternly warned not to pick these objects up). Winston Churchill occasionally took time off to view the battle from Dover—a favorite destination of his, since he had caused to be established there, despite opposition from the army and the navy, huge naval guns and howitzers preserved at his command since 1918, with which to shell German positions on the French coast—and to visit fighter airfields along the way. On this day of days, however, he would eventually be driven to Air Marshal Park's operations room at the headquarters of No. 11 Group at RAF Uxbridge, just outside London, to witness the greatest crisis of the day.

Strategically, the day got off to a bad start for the Germans. To begin with, despite Beppo Schmidt's optimistic estimate that the British were down to about 200 fighters, Fighter Command in fact began August 15, at 0900 hours, with 672 serviceable fighters, of which 233 were Spitfires and 361 Hurricanes. These were not a lot with which to hold off more than 1,000 enemy aircraft, but a lot more than

Göring supposed. Then too, when it finally arrived after the long flight over the North Sea from Norway and Denmark, the northern "jaw" of the pincer movement, the bombers of *Luftflotte* 5 attacking across toward the Newcastle-Sunderland area and the airfields of No. 13 Group, failed to do any major damage to either No. 13 or No. 12 Group, or to present Dowding with any serious challenge on his northern flank. Unfortunately for the Germans, Dowding had insisted, despite opposition, on the importance of extending his radar network to the northeast, so the force from Norway, consisting of sixty-five He 111 bombers of KG 26 and the thirty-four Bf 110s of 1/ZG 26 escorting them, as well as a separate unescorted raid by fifty Ju 88 bombers of KG 30 from Denmark, were all identified while they were still far out to sea, and it was ascertained that they were not accompanied by any single-engine fighters. Without an escort of Bf 109s both the bombers and the Bf 110s were sitting ducks for No. 13 Group, and there was no element of surprise to the attack, since Dowding's radar network extended farther north than the Germans expected—in fact, most of the British fighters were airborne early enough to attack the Germans well before they reached land.

Dowding had stoutly resisted intense pressure to strip No. 13 Group of pilots and aircraft to replace losses in the south, much to the chagrin of the pilots themselves, who felt left out of the action; but he was proved right in this decision too. At first visual contact, the British pilots were startled by the sheer volume of prey as the Germans approached the coast—there were so many German bombers that when a ground controller impatiently asked Flight Lieutenant Ted Graham, acting commander of No. 72 Squadron from RAF Acklington, "Have you seen them?" Graham, who suffered from a mild stutter, replied indignantly, "Of course I've *seen* the b-b-b-b-astards! I'm t-t-t-rying t-t-t-o w-w-w-ork out what to d-d-do!"[5]

But no fancy strategy was called for. In the end, Graham, and the rest of 72 Squadron, as well as 79 Squadron from Acklington, supported by a flight from 605 Squadron from farther north and by 41 Squadron from Catterick, simply attacked the dense pack of sixty-five Heinkels of KG 26, all flying in neat formation, from the side. In the absence of a fighter escort there was no need to maneuver, or to gain altitude and attack from out of the sun, so each British fighter just picked out a victim and opened fire at close range. It was like shooting fish in a barrel. "I saw two Huns simply disintegrate," one RAF pilot commented. "We hacked them about so badly, the formation split apart and they made for home." Many of the bombers jettisoned their bombs, causing one RAF pilot to remark, "The sea was churned white with bombs, as if a colony of whales had spouted."

The Bf 110s had an even harder time of it, and already running low on fuel and faced with the determined opposition of four squadrons of Spitfires and Hurricanes, they turned for home. The bombers they were supposed to escort that hadn't already jettisoned their bombs and fled for home plunged on inland in ragged formation and managed to destroy merely a dozen homes in Sunderland.

Slightly to the south a force of more than fifty Ju 88 bombers from Denmark was attacked by a squadron of Spitfires, a squadron of Hurricanes, and a squadron of the much-maligned Defiants, as well as a squadron of slow, unwieldy Blenheim twin-engine fighters. The Junkers managed to bomb a few houses in Bridlington, and to damage some hangars and destroy ten obsolescent Whitley bombers on the ground at RAF Driffield (once again, not a Fighter Command airfield), but at a cost of more than 10 percent of their force. All told *Luftflotte* 5 lost eight Heinkels, eight Junkers, and eight Bf 110 escort fighters, having inflicted minimal damage, none of it on any target of importance to Fighter Command. Not a single British fighter was lost. Even not counting the number of German aircraft that arrived home seriously damaged or obliged to crash-land on return, losses among the bombers and the twin-engine escorts were so high—approaching 10 percent, or twice what RAF Bomber Command would consider an "acceptable" rate of loss—that *Luftflotte* 5 never again attempted a mass attack in daylight.

Churchill, who was not by any means an uncritical admirer of Dowding, would later comment on this phase of the day's fighting,

> The foresight of Air Marshal Dowding in his direction of Fighter Command deserves high praise, and even more remarkable had been the restraint and the exact measurement of formidable stresses which had reserved a fighter force in the North through all these long weeks of mortal conflict in the South. We must regard the generalship here shown as an example of genius in the art of war.[6]

Of course this was written eight years later, when the Battle of Britain had already become the indisputable emotional high point of Britain's experience in World War II, and Churchill was anxious to present himself as having backed Dowding to the hilt, and also determined to paper over his eventual failure to protect Dowding from his enemies. That does not alter, however, the truth of Churchill's judgment. Nobody was a shrewder judge of generalship than Churchill, and Dowding, with slender resources, had outfoxed the Germans brilliantly on August 15, despite the criticism of Leigh-Mallory, Sholto Douglas, and Douglas Bader.

However, hours before the Germans' attack on the northeast failed, the sheer size of their attack on Fighter Command in southern England was causing even the usually imperturbable Dowding a degree of anxiety. In this attack, unlike the attack by *Luftfloffe* 5, the bombers were escorted with large numbers of Bf 109s, and the German raids were better aimed at targets that mattered. By mid-morning the forward airfields at Hawkinge and Lympne had been attacked by more than 100 Ju 88s; Lympne was put out of action completely for three days, its water supply and electricity cut off and its sick bay destroyed by a direct hit. Electricity to the coastal radar stations at Dover, Rye, and Foreness was cut off, putting them out of action and leaving a gaping hole in the defense; and two squadrons of British fighters were overwhelmed by superior numbers of Bf 109s. RAF Manston was strafed by Bf 110s and considerably damaged, and by the time the first waves of German aircraft began to withdraw new raids were already forming up. Fighter Command airfields all over southern England came under attack; the attacks were clearly visible to the radar plotters as a kind of electronic blur, too many to count. Not everybody's nerves were as steady under fire as those of the WAAF radar operators whom Dowding had praised—at Manston, and several other Fighter Command fields, a few of the RAF ground personnel were taking to the shelters and staying there, not surprisingly, given the number of bombs that were coming down. At RAF Martlesham Heath accurate low-level attacks by bomb-carrying Bf 109 and Bf 110 fighters (something of a novelty) put the airfield out of commission.

All over southern England No. 11 Group was struggling to keep going—pilots flew sortie after sortie, landing at emergency fields while their own were under attack or out of action, and sat exhausted in the cockpits of their fighters while equally exhausted ground crews hurried to rearm their guns and refuel the aircraft. Most of Park's pilots had been at their dispersal points since before dawn, and could no longer even count the number of times they had taken off, or the number of aircraft they had shot down. Those who were hungry sustained themselves on plates of lukewarm baked beans and mugs of hot, sweet tea from the dispersal hut, and if they were lucky cat-napped on the ground next to their aircraft, with a parachute for a pillow. Richard Collier, in his book on the Battle of Britain, lists some of the men who flew on August 15:

Warrant Officer Edward Mayne, Royal Flying Corps veteran, at forty the oldest man to fly as a regular combatant in the battle, young Hugh Percy, an undergraduate from Cambridge University who kept his log-book in Greek; New Zealander Mindy Blake, Doctor of Mathematics, who approached each combat like a quadratic equation, the Nizam of Hyderabad's former personal pilot, Derek Boitel-Gill, Randy Matheson, ex-Argentine gaucho; Johnny Bryson, a former Canadian Mountie; Squadron Leader Aeneas Mac Donell, official head of the Glengarry Clan; and Red Tobin from Los Angeles, with the [American] barnstormers, Andy and Shorty.

But these were the more glamorous exceptions, of course. Most of Park's pilots were ordinary young Britons, just out of school, commissioned pilot officers or noncommissioned sergeant pilots, tired, occasionally scared out of their wits, often sustained by a combination of adrenaline-producing excitement and a deep personal need "not to let the side down," many of them unexceptional marksmen only recently promoted from flying trainers to flying real fighters. Very few of them were old-timers who had seen a lot of combat, but it was taken as a rule of thumb that anybody who had come through three combat sorties unscathed was either naturally good at flying a fighter or just bloody lucky, which was even better.

Richard Hillary, who went straight from life as an Oxford undergraduate and intellectual to being a Spitfire pilot with 603 Squadron, and who would survive dreadful, disfiguring burns to write one of the most famous books about the RAF in World War II, *The Last Enemy*, before death finally caught up with him, wrote of his baptism of fire on August 15:

> We ran into them at 18,000 feet, twenty yellow-nosed Messerschmitt 109s, about 500 feet above us. Our squadron strength was eight, and as they came down on us we went into line astern and turned head on to them. Brian Carbury, who was leading the Section, dropped the nose of his machine, and I could almost feel the leading Nazi pilot push forward on his stick to bring his guns to bear. At the same moment Brian pulled back on his own control stick and led us over them in a steep climbing turn to the left. In two vital seconds they had lost their advantage. I saw Brian let go a burst of fire at the leading plane, saw the pilot put his machine into a half roll, and knew that he was mine. Automatically, I kicked the rudder to the left to get him at right angles, turned the gun button to "Fire," and let go in a four second burst with full deflection.* He came right through my sights and I saw the tracer from all eight guns thud home. For a second he seemed to hang motionless; then a jet of flame shot upwards and he spun out of sight. . . . It had happened. My first emotion was one of satisfaction. . . . And then I had a feeling of the essential rightness of it all. He was dead and I was alive; it could so easily have been the other way round; and that somehow would have been right too.[7]

---

* As bird shooters know, you don't aim at a bird in flight; you aim *ahead* of it, so that it will fly into your shot. The same is true of fighter marksmanship, but at vastly greater speeds and distances. In deflection shooting, a pilot aims not at the enemy plane but rather at the spot where he expects it to be when his "stream" of bullets converges there. Judging the lead or deflection is an essential skill for a fighter pilot or an air gunner. Note also that a "four-second burst" is about twice as long as that which a more experienced fighter pilot would consider necessary, or even prudent, considering how quickly a fighter plane's ammunition is expended, and how easy it is to overheat the gun barrels.

On August 15 young men died who had not been with their squadron long enough to get a change of sheets, or buy somebody a drink at the bar, or in some cases to unpack their suitcases. One pilot who was shot down and parachuted from his fighter suddenly realized that he was going to come down in the Channel, and unwilling to get his brand-new handmade shoes wet and ruin them, he united the laces and let them fall while he was still over land, and was astonished when they were returned to him at his mess, neatly wrapped in paper, a couple of days later. Another, wounded, with a crippled plane, glided out of the clouds and crash-landed in what he took to be an English field and was surprised to be lifted gently out of his cockpit by two German soldiers.

At noon Bf 109s attacked Manston again, destroying two Spitfires on the ground, and in the early afternoon two great attacks appeared, one of over 100 aircraft, the other of more than 150. Park was stretched so thin against these that he could put up only four squadrons of fighters, shortly followed by three more, and even so the British fighter pilots were now fighting at odds of two or three to one. Park brought in reinforcements from No. 10 Group, to the west, but his forces were still badly outnumbered, and groups of German aircraft seemed to be appearing all over Sussex and Kent. The Germans severely damaged the Short Brothers aircraft factory at Rochester, where the first of RAF Bomber Command's new four-engine heavy bombers, the Short Stirling, was manufactured—a severe blow, but not a direct blow on Fighter Command. As this attack ebbed, two more began, a total of 250 German aircraft coming in over the Isle of Wight against Fighter Command's airfields, particularly Middle Wallop, which had also been attacked the day before, and against which Park managed to put up eleven squadrons, one of whose pilots, Lieutenant J. Phillipart, a former pilot of the Royal Belgian Air Force, set the day's record by shooting down three Bf 110s. A separate German attack was made against four radar stations, showing that at last the importance of Dowding's radar system was beginning to sink in, though once again the aerials proved difficult to destroy from the air—the attempt was rather like finding (and destroying) a needle in a haystack.

The afternoon went by in constant fighting, then, just when it seemed that the day was over, a raid of more than seventy German aircraft was plotted coming in over the Channel to attack the Fighter Command airfields at Biggin Hill and Kenley. Attacked by two British fighter squadrons, the mass of German aircraft broke up. Some of them attacked the airfield at West Malling, Kent, but the most significant attack of the day was that of *Erprobungsgruppe* 210, which specialized in pinpoint, low-level attacks with a mixture of Bf 109s and Bf 110s, and which was aiming for RAF Kenley. Its commander, *Hauptmann* Walter Rubensdörffer, one of the most daring and dedicated bomber specialists in the entire *Luftwaffe*, brought his aircraft in so low that he could read the street signs and see the startled faces of pedestrians, relying for navigation on the railway lines he had memorized. He decided at the last moment to fly north of Kenley, and then turn back and attack the airfield from the direction where an attack would be least expected, but in the confusion of the heavily built-up suburban area beneath his aircraft he lost his way and seeing hangars, a runway, and aircraft—all airfields look pretty much alike from a few hundred feet up at 250 miles per hour—led his aircraft into an attack on RAF Croydon instead.

This was in every way the wrong airfield to strike. Croydon had until 1939 been London's major civil airfield, with a luxurious terminal for the day, and long runways built for the big aircraft that linked the capital with glamorous flights to the great cities of Europe and the far-flung empire, in the days when air travel was an expensive luxury. Now it housed several fighter squadrons, so it was in every sense a legitimate military target, except that Hitler had explicitly reserved for himself the decision about whether or not to bomb London. (Göring had passed this on to his commanders as his own order, embellished with angry threats against anyone who disobeyed it.) This was partly a matter of domestic policy—the Germans had so far been untouched themselves by the war they had begun, and neither Hitler nor Dr. Goebbels was entirely confident about how they would react to being bombed. The last thing Hitler and Goebbels (and the Nazi Party in general) wanted was a sharp decline in civilians' morale—like everybody else, the Führer overrated the effect of bombing, as well as the strength at the time of RAF Bomber Command. As for Göring, he had loudly and publicly promised the Germans that they would never be bombed, that his *Luftwaffe* was so strong that such a thing could never happen. Nobody in the German government doubted that so long as Winston Churchill remained prime minister, bombing London would produce some form of retaliation.

Hitler's hesitation at bombing London went beyond domestic policy, however, into the deeper realms of diplomacy and world strategy. Somewhere at the back of his mind he still nurtured the belief the British might yet be brought to the peace table, that the "right people" would eventually emerge to replace Churchill and his "gang," people who accepted that Britain had lost the war and were willing to talk terms sensibly; and he was anxious not to frighten such people off by bombing London, shrewdly sensing that such bombing would strengthen Churchill's hand. Even Göring still believed that time and patience were needed to deal with the British—along with a flair for diplomacy that he believed he possessed. Numerous amateurish private "peace feelers" were still being conducted, however ineffectively, by his agents in the neutral capitals of Europe.

Captain Rubensdörffer's daring, if mistaken, attack on Croydon had the misfortune of violating this policy—Croydon was undeniably part of Greater London. Not only had he attacked the wrong airfield; he had attacked it while some of its Hurricanes were still in the air nearby, and his aircraft were bounced from above by nine British fighters of No. 111 Squadron, whose home airfield it was, just as the Germans were about to release their bombs. In the ensuing melee, Rubensdörffer's *Erprobungsgruppe* 210 was not only surprised and scattered but badly mauled, and many of his pilots released their bombs early on nearby brick and mock-Tudor homes of suburban Croydon, now the site of office towers, shopping malls, and infamous traffic jams, killing more than seventy civilian Londoners. The Bf 110s tried to climb and form a circle to defend themselves against 111 Squadron and, shortly, No. 32 Squadron from Biggin Hill, which was quickly directed to the scene. The 111 Squadron armorers tried to fight back from the ground with a machine gun mounted on a homemade tripod, but a number of aircraftmen as well as Gangster, a much-loved dog of No. 111 Squadron, were killed by a bomb. As for Rubensdörffer, the *Luftwaffe* expert on low-level flying was pursued across picturesque Surrey and Sussex at rooftop height, and finally brought down just outside a small English village, the aircraft, Rubensdörffer, and his gunner shattered into tiny, flaming fragments. The Führer, when he was informed of the raid on Croydon, was appalled and enraged.

So were field marshals Kesselring and Sperrle when they finally arrived back from Karinhall at their headquarters, with the warning from the *Reichsmarschall* no doubt still ringing in their ears—and they could not have doubted that it had been passed on directly from Hitler himself.

Hitler was not the only major political figure following the day's fighting closely. In London, the Cabinet had been meeting at 10 Downing Street throughout the morning, its discussions interrupted from time to time as news of the great raids were brought to the prime minister. When, at last, the Cabinet was concluded, Churchill and Anthony Eden, Secretary of State for War, sat for some time in the Cabinet Room, trying to make sense of the somewhat scrappy news they had been brought so far, which seemed to indicate that Park had already committed his entire strength and that the Germans were still coming in great numbers. Obviously, a crisis was building, and, in Eden's words, "At last Churchill announced that he would drive to Fighter Command HQ and I went back to the War Office, neither of us yet knowing that this was to be one of the most critical days of the war."

Churchill was in a grumbling mood when he arrived at Dowding's headquarters. American correspondents had been busy driving back and forth over southern England, counting the number of German planes that had crashed, and had come to the conclusion that the RAF was exaggerating the figures. This was true enough, for reasons we have seen, and the prime minister knew it, but he deplored attempts being made to persuade the American journalists otherwise. "There is something rather obnoxious in bringing correspondents down to air squadrons in order that they may assure the American public that the fighter pilots are not lying and bragging about their figures,"[8] he wrote to his old friend (and former adjutant when he had commanded an infantry battalion in the trenches in World War I) Sir Archibald Sinclair, Secretary of State for Air. "We can, I think, afford to be a bit cool and calm about all this."

Dowding, typically, was neither shaken nor apologetic when the prime minister brought the matter up, and simply replied, in his usual cool, thoughtful way, that if the Germans' claims about the number of British aircraft they had brought down were true the German army would already be here. [9] The news that Dowding's bold decision to retain his fighter strength in the north of England had led to the defeat of the attacks there, and that so far more than 100 German aircraft had been shot down, eventually cheered the prime minister, and when he returned in the evening to 10 Downing Street he put in a call to Neville Chamberlain, who was at home recuperating from cancer surgery, to tell him the good news. Churchill's Junior Private Secretary John Colville (who had been Chamberlain's secretary, and who would soon join the RAF himself) noted, "I . . . found Mr. Chamberlain somewhat cold at being disturbed in the middle of dinner. However, he was overcome with joy when he heard the news and very touched at Winston thinking of him. It is typical of W. to do a small thing like this which could give such great pleasure. 'The Lord President [this was Chamberlain's present position in the Cabinet] was very grateful to you,' I said to Winston. 'So he ought to be,' replied W, 'this is one of the greatest days in history.'" [10]

At the end of the day, the RAF claimed 161 German aircraft "destroyed," sixty-one "probable," and fifty-eight "damaged," with a loss of thirty-four British aircraft and eighteen pilots killed or missing. In fact, the British had shot down seventy-five German aircraft, but that was still better than two for one. The *Luftwaffe* claimed to have shot down 101 British aircraft, approximately three times the actual number. By now, bookies and the porters in hotels and clubs were taking bets on the number of planes the RAF would shoot down versus the *Luftwaffe*, as if it were a sporting event, and newspaper vendors scrawled the latest "score" on their boards as the news came in.

Any way one looked at it, it was a British victory—and a victory for Dowding's strategy. His object, like that of General Kutuzov against Napoleon in 1812, was to keep his force in being. Kutuzov was widely criticized for letting Napoleon take Moscow after the stalemate of the Battle of Borodino—a profound humiliation for the czar—but he understood that the winter and starvation (and eventually the burning of Moscow) would force the French to retreat, and that if he kept his army in being long enough he would beat the emperor. In order to save England Dowding had only to keep Fighter Command in being and keep shooting down the Germans until the autumn weather finally put an end to the invasion season.

In the meantime, the shock to the Germans of the continuing strength of Fighter Command, and their own losses, persuaded Göring to issue two fatal orders. First, henceforth the fighters would no longer be allowed to roam free over England seeking out and attacking the enemy; they would stick close to the bombers at all times. Second, since he considered it "doubtful whether there is any point in continuing attacks on radar sites," none of them apparently having been put out of action, they were taken off the target list.

Perhaps even more significant was his order that henceforth no more than one officer would serve in any aircrew, in order to cut down on the casualties of trained officers.

Whatever else the day had accomplished, it was no longer possible to believe that Fighter Command was on the verge of being destroyed. The German attacks would have to be increased in strength and number—what remained of *Luftflotte* 5 in Norway and Denmark was used to reinforce the two air fleets in the Netherlands, Belgium, and France—and continued on a daily basis.

For both sides, the hardest and most brutal fighting was still to come.

CHAPTER 9

The Hardest Days—
August 16 Through September 15

Any notion that the Germans would pause for a day of rest after their losses on the 15th was dispelled the next day, when a raid of over 250 aircraft flew up the Thames estuary at noon to attack RAF Biggin Hill again, and when bombs fell for a second time on the suburbs of London, including Wimbledon, whose only major target was the famous tennis club.

The weather was warm and sunny, with a slight haze over the Channel—almost ideal for the attackers. The day was to be marked by three notable events. The first would be the award of Fighter Command's first Victoria Cross to Flight Lieutenant J. B. Nicholson of 249 Squadron, who, though badly burned and wounded, kept on pursuing a Bf 110 and destroyed it before bailing out of his flaming aircraft (and then was mistaken for a German and wounded again by the Home Guard when he landed). The second event was the crash landing at RAF Tangmere, after a brisk fight with German dive-bombers, of a Hurricane flown by Pilot Officer W. M. L. "Billy" Fiske of No. 601 Squadron, the dashing, wealthy former captain of the U.S. bobsled team at the winter Olympics of 1928 in Saint-Moritz and of 1932 in Lake Placid. He died of his burns two days later, becoming the first American killed in action during the war. (A plaque was placed in Fiske's memory in Saint Paul's Cathedral; it reads, "An American citizen who died that England might live.") The third event was the historic visit of Winston Churchill to Air Vice-Marshal Park's Operations Room at No. 11 Group headquarters in Uxbridge, outside London.

Countless young pilots shared the experience of Pilot Officer Nigel Rose, a twenty-two-year-old Spitfire pilot with No. 602 City of Glasgow squadron, which had flown down from Scotland the day before. Rose saw action for the first time that day, and survived to write home to his parents, "Six of us on patrol at 16,000 ft ran into about 50 Jerries and I had my baptism of firing. I made three attacks, and on the last I believe I may have got my man for he went into a vertical dive and hadn't pulled out by the 10/10 clouds at 6,000 ft. It was terrifically exciting and I'm darned if I can remember what happened at the time."[1]

Although slow to start after the huge effort of the day before, the *Luftwaffe* was back over England in force by the middle of the afternoon. Three separate big raids were aimed at the Portsmouth area and at RAF Tangmere. (Nigel Rose happened to witness the bombing of Tangmere, and wrote to his parents, in the spirit and style of *Biggles*, "We had a magnificent view of the whole affair and it was most thrilling to watch."[2]) More than 170 aircraft were plotted approaching Hornchurch and Debden; in all, there were more than 350 German aircraft attacking Fighter Command airfields during the course of the afternoon. There were fierce fights all over southern and southeastern England, and Tangmere, one of Dowding's most important airfields, took a repeated pasting. The runway was pockmarked with bomb craters and buried delayed-action bombs; aircraft caught on the ground were destroyed; hangars and workshops were set on fire; the sick quarters and the officer's mess received direct hits. Ground crews were shaken by the repeated bombings, but cheered up when a van from the Women's Voluntary Service (WVS) appeared in the middle of the bombing to serve tea.

The radar station at Ventnor was put out of action again, despite Göring's order to ignore these, and by the late afternoon every one of Park's squadrons—and by now all his squadrons were short of aircraft and pilots—was fiercely engaged. This moment was indelibly captured by General Hastings Ismay, Churchill's chief of staff in his self-appointed (and self-created) second capacity as "Minister of Defence," who had accompanied the prime minister to Uxbridge:

> There had been heavy fighting throughout the afternoon, and at one moment every single squadron in the Group was engaged; there was nothing in reserve, and the map table showed new waves of attackers crossing the coast. I felt sick with fear. As the evening closed in the fighting died down, and we left by car for Chequers [the country residence of British prime ministers], Churchill's first words were: "Do not speak to me; I have never been so moved." After above five minutes he leaned forward and said, "Never in the field of human combat has so much been owed by so many to so few." The words burned in my brain and I repeated them to my wife when I got home. [3]

The prime minister was to make this line immortal in a long speech on the war situation given four days later in the House of Commons, and it has since been burned into many brains and has come to represent the spirit of the Battle of Britain, and of the Royal Air Force as well. It is a statement of British patriotism right up there with Nelson's signal before the Battle of Trafalgar, "England expects that every man will do his duty," and Wellington's "Up, Guards, and at 'em," at Waterloo. As a result of it, those who flew in the Battle of Britain will be forever remembered as "the Few."

On that day, the RAF claimed seventy-five enemy aircraft destroyed, twenty-nine probables, and forty-one damaged, with a loss of fourteen fighters and eight pilots, as well as sixteen RAF personnel killed on the ground, and seventy-two civilians. (In fact, the *Luftwaffe* had lost only forty-five aircraft, but that is still three for one, and since most of the German aircraft were bombers it was more like twelve to one in terms of irreplaceable trained aircrew personnel.)

The 17th was another day of partial haze, with scattered clouds— good weather for the Germans, but the exhausted British pilots waited by their aircraft sunbathing, playing cards, and in at least one case, playing cricket, for nothing—only a few German aircraft came over, and those were mostly reconnaissance flights, providing a good clue that preparations were being made on the other side of the Channel for another big attack. Dowding spent the day continuing to press the Air Ministry to transfer pilots from the so-called "light bomber squadrons" (equipped with the infamously slow and ineffective Fairey Battle) and the "army cooperation squadrons" (equipped with the even less effective Westland Lysander), both of which had failed so dismally in France, but which the Air Staff was reluctant to give up on in case of a German invasion. In the last nine days Fighter Command had lost 156 pilots, and the operational training units (OTUs) were turning out new ones at a very slow rate. New fighter pilots were coming out of the OTUs at about one-third of the rate at which

Fighter Command was losing them. Dowding managed to persuade the Air Ministry to let five pilots volunteer for Fighter Command duty from each Battle squadron and three from each Lysander squadron, and managed to get fifty-six Royal Navy Fleet Air Arm pilots as well (hence the occasional presence of a pilot in naval uniform in photographs taken of fighter squadrons in 1940), but this was a drop in the bucket, compared with his needs. His supply of aircraft was holding up well enough, in part thanks to Lord Beaverbrook, in part thanks to an ambitious scheme in which damaged aircraft were repaired overnight and the parts of badly damaged aircraft "cannibalized" (to use a later word from the USAAF) to build a whole new one; but he was now in acute danger of running out of pilots. Even the pilots he managed to squeeze out of the light bomber squadrons, the army cooperation squadrons, and the Fleet Air Arm were of no immediate use to him—they required at least two to three weeks at an operational training unit to learn how to fly Spitfires or Hurricanes, and even then they would still be "new boys" rather than the experienced, battle-hardened fighter pilots they were replacing.

Most of the 17th was devoted to pick-and-shovel work, as station commanders all over southern England tried to fill in the bomb craters in their airfields, while the army's bomb disposal units removed unexploded bombs. (Bomb disposal was perhaps the most hazardous job of all, since the Germans were already expert at building into their bombs ingenious, hidden fuses triggered by timers, by movement, or by a combination of both, so that not every unexploded, buried bomb—or UXB, in the service jargon of the time—was a dud). Churchill, with his usual keen eye for detail, noted that this process was slowed by a lack of earth-moving machinery, and proposed appropriately equipped mobile units to rush to each airfield that was bombed and not only fill in the craters, but create camouflage holes so that from the air the runways would still look unusable. But in the meantime the airmen and whatever civilian laborers could be found did what they could with spades, plenty of grumbling, and an occasional mug of tea from the urn of the WVS van.

Sunday, August 18, dawned clear. "Fine and fair early," the RAF meteorologists would later report. "Rest of day cloudy." By now Beppo Schmidt was reporting that Fighter Command had no more than 200 fighters left, although Dowding's records indicate that he began the day with 706 serviceable aircraft, of which 228 were Spitfires and 396 Hurricanes. The No. 310 (Czech) Squadron was made operational at last, although Dowding and Park had some reservations about "foreign" pilots. The chief objections were that most of them couldn't yet speak or understand English, a big problem for the air controllers and also for their British squadron commanders; that they had poor flying discipline in the air (mostly because they failed to understand orders rather than because they were deliberately disobedient); and that they chattered too much to each other on their radios in Czech, French, or Polish. (Dowding's decision was quickly proved right— a Czech, Sergeant Joseph František, would become the second-highest scoring ace in Fighter Command during the Battle of Britain, with a total of seventeen kills before he was killed himself on October 8, 1940.) A Canadian squadron was declared operational as well, though the two Polish squadrons were being held in reserve. Still, on August 18, Dowding was short 209 pilots, a matter of increasing concern to him—and it had concerned Churchill for many weeks, in part because the Air Ministry's figures changed continually. He had already expressed his distress at "this particular admission of failure, on the part of the Air Ministry" to Sir Archibald Sinclair, the Secretary of State for Air, commenting that "it would be lamentable if we

have machines standing idle for want of pilots to fly them,"[4] a senti-
ment with which Dowding would surely have agreed.

There was no doubt that the entire system for training pilots remained slow and resistant to change, as opposed to the dramatic
improvements that Lord Beaverbrook had made in fighter production—this was a severe indictment of the Air Ministry's policy, and
had for some time been a bone of contention between Dowding and
Sholto Douglas. It was another of those disagreements that made
Dowding increasingly unpopular with his colleagues on the Air Staff
at just the moment when he was fighting (and winning) the country's
most important battle.

The flight training establishment was still working peacetime
hours, and responded to pressure for more pilots simply by shorten-
ing the courses, so that a lot of young pilots (their average age was
seventeen) reached their squadrons having logged only a few hours
in a Spitfire or Hurricane, and without ever having used a reflector
sight or learned deflection shooting. In the "old days," it had been up
to the squadrons to give new pilots a little polish and experience, but
in the summer of 1940, nobody had the time—the most a young pilot
reaching a squadron could expect was a couple of hours flying a
fighter behind a tired, irritable flight commander not much older
than himself, just to make sure the "new boy" remembered to put his
wheels down before landing. No matter how often a new pilot was
warned to keep looking behind himself, to stick "close as glue" to his
leader, and never to fly straight and level for more than twenty seconds, the first few operational flights (if he survived them) were
terrifying. One newcomer to a fighter squadron, intent on holding his
position in the formation on his first operational flight, recalls hearing his squadron commander shout, "Jerries behind, break right!" on
the wireless, reacted too slowly, and suddenly found himself alone in

the sky surrounded by German fighters. By some miracle they ignored him, and he was soon flying all by himself at 20,000 feet, with no idea where the rest of his squadron had gone—perhaps an even more frightening situation. Things happened in a fraction of a second, and the life expectancy of a new fighter pilot was measured in minutes or, if he was lucky, hours. A veteran fighter pilot voiced the common complaint that the new pilots reaching his squadron scared him a lot more than the Germans did. Though Churchill and Dowding could not have known it, the same complaints about pilot training were being made to the Air Ministry in Berlin by the German commanders in the field.

Neither Dowding nor anyone else could have guessed that the 18th would produce an air battle so intense and prolonged that at least one book has been written about this day alone (*The Battle of Britain: The Hardest Day*, by Alfred Price, Macdonalds and Jane's Publishers, 1979). The day was to see a sudden change in *Luftwaffe* tactics. Instead of scattered attacks against many airfields, this time the entire strength of the two German air fleets would be aimed at two of Dowding's most important airfields: Biggin Hill and Kenley. Both were "Sector" airfields—each Group was divided into Sectors, six of them in both No. 11 Group and No. 12 Group, with one airfield controlling the Sector, and usually with a varying number of smaller, alternative airfields within the Sector. Sector airfields like Biggin Hill and Kenley usually had four squadrons of fighters each, though two of the squadrons might be stationed either at more "forward" airfields like Gravesend and Manston in the case of Biggin Hill, or at nearby Croydon in the case of Kenley, on the principle of not putting all one's eggs in one basket in case the Sector airfield was attacked and put out of action.

Both these Sectors were shaped a little like roughly cut slices of pie, with the Sector airfield in both cases on the outskirts of London, at the sharper end of the slice, and the other end on the Channel. Biggin Hill and Kenley thus dominated the shortest and fastest approach from the Channel across southern England to London, and in order to attack London effectively (or to invade, if it came to that), they would have to be put out of action completely. The Germans understood this; what they did *not* understand was that the Sector operations rooms, each of which was like a miniature version of Park's operations room at No. 11 Group headquarters in Uxbridge, were in fact far more important targets than an airfield's hangars, its fuel supply, its runways, or even the aircraft on the ground.

The flow of information was channeled and centralized as it made its way from the radar posts and the Observer Corps to Dowding's headquarters at Bentley Priory. But once it had reached there, it was "filtered" so that personnel at each Group headquarters received only what they needed to know as quickly as possible and passed it on in turn to Sector headquarters, from which it would be transmitted to the Sector's fighter squadrons, leaving the Sector commanders free to devise their own tactics. On paper, the system looked inflexible and overcentralized, but in practice it gave each Sector and that Sector's fighter squadrons almost complete freedom of action in determining how to meet the approaching threat, and as much information as possible in precise, coherent form, and in what we now call real time. This was a vital factor for squadron commanders in the air, who measured time in seconds and wanted an instant reply to the basic questions: "How many? What height? What direction? What course do I have to fly to meet them? How far away are they?

This information was spoken to them by their Sector ground controller and his staff ("tellers," as they were called, many of them young women), who got it from the Group controller, who got it in turn directly from the Fighter Command controller at Bentley Priory, where the "big picture" of German attacks was being continually plotted on the map table by the WAAFs as they received the information through their headphones. (The controller at No. 11 Group was none other than Lord Willoughby de Broke, future steward of the Jockey Club, whose firm, clear, authoritative voice, a prerequisite for a fighter controller, and total unflappability were admired even by so critical a judge of these qualities as Winston Churchill.) Since all this depended on secure telephone lines, Dowding's insistence in 1937 on having them buried underground and protected by concrete shielding against bombs was justified over and over again.

Life was a good deal rougher on the forward airfields than on the larger Sector airfields, in terms of comfort and facilities—practically speaking, they were satellites of their Sector airfield, and very few of them had its creature comforts and resources in terms of messes and buildings. In both places, the pilots spent their day, from before dawn to sunset, in their squadron "dispersal hut," usually a wooden barracks building at Sector airfields, sometimes no more than a camouflaged caravan (trailer) on the more primitive forward airfields, never more than a minute's run from their aircraft. Pilots wore their second-best uniform ("battle dress" had not yet been issued in the RAF), a Mae West inflatable life jacket at all times (since this jacket was difficult to put on in a hurry, and easy to forget), and calf-high black leather "flying boots." In the less formal surroundings of the forward airfields they might wear a white roll-neck sweater under the tunic, but this practice was discouraged at Sector airfields, where a collar and tie were insisted on by most station commanders. (The station commander was normally referred to by all ranks, though never to his face, as the "Groupie," short for Group Captain). In the more glamorous Auxiliary Air Force squadrons, whose pilots were often wealthy or sporty types, it was often the custom to wear a silk scarf and leave the top button of the tunic open. A few of the older, regular, prewar RAF pilots, NCOs and officers alike, still wore the bulky "Sidcot" flying suit, a heavy, canvas-like one-piece overall, with many zips, pockets, and flaps, that was a relic of open-cockpit flying. Normally, a pilot placed his parachute on the port stabilizer or wing of his aircraft first thing in the morning, so he could grab it quickly as he ran to "scramble." There was no time to put it on before entering the cockpit—the pilot simply threw it onto the seat as he stepped up onto the wing (it served as his seat cushion), jumped in after it, then buckled the parachute straps on tightly as soon as he was seated. One of the ground crew usually helped the pilot fasten the Sutton harness that secured the pilot to his metal bucket seat—the straps were usually draped carefully over the sills of the cockpit, to avoid any risk of their getting caught up in the straps of the parachute harness—while the pilot pulled on his flying helmet, with the oxygen mask and flying goggles already attached; plugged in the cord of his microphone and headphones; then twirled his right index finger in a wide circle, as a signal to the ground crew to start the engine. From the dispersal hut to takeoff took less than a minute. (Once in the air and going into combat, the first thing a pilot did was to lower his seat, giving himself a better view of his reflector sight, then tighten his Sutton harness even more, so he would be firmly held in his seat even in the most extreme maneuvers at high speed.)

The dispersal hut was the pilot's private, clublike world, one in which rank counted for less than a pilot's wings sewn on the left side of the tunic. Here, sergeant pilots and officers were still not quite equals, but they were as close to equality as they ever got on the ground. The atmosphere was a combination of the locker room in an athletic facility and the run-down, messy, untidy common room of a boarding school, with odd pieces of furniture scrounged from anywhere, big worn-out leather armchairs, a ratty old sofa on which a pilot or his dog was always sleeping, sometimes a Victrola and a stack of records, old magazines, newspapers, cards, a chess set (or draughts, the British equivalent of checkers, for the less "brainy"), untidy piles of raincoats and flying clothes (many of them belonging to dead pilots) hung from hooks on the wall, peeling strips of "sticky tape" on the windows to prevent the glass from imploding in splinters in case of attack, and a few dog-eared paperback books. (James Hadley Chase's hard-boiled, risqué thriller *No Orchids for Miss Blandish* was a favorite, with a sexy blond on the cover. Also popular were the doings of "Jane," another bosomy, sexy blond who was always coming out of her clothes or having them torn off her in the famous *Daily Mirror* cartoon strip of the same name. Many people, including the prime minister, considered Jane the biggest morale booster of all for British servicemen.) The air was a thick fug of cigarette and pipe smoke—this was an age when almost everybody smoked, and in any case fighter pilots knew that it probably wouldn't be smoking or drinking that would kill them. There were the obligatory cork bulletin boards, thick with notices, lists, and warnings; a blackboard with the daily list of aircraft and pilots in chalk; and dusty air recognition models of German aircraft hanging from the ceiling. In the warm summer months the pilots scrounged canvas deck chairs and sat outside in the sun, or lay in the grass, smoking and waiting. An aircraftman sat at a desk near the door to answer the telephone, and every time it rang, the pilots tensed. Often it was a harmless message like "The tea van is on its way," or a routine order or inquiry from the station bureaucracy, which was proceeding on its stately way, filling out forms and holding inspections as in peacetime, and the pilots would go back to whatever they had been doing to calm their nerves and deal with the stress of waiting for the call to scramble. The sharp, loud noise of a telephone ringing was enough to make some pilots go outside and throw up, and haunted many pilots for years to come.

In some of the most exposed forward airfields at least one flight might be kept manned from first light on, with the pilots sitting uncomfortably in their aircraft, ready to take off at a moment's notice—for the distance from the lighthouse at Beachy Head on the Channel to RAF Biggin Hill was less than sixty miles, or about fifteen minutes' flying time for German bombers, and if they elected to come in low over the Channel the radar operators might not pick them up until it was too late to intercept them.

This thought had occurred to the Germans as well, and it was to form a major part of their strategy for the 18th.* This was to be a precise, surgical strike on two vital parts of Fighter Command, the first by Field Marshal Kesselring's *Luftflotte* 2, and the crews were briefed with more than the usual attention to detail. German reconnaissance aircraft had brought back photographs of Kenley and Biggin Hill, and pilots and bombardiers were told exactly what to hit. The bomber crews themselves were impressed by the clarity of the photographs, eight-by-ten-inch glossies, which everyone agreed were superb, and which were studied carefully and passed around from hand to hand at the briefings.† Every building was clearly shown, and crews—especially

---

*I am indebted to Alfred Price's *The Battle of Britain: The Hardest Day* for his detailed, minute-by-minute account of the battle of August 18, both in the air and on the ground.

† The *Luftwaffe* mostly used standard German bombers, as well as the Bf 110 twin-engine fighter, for photo reconnaissance, but there is some evidence that they had also been using, over England, the futuristic, high-altitude, diesel-powered Ju 86P, which flew at over 38,000 feet, well above the reach of British fighters, and carried two cameras, each weighing nearly 200 pounds, and a crew of two in a pressurized cabin.

those of the dive-bombers—were assigned specific targets, as well as carefully planned approach routes. The attack was to consist of a combination of heavy bombing from twin-engine bombers and pinpoint, low-altitude bombing by dive-bombers, with large fighter sweeps to draw British fighters away from the bombing forces. It was hoped that the low-altitude attacks would go undetected by the British until it was too late, and that Fighter Command would have to divide its forces in order to deal with the simultaneous attacks. The low-altitude attacks were to go in literally at "rooftop level," the crews navigating by road and railway maps, and stay where it would be hard for British fighters to spot them or shoot them down. The plan called for a simultaneous raid by sixty He 111s on Biggin Hill, and an attack on Kenley by forty-eight Do 17s and Ju 88s. The attack on Biggin Hill would be a conventional high-altitude attack; that on Kenley would be more complex, and split into three separate phases—first there would be a "precision" dive-bombing attack carried out from a high altitude on the vital structures of the airfield, then a high-altitude raid to destroy the runways and the airfield's defenses, and finally an attack at rooftop level to destroy whatever was left standing. The exact timing of the attacks and the approach routes were worked out with exemplary precision, and were intended to surprise and overwhelm both the British fighters and the antiaircraft guns around the airfields.

As it happened, there were two surprises in store for the *Luftwaffe*. The more serious one was that nobody in *Luftwaffe* intelligence had picked out the site of the Sector operations room at Biggin Hill or Kenley, the destruction of which would indeed have paralyzed the fighters of Park's No. 11 Group for a time. The Germans had no idea that each Sector had its own operations room, linked by underground telephone cables to the Group operations room, and from there to Fighter Command, or that radar information was flowing constantly down to the level of the Sector airfields. The fact that the operations room in every Sector airfield was merely in a wooden hut above-ground,* protected at best by a blast wall, haunted Dowding, but there had been no time to put them underground like those at the Group level, and once the battle had started it was too late to do anything more about this. Thus, the one absolutely vital (and unprotected) target at each of the Sector airfields, aboveground and vulnerable, was unknown to the German planners.

The other was the existence, at Kenley, of six parachute and cable launchers (also referred to as UP, for unrotated projectile, and as PAC, for parachute and cable device), one of Churchill's most cherished secret weapons.† This was the brainchild of his long-term scientific adviser and friend Professor Frederick Lindemann (later Lord Cherwell, but always referred to by those around the prime minister as "the Prof"). The Prof and Dowding had clashed sharply on numerous scientific and technical matters in the past, but in the case of the parachute and cable launchers, which everybody in the RAF and the Royal Artillery dismissed as a waste of time and money, Churchill's will prevailed (as it had over the big guns at Dover), at least to the extent that the system was installed on a trial basis at Kenley, despite Dowding's objections, which prompted Churchill to remark, "Dowding has the reputation of . . . not being receptive to new ideas."[5] A weapons system that might have been conceived by Rube Goldberg or Heath Robinson at their most whimsical, UP consisted of a rocket,

---

* The possibility that the Sector operations room at Kenley might be destroyed had led to the preparation of an "alternative site" in a vacant butcher shop in nearby Caterham, on Caterham High Street, less than a mile from Kenley. It had been chosen because it was directly over the GPO's main underground telephone cable for the entire area.

† Others included the "sticky bomb" to be thrown or launched at enemy tanks (not a success), and the "proximity fuse," which exploded an antiaircraft shell when it passed near an enemy aircraft, and which would turn out to be one of the Allies' most significant "wonder weapons" of the war.

which, when fired, rose 600 feet high and released a small parachute suspending a 480-foot-long stout wire cable in front of enemy dive-bombers. In the event an enemy aircraft ran into the wire, a second, smaller parachute opened at the bottom end, ensuring that the wire, even if didn't tear off a wing or do other structural damage, would drag the aircraft to the ground. It was, in effect, a more sophisticated development of the barrage balloon, a device first used early in World War I, which dangled a cable from a height of about 500 feet to discourage low-flying enemy aircraft. Some 1,500 barrage balloons were then in service at important sites throughout Britain. The difference between them and the UP was that the barrage balloon was a passive defensive device—the balloon itself was clearly visible, and low-flying aircraft could simply avoid it—whereas UP was an aggressive device, more in keeping with the prime minister's nature, just the kind of "dirty trick" he liked to play on the Germans, and in theory it could be used to ensnare enemy bombers by night or day, dragging them down out of the sky. The problem was statistical, as the Air Staff instantly perceived—it would require a phenomenal number of UPs to have any chance of working; you would have to throw a haystack up into the sky to catch a needle. Nevertheless, judging from the number of testy "Action This Day" minutes that Churchill wrote on the subject in 1940, and the fact that he was often willing to interrupt his busy day to observe tests of the UP, most of them disappointing, it remained dear to his heart, a hobbyhorse from which the prime minister was unwilling to dismount.

As was so often the case, the meteorologists got it wrong. The weather looked perfect, as predicted, but no sooner had the German aircraft taken off in the early morning of August 18 than they were recalled because a layer of haze over the targets was discovered that would make the low-level attacks impossible. The bomber crews were obliged to land their aircraft with a full load of fused bombs, never an easy task. Keyed-up, fully kitted, and ready to go, the German aircrews were then obliged to hang around their aircraft until shortly before noon, when they reboarded them and started out again, reconnaissance planes having reported that the haze over the targets had lifted.

A few of the British fighter pilots had been scrambled in pursuit of the German reconnaissance aircraft, one of which was shot down, but most of them passed an uneventful morning, and were beginning to hope there was a chance for a peaceful lunch. By noon, however, British radar operators were becoming aware that something big was happening, and by twelve-forty-five they were reporting to Fighter Command that at least six major concentrations of enemy aircraft were forming up over France and heading for the coast, estimating the total number at 350. This was about 100 more than the Germans were actually sending—108 bombers and 150 fighters—but radar was still undependable at estimating enemy numbers. Either way it was enough to start Air Vice-Marshal Park getting his fighter squadrons into the air.

On the German side, however, the problem of organizing a complex, multilayered attack on two targets, to be carried out at very different altitudes, and composed of aircraft flying at different speeds and gathered from more than a dozen airfields, was proving to be a more difficult task than anybody had anticipated. Despite the generally good weather there were clouds over the Calais area from about 6,000 to 10,000 feet, so inevitably some of the bomber formations missed each other and their fighter escorts were unable to find them. The attack was a brilliant piece of planning, but it depended on the perfect synchronization of its various elements, and this is hard to achieve in the air. Sixty of the German fighters were supposed to sweep over southern England from Dover to Kenley and Biggin Hill, a distance of about forty miles, and engage British fighters before the bomber formations appeared, while the remainder stuck close to the bombers to protect them. RAF Kenley was supposed to receive first a concentrated, precision dive-bombing attack on its vital buildings; then, immediately afterward, a conventional high-altitude bombing attack to destroy the runways; finally, as the coup de grâce, a daring and unexpected rooftop-level attack to destroy anything that remained undamaged. This whole rapid and carefully choreographed succession of separate attacks would be over in ten minutes, and was intended to leave Kenley a smoldering ruin. In the meantime, the force of sixty He 111s would attack Biggin Hill from a high altitude, putting it out of action, while the speed of the combined attacks, the fact that they were aimed at two separate targets, and the sheer number of German fighters overhead would overcome or distract the British fighter squadrons. On paper it seemed like a sure thing.

That it was not was shortly made apparent by the appearance of no fewer than nine squadrons of Spitfires and Hurricanes, nearly 100 British fighters—almost half Dowding's total force, if you believed Beppo Schmidt's numbers, as Göring evidently did. Park prudently kept half of them to the northeast of Kenley and Biggin Hill, to cover the Thames and Dover. Although the Germans had no way of knowing it, Park also had three more squadrons in reserve at RAF Tangmere and six more he could draw on if he needed them. Further evidence that the day was not going to go as smoothly as planned became rapidly obvious to the leader of the Ninth *Staeffel* of Do 17s, which had been sent on a different course from that of the main force, crossing the English coast farther east at Beachy Head to deliver the third, low-level attack on Kenley. The commander, Captain Joachim Roth, had led the aircraft in so low over the Channel that the wash of their propellers left a wake on the sea—in fact, as they approached England they were well below Beachy Head, looking *up* at the chalk cliff face, on top of which was an Observer Corps post! As it happened, a war photographer was with them, and shooting with an ordinary Leica, he was able to capture pictures of English civilians sprinting for cover in the small town of Lewes, north of Brighton, as the German planes flew over them (one man is running while carrying a shopping bag; another is looking up in amazement). The German fliers observed cyclists on the roads below them hastily abandon their bicycles and run for the nearest ditch. The startled observers on Beachy Head had been looking *down* on the German bombers, rather than up at them, and reported that they had crossed the coast at "zero altitude," and indeed Roth maintained an altitude of about fifty feet as he followed the railway line from Southease to Blechingley, a brilliant piece of navigation, though from time to time he had to pull up a bit, to avoid hills and electricity lines. Flying a bomber at an altitude of fifty feet and a speed of 250 miles per hour requires intense concentration, so it was not until Roth passed over the village of Blechingley, less than six miles south of his target, that he became aware of what he was *not* seeing ahead of him: there was no huge column of smoke rising from the airfield.

Owing to a muddle and the scattered cloud cover over the French coast, Roth's aircraft were the first to strike Kenley, instead of the last. Although, as the Germans had guessed, they were too low to be picked up by radar, thanks to the Observer Corps they were going to receive a warm welcome. Kenley, like all the Sector airfields, was strongly defended. Detachments of infantry were present at all of them—in the event of an invasion, it was recognized by everybody except Winston Churchill that RAF ground personnel would be no substitute for trained infantry—and in Kenley's case they were from the Scots Guards, one of the five foot regiments of the Brigade of Guards, and one of the oldest and most prestigious regiments in the British Army. In addition, there were both heavy and rapid-fire anti-aircraft guns (Bofors forty-millimeter quick-firing cannon), manned by the Royal Artillery; large numbers of machine guns; and the much maligned UP projectors, manned by airmen. Despite the short warning period, Kenley, Biggin Hill, and Croydon had all scrambled their remaining fighters, and also had time to broadcast the alert, warning everybody to take cover immediately. The personnel in the Kenley operations room, men and women, having donned their steel helmets, stayed at their posts, however, and watched as the plotters moved the air-raid markers across the map until they converged on their own airfield, then braced themselves for the bombs they knew were coming.

Roth's low-level attack destroyed three hangars and many other buildings, and briefly severed the electricity cable to the operations room, but at a terrific cost to his own unit—he would lose almost half his aircraft, and he himself would be taken prisoner, after being badly burned along with his pilot, crash-landing in a field close to Kenley. Ironically, the UP projectiles helped bring Roth down—his pilot was so startled by the long rows of bright orange flashes ahead of him as the rockets were launched at the northwestern end of the airfield that he pulled the aircraft up to clear them, giving the Bofors gunners a perfect chance to hit him as he climbed. Another German bomber banked sharply to avoid whatever was ahead, with the result that one of the suspended wires snagged a wing, then slid off without the parachute opening, puzzling the crew. A third UP did exactly what it was supposed to do and pulled a Dornier out of the sky, bringing it down on a nearby house with an explosion that killed everyone on board, including a full colonel who had been flying as an observer.

The UP had created consternation in the air and on the ground—to the German pilots it looked as if they were flying into an inexplicable, lavish daytime fireworks display; but to the British airmen, gunners, and infantrymen on the ground the sight of what seemed like a cloud of white parachutes in the sky led to the conclusion that German paratroopers were landing in what must be the first act of the invasion. One consequence was that throughout the day RAF fighter pilots who were shot down and landed by parachute found themselves being held at gunpoint by the Home Guard or by a farmer armed with a shotgun. Usually, a burst of angry swearing was sufficient proof of British identity, but this did not help Poles, Czechs, or, in one case, an enraged New Zealander.

The low-level raid was over in a couple of minutes. Ironically, *Hauptmann* Roth, his hands and face badly burned, and his pilot were brought to RAF Kenley as prisoners just in time to be bombed by what should have been the first wave of the attack. One WAAF described the scene as she took cover: "Beyond our trench—perhaps 50 yards away—the hangars were ablaze; everything seemed to be burning fiercely in a pall of black smoke blowing across to the right." For a moment, the only noise heard was the crackling of burning hangars and the occasional explosion of an oxygen cylinder; then the antiaircraft guns opened up again as the twenty-seven Dorniers of the high-altitude force and their fighter escorts appeared over the airfield, subjecting Kenley—and the surrounding villages—to a heavy pasting. The Ju 88 twin-engine dive-bombers, which should have been the first to attack Kenley, did not turn up until the airfield, seen from the sky, seemed to have been demolished, and therefore flew on to their alternative target, at RAF West Malling. The entire attack had taken a grand total of eight minutes, and with the hangars and buildings on fire, the runways pockmarked with bomb craters, and so many fire engines responding to the blazing RAF station and the homes nearby hit by stray bombs that the surrounding roads were blocked, the Germans concluded they had succeeded, albeit with heavy losses. In fact, Kenley would be ready for action again in two hours—the operations room was moved to the vacant butcher shop, a runway was marked out that avoided the bomb craters, and the fires were brought under control. Twelve airmen had been killed, and there were many RAF and army personnel and civilian wounded, but at the end of the day Kenley was still usable.

The high-altitude bombing of Biggin Hill by sixty He 111s was more conventional, but had even less effect. Most of the bombs missed the airfield, and exploded harmlessly in the woods and fields. From the air, the smoke and dust made it look to German aircrew as if the airfield was destroyed, but on the ground the RAF personnel and soldiers moved quickly to make the airfield usable as soon as the bombers had left. Perhaps the most memorable moment of the raid on Biggin Hill was the defusing of an unexploded German bomb by a WAAF sergeant, who would become the second airwoman in the Battle of Britain to be awarded the Military Medal for courage in action. (Another WAAF and two Wrens—members of the Women's Royal Naval Service—would win awards for courage under fire on August 18, as did one army lieutenant and five NCOs and soldiers. It was a day when the ground personnel, men and women, acted with the same heroism as the fighter pilots.) As the Germans streamed back across Kent and Sussex toward the Channel, they were fiercely attacked by British fighters, and losses on both sides were high.

The day was not yet over—in fact, it had hardly begun. The aircraft of *Luftflotte* 2 had scarcely landed back at their bases (the survivors of the ill-fated low-level attack on Kenley were disbelieved and ridiculed when they described the mysterious fireworks display and the tangle of cables into which they had flown) when those of Field Marshal Sperrle's *Luftflotte* 3 took off from their bases west of the Seine to attack Gosport, Ford, and Thorney Island, all clustered around Portsmouth and the Isle of Wight.

This was the largest concentration of Ju 87 Stuka dive-bombers ever assembled for a single raid on Britain, and it was protected by no fewer than 157 fighters. The ambitious attack had several flaws, however. First, the Stukas had already demonstrated that they were sitting ducks for British fighters. Secondly, although the attack might have contributed to overwhelming No. 11 Group by sheer numbers had it been made at the same time as the attacks on Kenley and Biggin Hill, it would actually begin more than half an hour later. Consequently, Park had a slim opportunity (or as we would now say, a window of opportunity) in which to get his squadrons refueled and rearmed, while sending up whatever he had left to meet the new threat. Third, thanks to another failure of German intelligence, none of the three airfields being attacked was used by Fighter Command. Gosport and Thorney Island were both naval airfields (Thorney Island's official name was HMS *Peregrine*, since all permanent shore bases belonging to the Royal Navy are named like ships, something which Beppo Schmidt's staff could have discovered by looking at an AA road map); and RAF Ford was a Coastal Command airfield. All three targets were also well defended, and very close to RAF Tangmere and several other Fighter Command airfields. A look at the map should have warned Sperrle and his bomber commander, Major General Baron Wolfram von Richthofen (a cousin of the famous Red Baron of World War I), that Fighter Command would be able to dominate the sky above the targets.

The Stukas came over in perfect, massed formation, wingtip to wingtip as if they were flying at the annual Hendon Air Show, an enormous, tightly packed display of aircraft that impressed everybody who observed it. Each Stuka carried a 500-pound bomb under the fuselage and four 110-pound bombs under the wings, a powerful bomb load for a single-engine, two-seat aircraft, and one that a good dive-bomber pilot could aim with pinpoint accuracy. Since this area was to the south of England, Park could draw on the fighters of No. 10 Group to his west when he needed them. This option had an additional advantage: there was no bad blood or friction between Park and Air Vice-Marshal Sir Christopher Brand, as there was between Park and Air Vice-Marshal Leigh-Mallory of No. 12 Group. By the time the Stukas, now joined by their fighter escort (because of their greater speed, the fighters had taken off later), were approaching the coastline, Park had nearly seventy British fighters in the air. That still left him at odds of two to one with the German fighters, but it was not an insignificant number, and the German fighter pilots were once again faced by two insoluble problems—how to protect the slow, lumbering dive-bombers at low altitude in a plane that could fly almost 150 miles per hour faster and was at its best above 20,000 feet, and how to fight a prolonged battle with one eye on the fuel gauge or the "low fuel" warning light.

At two-fifteen that afternoon the Stukas split into four groups as they passed the Isle of Wight, one bound for Thorney Island, one for Gosport, one for Ford, and one for the radar station at Poling. The natural assumption on the ground, considering the persistent efforts the Germans had made in the past few days to destroy Tangmere, was that it would be once again the target, and given the short distances involved, it is not surprising that the real targets were caught by surprise. Nor is it surprising that the Stuka attacks were more deadly than those of the more conventional bombers at Biggin Hill

The fatally damaged Hurricane of Billy Fiske—the first American
killed in action in World War II—about to crash-land.

The Battle of Britain, painting by Paul Nash.

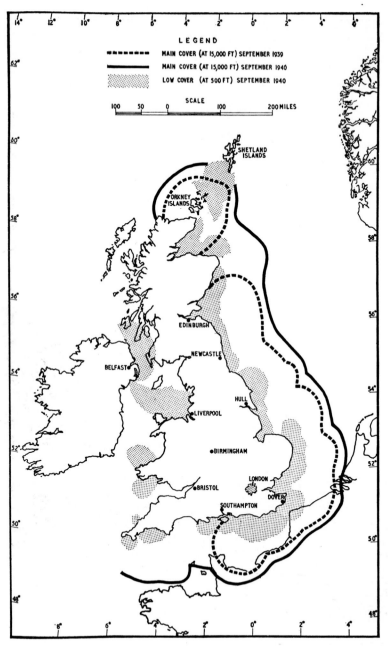

Radar cover, September 1939 and September 1940.

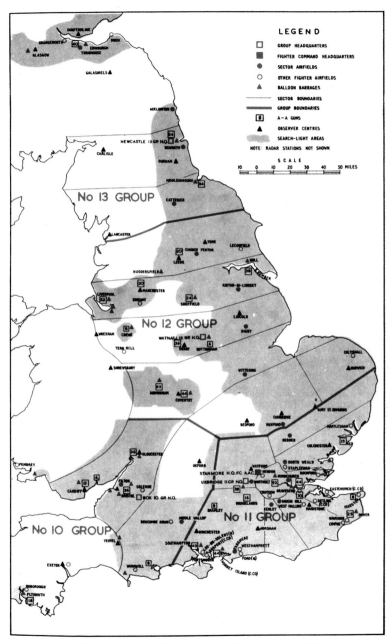

The air defenses of England and Wales, August 1940.

A Hurricane Mk I (foregound) and two Spitfire Mk I's
in the sky over England, summer of 1940.

A Spitfire rolls below a Heinkel 111 bomber in the air above Kent,
seen from the bomb aimer's position in another Heinkel.

and Kenley. Stuka pilots were still the elite of the *Luftwaffe*. They did not attack at low levels—instead, they climbed to 13,000 feet, and from that altitude went into a steep dive, of between seventy-five and ninety degrees, aiming directly at their target. The side panel of the pilot's windscreen was etched with lines that allowed the pilot to check exactly the angle of his dive. Every variable had to be carefully calculated—the aircraft had to bomb directly into the prevailing wind, which of course determined for the pilot the direction of the attack. The speed and the angle of dive had to be held exactly, and a horn sounded automatically in the cockpit to warn the pilot four seconds before it was time to release the bomb load, usually at a height of 400 meters (just over 1,200 feet). This was a method of bombing with pinpoint accuracy that no other air force could match at the time.* However, one defect was that during the dive the Stuka's only protection was from the wireless operator–rear gunner seated behind the pilot, who had only one machine gun with which to hold off fighters armed with eight guns. Another defect was that when the pilot pulled out of the dive and climbed away steeply, having released his bombs, his airspeed slowed to the point where he was an easy target for antiaircraft fire from the ground, or for British fighters. Although the Stuka had originally been equipped with an external siren that gave off a banshee wail when the aircraft dived, intended to strike terror into the hearts of those on the ground, by the time of the Battle of Britain these had mostly been removed, as one more object that increased drag and slowed the plane. Besides, the targets were no longer masses of terrified, traumatized refugees or

---

* As late as 1943 RAF Bomber Command, despite the help of radar and "Pathfinder" Mosquitos laying a flare path to the target, was still capable not merely of missing a specific target but of hitting the wrong city (see *Bomber*, by Len Deighton). The same was true of the USAAF bomber force, which in broad daylight managed to bomb Schaffhausen, in neutral Switzerland, twice, in 1944 and 1945.

fleeing troops on the roads, as had been the case in Poland and France, but military installations, in which discipline was likely to prevail over fear. At the Poling radar station the WAAF plotters kept on at their work even when they had plotted the enemy aircraft as right above them, and when they could hear the whistle of the descending bombs. (One of them, Corporal Joan Avis Hearn, would win the Military Medal for her courage under fire.) At Ford Naval Air Station, sailors fired back at the Stukas with World War I Lewis guns, and one officer used his revolver; and Wren stewards and cooks helped to rescue and tend to the wounded as bombs went off around them. Of the targets, Ford was hit worst, with twenty-eight killed and eighty-five wounded—it was a scene of "mutilated bodies and wrecked buildings," over which a dense cloud of burning oil from the flaming fuel tanks hung ominously. Gosport and Thorney Island were the least badly damaged. The radar station at Poling was put out of commission—one of the wooden receiver towers had been damaged. The Stuka force lost sixteen aircraft, and eight of the escorting Bf 109s were destroyed, for a total loss of five British fighters.

The day was still not over. At five-forty-five *Luftflotte* 2 attacked again, flying up the Thames estuary, this time to attack Croydon, while Manston was attacked at ground level by fighters. Further raids took place during the night. In the meantime, each side counted its losses. The RAF had lost twenty-seven fighters, with ten pilots killed; the *Luftwaffe* had lost a total of seventy-one aircraft, of which thirty-seven were bombers and eleven were Bf 110s. Forty-four civilians had been killed and 108 wounded. On no other day in the Battle of Britain did German and RAF losses mount so high, or in the case of the *Luftwaffe* ultimately serve so little purpose. It was not so much the number of aircraft that mattered—they could be replaced—

but the irreparable loss of so many highly trained bomber crews. Even more important, although the fact was not yet clear to anybody in the *Luftwaffe* high command, at no point had the Germans in any way endangered RAF Fighter Command, or even tempted Dowding to make a tactical mistake. Certainly, the loss of twenty-seven fighters was worrisome, but thanks to Lord Beaverbrook's efforts they could be replaced overnight; and although Dowding's concern over the supply of fighter pilots was still intense, the immense effort the two German air fleets made on August 18 had merely put two of his major Sector airfields out of action for a few hours at most, and knocked out one radar station, which could be replaced with a mobile unit until repairs were made. Dowding could look at the day with a certain grim satisfaction. This was exactly how he had planned to fight and win the battle—the Germans were making huge efforts to destroy Fighter Command, at a great cost in life and machines, while Dowding, without ever revealing his real strength, was inflicting more and more casualties on them. Eventually, it would dawn on them that they were battering their heads against a brick wall, but in the meantime, as long as they continued to do so, there would be no invasion.

Unlike most battles, this one was being fought in full view of the public and of war correspondents from all over the neutral world, like a spectator sport on a vast scale, and with the involvement of countless numbers of civilians—as well as firemen, policemen, and the Home Guard, many of whom were more than happy to talk to the press. It was, to be blunt—and although the thought does not ever seem to have crossed Dowding's mind—great propaganda. The fighter pilots were young, photogenic, clean-cut, cheerful, and enthusiastic. There was no equivalent here to the hundreds of thousands who had died in the mud, barbed wire, futile mass attacks, and gas clouds of World War I. The fighting took place in the air, watched by thousands, sometimes at low altitudes; aircrews on both sides parachuted down onto English fields, villages, golf courses, and gardens; damaged aircraft crashed in bucolic spots or urban streets, or made forced landings in parks and on the lawns of stately country mansions; bombs fell not only on the airfields and radar stations but on the homes of ordinary people, more by accident than by design at this stage of the war, and not in the numbers of the Blitz, when the cities and those who lived in them became the targets of the *Luftwaffe*.

This was not a war people merely read about in the newspapers or heard about on the nine o'clock BBC news—it was fought right overhead, and, interestingly, the effect was to raise British morale, and to capture the attention and admiration of many people in America who in other circumstances might have been indifferent or hostile to what was happening on the other side of the Atlantic. The British Army had been badly beaten in Norway, and had lost again in France, but now, quite unexpectedly, the British found that Dowding's "chicks," few and young as they might be, had proven themselves heroes in the eyes of everyone in the world except the Germans. Even the Soviet Union's spies in the United Kingdom sent accurate, admiring messages back to Moscow, including one from a spy who managed to get into Croydon on August 16 to report on the damage there, and also got very close to Kenley on the 18th, and reported correctly that there was no panic in the surrounding civilian population, and that Kenley's Hurricanes were back in the air—although whether Stalin saw this, or was informed, is unknown.

During this battle, unlike other great battles in history, life went on as usual close to the fighting, despite the bloodshed in the skies above, bringing to mind W. H. Auden's lines:

About suffering they were never wrong,

The Old Masters; how well they understood

Its human position; how it takes place

While someone else is eating or opening a window or just walking
    dully along. . . .

In Breughel's *Icarus*, for instance: how everything turns away

Quite leisurely from the disaster . . .

Something amazing, a boy falling out of the sky . . .

"A boy falling out of the sky . . ." People went on with their lives, picnicking, playing tennis, having lunch outdoors in the glorious (and
very un-English) summer weather, while young men four miles above
their heads fought and died, or did indeed fall out of the sky. Occasionally they looked up from what they were doing at the maze of
contrails in the blue sky, or more rarely, saw an orange flash and a
puff of black smoke as an aircraft was hit, and from time to time
watched a parachute slowly descend, and wondered whether it was
one of theirs or one of ours. No less important a figure than Anthony
Eden, the debonair Secretary of State for War, saw a Spitfire and a
Messerschmitt flash past at rooftop level as he stepped out of his bath,
and later remarked on how strange it was to see the fighting going on
in the sky as he and his guests played tennis. Harold Nicolson, the
writer and member of Parliament, and his wife, poet and novelist Vita
Sackville-West, watched the air fighting high above their heads day
after day from their famous garden at Sissinghurst. People grew accus-
tomed to having the war drop in on their lives suddenly and unexpectedly—literally out of the blue—as bombs, pilots, aircrews, empty
cartridge cases, flaming fragments of damaged aircraft, and even whole
airplanes streaming smoke, flames, or white clouds of glycol, descended
on them out of the sky. One RAF pilot who had been shot down and

wounded was helped by friendly golfers to a nearby golf club, and parked at the bar in his bloodstained shirt while an ambulance was summoned, only to hear one member say to another, "Who's that scruffy chap at the bar? I don't think he's a member." The rousing patriotic popular song of the period "There'll Always Be an England,"* (played almost as frequently as "The White Cliffs of Dover"), comes to mind when we read about incidents like this. However long England might last—and the issue was still in doubt—there were some things about it and the English that would never change, even at the supreme moment of national crisis: in the ironic words of John Betjeman's poem,

> Think of what our Nation stands for,
> Books from Boots' and country lanes,
> Free speech, free passes, class distinctions,
> Democracy and proper drains.

The England that was being fought over in August 1940 was not yet that of the Beveridge Plan, the nationalization of industries, and the National Health Service that the Labour Party would introduce in 1945, still less that of our own day, when it has become, with whatever reluctance and mental reservations, crisscrossed with six-lane motor highways and part of Europe. It was still, at any rate south of London, in Kent and Sussex, slightly stuffy, dotted with neat suburbs and beyond them deliberately and self-consciously "picturesque" rural villages, then open fields rolling down to the old-fashioned seaside resorts, the shingle beaches and the famous white cliffs. The swashbuckling young airmen, whether German or British, seemed,

---

* "There'll always be an England / And England shall be free / If England means as much to you / As England means to me."

on landing, to be out of place in their flying kits, warriors from a futuristic and technological world. H. G. Wells had imagined it vividly, but its impact had not yet been felt in this tidy, prosperous corner of Britain, with its narrow roads, its flocks of sheep, its yearly hop picking, and its tidy fields full of horses and ponies. This was the part of England that the Germans proposed—improbably, as many people thought—to invade the moment Göring succeeded in sweeping the skies clear of British fighters.

Perhaps the most important event of the day, therefore, occurred many miles away, and unbeknownst to the British. Given the severe losses of the *Luftwaffe* and the continuing resistance of Fighter Command, Hitler postponed the date for Operation Sea Lion to September 17.

In fact, the events of August 18 led to some further thinking on both sides of the English Channel. On the German side, it was now abundantly clear that whatever promises Göring had made to the Führer, Fighter Command was not going to be eliminated in two weeks. The Germans finally bit the bullet on the subject of the Stuka and the Bf 110, in view of their high rate of loss—Stukas were at last taken out of the order of battle altogether for the time being, and Bf 110s were restricted to combat in areas where they could be protected by Bf 109s, a plan that made no sense at all, since it essentially involved using one fighter to protect another, and limited the use of the big, twin-engine fighter to the short range of the single-seat fighter. Also, the decision was made to concentrate the attacks on Fighter Command airfields and the factories in which the Spitfire and the Hurricane were manufactured, to the exclusion of everything else.

In Britain, Dowding ignored the triumphant headlines in the press regarding German losses—which announced that as many as 165

German and only twenty-seven British aircraft had been shot down, more than twice the actual number of aircraft the Germans lost. Instead, he concerned himself with his dwindling resources. If the Germans continued attacking in the strength they had shown on August 18, and if they concentrated their attacks on the aircraft factories, as he had already guessed they would, Fighter Command might soon be reduced to the point where it could no longer hold its own against them. Despite the admiration that was being showered on his fighter pilots, their actual number was now well below 1,000, and the rate at which new fighter aircraft were being built was leaving him with an increasingly slim reserve of machines. His margin of strength was paper-thin. Dowding could do the numbers better than anyone else, and what they told him was that the rate of attrition was now in danger of working against him faster than against the *Luftwaffe*. In No. 11 Group, which had borne the brunt of the casualties so far, it was decided to move those squadrons in which the casualties exceeded 50 percent "to quieter areas for a rest and a refit," and to replace them with squadrons from the west and the Midlands. Air Vice-Marshal Park gave his controllers orders not to send fighters out over the sea in pursuit of German reconnaissance aircraft or small numbers of German aircraft, and to avoid sending up large numbers of aircraft against German fighter sweeps. In short, Dowding and Park were pursing (and intensifying) a strategy that was the exact opposite of what Leigh-Mallory was demanding with increasing vehemence (and with Bader as spokesman for the fighter pilots of No. 12 Group), which was to engage the enemy over the Channel with "big wings" of fighters, instead of single squadrons.

On August 19 the weather took a turn for the worse—"Mainly cloudy, occasional showers in the east," the RAF report notes—and poor weather continued until August 23, to the great irritation of *Reichs-marschall* Göring. The Germans were not idle for five days, of course. They carried out massive "fighter sweeps," hoping to provoke No. 11 Group's fighter squadrons into the air, where they would be outnumbered, and also undertook random bombing, particularly at night. In fact, Göring had ordered an increase in night bombing against industrial targets, since the stretch of bad weather predicted for the next few days made daytime bombing impractical. He sensibly ordered a list to be drawn up of likely targets (a little late, one might think), including aluminum and aircraft engine plants, reserving to himself the decision to bomb targets in London and Liverpool by night.

In this area, at least, the Germans were formidably well prepared, and light-years ahead of the British. As long ago as June, Churchill had been startled by the surprising accuracy of German night bombing, which argued for the existence of a "secret weapon." Although the Air Ministry was reluctant to admit it, the *Luftwaffe* in fact benefited from an advanced system of radio beams code-named *Knickebein*, enabling bombers to fly a course along a given beam until a crossbeam, aimed at a specific factory or location, told them exactly when to drop their bombs. The most knowledgeable man on the subject turned out to be a twenty-eight-year-old scientist, R. V. Jones, then on the Air Ministry staff. Churchill summoned Jones to 10 Downing Street on June 21 to explain the bad news to him and the War Cabinet. It was, for Churchill, as he would later remark, "one of the blackest moments of the war," when he realized that the Germans could bomb as accurately by night as by day, knowing as he did that radar-equipped night fighters were still in their infancy—indeed, Fighter Command's inadequacy in this area was very soon to become a major issue, ostensibly *the* major issue between Dowding and his colleagues.

Dowding took the sensible but pessimistic and unpopular view that only the introduction of radar-equipped, twin-engine night fighters, with a trained radar operator on board as well as a pilot, would enable Fighter Command to intercept German bombers successfully at night, and that until such time as he had enough of them (and the bugs in the airborne interception, or AI, radar equipment were eliminated), the German night raids could not be stopped. Sholto Douglas, his old antagonist in the Air Ministry, wanted him to send up large numbers of Spitfires and Hurricanes at night to intercept the German bombers. This was a tactic which, as Dowding pointed out, was bound to fail—his pilots had no practical way to find an enemy aircraft by night, and since most of them were in any case woefully inexperienced at taking off and landing in the dark, large numbers of fighters and pilots would inevitably be lost in accidents. Originally, both the Hurricane and the Spitfire had been optimistically designated by the Air Ministry as "day and night fighters," but nobody had taken that seriously—the only modification made to them for night fighting was to rivet a piece of sheet metal above the exhaust stubs on either side of the engine cowling so as to prevent the pilot's night vision from being blinded by the flames from his own exhaust. Come to that, the only way for a fighter pilot to aim at an enemy bomber at night—if he could find one in the first place—was to search in the darkness for the telltale bluish-red flare of its exhausts.*

---

* The legend that eating raw carrots improves night vision came about in part as a propaganda cover story invented to conceal the existence of AI—a small radar set mounted in an aircraft. Raw carrots were placed conspicuously on the table at every meal for night fighter pilots, and the story about their effect on eyesight was skillfully spread by the Ministry of Information—so skillfully that parents today are still urging children to eat carrots. The famous night fighter ace Squadron Leader John "Cat's Eyes" Cunningham was said to eat them in large quantities, but whether he did or not, the truth was that even Cunningham never managed to achieve a single kill at night until he began flying a twin-engine Beaufighter, with a radar operator and a working AI set.

The gloom at the War Cabinet on June 21 about *Knickebein* had been lifted somewhat by Jones's breezy, youthful optimism; he believed that countermeasures could be developed to "bend" the second beam so that the German bombers would miss their target and drop their bombs over open country. But in August 1940 *Knickebein* was still functioning well enough, and in the event, the *Luftwaffe* more than justified Churchill's apprehension, virtually destroying at least one aircraft factory and hitting the Dunlop tire works in Birmingham with night raids.[6] This was pinpoint accuracy with a vengeance, and Fighter Command was virtually powerless to prevent it. The single-engine fighters were unable to find an enemy aircraft in the dark, and the only twin-engine fighter available was a conversion of the now venerable Bristol Blenheim bomber. The night fighter version of the Blenheim was slower than the German bombers it was supposed to hunt, and no more maneuverable—even equipped with the early AI radar set it was not much of a threat.

From August 19 through 23, the *Luftwaffe* demonstrated just what it could do by night using *Knickebein*, striking Portsmouth, Bristol, Liverpool, Hull, Newcastle, Glasgow, and Edinburgh with the loss of only six aircraft on the night of the 19th. On the night of the 20th the Germans managed to put more than 150 aircraft over England, despite very poor weather, and again on the 21st. On the night of the 22nd more than 230 aircraft attacked, rendering the airfield at RAF Manston unserviceable, and hitting the Bristol Aero factory, as well as the somewhat unlikely targets of Harrow and Brighton. On the night of the 23rd there were smaller but still damaging raids over Bristol, Cardiff, and Birmingham. Many of these, of course, inevitably hit civilians rather than military or industrial targets—a typical example, chosen at random, was the bombing of a café in Bridlington, Yorkshire; several people were trapped and four of them were killed.

No matter how accurately the *Luftwaffe* bombed by night, bombs were bound to go astray, and in any case, bombers jettisoned their bombs, or dropped bombs at random if they were damaged, lost, or unable to find their target. This was not, as yet, the deliberate, whole-sale attack on cities, intended to break civilians' morale, of the Blitz to come, but it was a big step down the slippery slope toward it.

It is worth keeping this firmly in mind, for most accounts of the Battle of Britain concentrate on the pilots, but no twenty-four-hour period in the official RAF "Campaign Diary" is without its sad little note at the end of each day of "Casualties on Ground," split into "RAF Ground Personnel" and civilians (the latter referred to, typi-cally, as "Others"). On August 15 civilian casualties were twelve killed, forty-one injured; on August 16, seventy-two killed, 192 in-jured; on August 17, a day when the RAF described enemy activity as "very light," ten killed, sixty-six injured; on August 18, forty-four killed, 108 injured. So it goes day by day throughout the Battle of Britain—twenty-three killed, seventy-four injured on the 19th; twen-ty-three killed, 135 injured on the 20th; four killed, 178 injured on the 21st; three killed, thirty-six injured on the 22nd; thirty-four killed, 107 injured on the 23rd. Even when there was, according to the RAF, "little" or "light" enemy activity, civilians—men, women, and children—died, blown to bits by bombs, or buried under the rubble of their homes, shops, schools, and workplaces, or—on rare occasions—even machine-gunned by a low-flying German plane. Casualties on the ground almost always exceeded those among fighter pilots. To pick a day at random, on August 15 Fighter Com-mand lost thirty-four Hurricanes and Spitfires, with eighteen pilots reported killed or missing, while on the ground twenty-five civilians were killed and 145 injured. This is not to denigrate the fighter pi-lots—it took extraordinary courage to go up and fight, often several times a day, as well as youth, physical fitness, good reflexes and eye-sight, and hundreds of hours of training—but day after day the sad, inglorious little toll of the civilian dead mounted up, a toll of those who died not because they were in combat four miles above the ground but because they were in the wrong place at the wrong time, even if it happened to be their own bed.

On August 24, the weather cleared at last, and the Germans' air offensive resumed at full strength. It would shortly be apparent that their strategy was simple and effective—to bomb the major RAF Fighter Command airfields in the south by day, rendering them unusable; and to bomb specific industrial targets by night, with the aim of bringing the production of components for fighter aircraft to a halt. With this in mind, Göring moved most of the fighter strength of *Luftflotte* 3 to the *Luftflotte* 2 area, in the Pas-de-Calais, within closer range of England, to give the maximum protection to his bomber force, and ordered frequent sweeps over the Channel to confuse and distract the British.

The 24th was a day of heavy fighting and losses on both sides. Between six in the morning and noon the *Luftwaffe* sent large numbers of aircraft over Kent, some of them feints to draw the British fighters away from a major raid on RAF Manston. The airfield at Manston was bombed so heavily that the RAF was obliged to evacuate it by one in the afternoon—all the buildings were destroyed or ablaze, the runways were made unusable by bomb craters and unexploded bombs, and the telephone and teleprinter lines were cut. "Forward" airfields nearer the coast had been attacked so heavily that many of them were put out of action. Sheer numbers were beginning to tell—the *Luftwaffe* sent more than 500 aircraft over the south of England during the course of the day, putting a huge strain on No. 11

Group's squadrons. Park was obliged to ask Leigh-Mallory for help, and Leigh-Mallory obliged him with two squadrons; but since these squadrons proved unable to do much to protect Park's airfields—it would have taken much more than their number to have made a significant difference—the antipathy between Air Officer Commanding No. 11 Group and Air Officer Commanding No. 12 Group was only sharpened. Part of this may have been caused by Leigh-Mallory's attempt to form a "big wing" from the three squadrons at RAF Duxford, which, just as Dowding and Park had predicted, took so long to form up that the Germans had already left for home by the time it arrived. At every airfield in No. 11 Group, ground personnel worked under constant bombing—ground crews had been ordered to dig slit trenches next to their aircraft so they could take cover when attacked, but many continued to refuel and rearm their aircraft even when being bombed. Throughout No. 11 Group's area, hangars, mess halls, sick bays, and living quarters were severely damaged or destroyed. The airfields at Hornchurch and North Weald were heavily attacked, and several cities were bombed, mostly by errors of navigation, Ramsgate and Portsmouth among them. The end of the day brought no relief. Practically speaking, the Germans appeared to have settled on a division of labor—*Luftflotte* 2, with its reinforced fighter force, would attack by day; *Luftflotte* 3 would attack by night. London was heavily bombed for the first time, and in addition Birmingham and Cardiff were hit. The night raid on Birmingham was the most dangerous, since it was aimed at the "shadow" Spitfire factory at Castle Bromwich, but the scattered attacks on London were to have the most serious effect on the battle.

The fighting on August 25 does not appear to reflect great credit on Dowding, and it is certainly true that this might have been the right moment for him to have knocked Park's and Leigh-Mallory's heads together. The *Luftwaffe* lost twenty aircraft, and the RAF lost sixteen, with nine pilots killed; civilian casualties on the ground soared to 102 killed and 355 injured, and German aircraft had bombed places as far apart as the Scilly Isles and Aberdeen. Certainly many of Dowding's pilots seem to have felt that he was a remote figure, and this was true; but Leigh-Mallory also had detractors, most of whom resented the fact that he had never been a fighter pilot himself—among the senior leaders of Fighter Command only Park, who flew everywhere in his own Hurricane to see for himself what was happening, was admired by the pilots. Dowding's more devoted biographers note that he was preoccupied with the problem of night fighters at this point in the battle, and this too was doubtless true; but the truth is also that Dowding's focus remained fixed on the essentials of what was taking place. The critical factor remained what it had always been—the weather in the Channel. He understood perfectly, as did Hitler and Churchill (the latter reluctantly), that the calendar, not the number of enemy aircraft shot down, would determine the outcome. Already, Hitler had postponed Operation Sea Lion to mid-September, but he could not hope to carry the invasion off if he waited much longer than that—a fact of which his admirals reminded him constantly. By the end of September the Channel storms would be coming through, bringing with them high seas and bad weather. Early to mid-July would have been the ideal time for the invasion; mid-August was possible; mid-September would be risky; and once October arrived an invasion would be madness. In October, even if the weather allowed the troops to get ashore with their heavy equipment (and they would need to seize the Channel ports in working condition for that, since they had no equivalent of the LSTs Eisenhower would have in 1944), bad weather could cut off any chance of supplying or reinforcing them for days on end.*

Dowding, therefore, saw his main task as keeping his force in being until the weather and the calendar made the invasion of Britain unlikely or impossible, and by that standard he did not need to win a spectacular victory over the Germans in the air; he merely needed to keep his squadrons flying and attacking the German bombers through the first week of October. He did not anticipate that the German air offensive would end then—it might continue for months, or even years—but there would be no further risk of invasion in 1940.

To those who looked for a visible, clearly defined victory, like that at Waterloo or Trafalgar, this was not easy to accept, but Dowding, if he looked to history at all for examples, was following the example of Elizabeth I, who understood that the defeat of the Armada, while it was undoubtedly a great victory, would not end the war between England and Spain, still less the war between Protestantism and the Catholic Church. It would merely demonstrate for some time to come, perhaps permanently, that Spain was unable to invade England. It had not been complete victory, but it was enough.

Though it did not seem so at the time, August 25 was to prove a critical day of the Battle of Britain, a day that would show, in hindsight, just what a precarious undertaking war is, and how even small errors and events in warfare can have momentous and far-reaching historical consequences that are unimaginable at the time. On the

* It was for this reason that the planners of Overlord (formerly Round-Up), the Allied invasion of Europe in 1944, chose mid-May as the date. Eisenhower postponed the invasion to mid-June because of the shortage in landing craft, and would have been prepared, but reluctant, to postpone until mid-July; but he regarded the weather and the decreasing daylight hours as making even the first week of September undesirable. As it was, even in mid-June the weather was bad enough to make the Normandy invasion one of the riskiest operations in military history.

night of August 24–25, German bombs had fallen on the City of London, the famous "square mile" of old London, its historical and financial center, which had not been bombed since the Gotha raids of 1918. As it happened, this was not intended as a German challenge to the British; it was due to a simple error in navigation on the part of bombers bent on destroying the oil storage facilities at Thameshaven. Also, it was against the orders of Göring, who had reserved the decision to bomb London to himself (though, in fact, he would not have done so without an order from the Führer, for whom it remained a political rather than a military matter). In any event, careless navigation by the bomber pilots of Sperrle's *Luftflotte* 3, rather than any change in policy at the top, decided the matter.

Churchill had no way of knowing this, however, and was outraged, though not surprised, and in no doubt that retaliation should take place immediately. This was neither easy to do, given the distance to Berlin and the very primitive navigational aids available to Bomber Command, nor anything the Air Staff wanted to do, since it would deflect them from nearer, and in their view, more important industrial targets, but nobody was prepared to argue the point with the prime minister. Churchill, whose threshold of patience with the Air Ministry was already very low, had anticipated these objections by asking how long it would take to prepare for a bombing raid on Berlin. He had been told that no more than twenty-four hours' notice would be required, and on the night of the 24th, once bombs began to burst around the old Roman walls of the City of London, he therefore gave orders for the raid to be set in motion, weather permitting, for the night of August 25.

More than seventy-five twin-engine Wellingtons and Hampdens attacked "industrial targets" in Berlin that night, and these attacks were repeated on three of the next four nights (on one night the weather

prevented a raid). There is no evidence that the British bombers managed to hit anything of consequence—given the standards of night
navigation and bomb aiming of Bomber Command in 1940, they
were fortunate to reach the right city—but ten civilians were killed,
and on four nights Berliners heard the sounds of sirens and were told
to take shelter.*

This had a disproportionate effect on the Berliners, however—
Göring had not only promised them that this *Luftwaffe* would ensure
they would never be bombed, but had famously joked that if a single
British bomb ever fell on Berlin "my name is Meyer." They had believed him. Now the unthinkable had happened, and not a few Berliners guessed that these raids might be merely the start, and that more
would soon be coming. Many of them had cheered and applauded
when the *Luftwaffe* had devastated Warsaw and Rotterdam, events
that were shown to the German public in triumphant newsreels, but
nobody had seriously expected retribution, least of all the Führer
himself. He had, from his point of view, made every effort to extend
the hand of peace to the British, he had refrained from bombing London (there is no evidence that Sperrle had passed the unfortunate
consequences of his pilots' navigational mistakes back up the chain
of command to Hitler), and apparently all he had gotten for his pains
was the bombing of the Reich's capital by the RAF. He seethed. The
question of bombing London was no longer a matter of foreign policy, however woollily conceived; it had moved into the realm of the
Nazis' domestic policy—there was no way Hitler could fail to respond to the bombs falling on Berlin without running the risk of

---

* A more sensible use for Bomber Command might have seemed attacking the *Luftwaffe*
airfields in the Netherlands, Belgium, and France, but the bombers had no way to find
them by night, and no way of defending themselves effectively over enemy-held territory
by day.

shaking the German people's morale and, more important, their belief in him. Five days later he would meet with Göring, who was himself humiliated and shaken by the bombing of Berlin, and order him to begin the immediate bombing of London, and four days after that he would announce to a wildly cheering crowd at a rally at the Berlin Sportpalast, "Since they attack our cities, we will extirpate theirs!"

Thus, inadvertently, a major change in strategy was forced on the *Luftwaffe*. Though the British had no way of knowing it, the concentration on Fighter Command's airfields and on the aviation industry, which was beginning to pay dividends, was about to be weakened by the beginning of large-scale "revenge attacks" on London. Even the *Luftwaffe* had only so many bombers, particularly once the Stukas had been removed from the front line, and there were certainly not enough of them to pursue two entirely different strategies at the same time.

Opinion on the wisdom of this change in plans was divided, although nobody in the *Luftwaffe*, least of all Göring, was about to question a decision of Hitler's. Field Marshal Kesselring was in favor of bombing London, reasoning that this would force Fighter Command to put up its last remaining fighters, estimated now at less than 200, for defense, and thus give the German fighters a chance to destroy them. Field Marshal Sperrle was more pessimistic. He did not think that Fighter Command had been sufficiently weakened yet, and would have preferred to keep on attacking its airfields and the aviation industry. Besides, there were two serious problems in attacking London. First, although it was certainly an easy target, being then the largest and most populous city in the world (about 600 square miles and more than 8 million people), London's very size made it difficult to destroy (unlike Warsaw and Rotterdam). In short, it could absorb a lot of punishment. Second, the German single-engine fighters would have at most ten minutes of combat time over London in which to defend the bombers if they were to make it back to their bases in France. The short range of the Bf 109 was, once again, a serious problem, to which there was no immediate solution.

In deciding to bomb London, and other British cities, the Germans, without giving the matter much thought, had stumbled across the same kind of question that was to face the Allies when, in 1942, they began to bomb Germany on a much larger scale: What level of destruction is necessary to break the will of a people? How many civilian deaths does it take to convince a people that a war is not worth fighting? Ironically, as matters turned out, the Germans themselves would eventually provide the answers to these questions—they continued to fight on even when their major cities were reduced to smoking rubble, and the only thing that would persuade them to surrender in the end was the death by his own hand of their Führer.

The destruction of Cologne by the RAF in 1942, the firestorm in Hamburg in 1943 that killed at least 50,000 people in one night, the wholesale destruction of Dresden in 1945—none of these was sufficient to break the German people's will to resist, despite elaborate research on the subject by the many psychologists, zoologists, statisticians, economists, historians, and presumed experts on Germany who were consulted or put into uniform by the Allied air forces—indeed, it is possible that the bombing campaign against Germany may have had exactly the opposite effect to what was intended.

The Germans, by contrast, began their bombing campaign against British cities without having given any serious thought to what the effect would be, and without assembling teams of learned academics to tell the *Luftwaffe* what to bomb. Some Nazi leaders believed that bombing the West End of London—where wealthier Londoners lived and shopped—would break the will of the upper classes and persuade them to oust Churchill and his supporters and bring in a new government, perhaps including such old appeasers as Lloyd George, Lord Halifax, and the marquess of Londonderry, who were thought to be pro-German, or at least pro-peace. Others—including Foreign Minister Ribbentrop, Germany's odious, vain, arrogant former ambassador to the Court of St. James's, whose knowledge of Britain was taken seriously only by Hitler and dismissed by everybody else—favored bombing the East End of London, in the hope of stirring up social discontent among the working classes, the poor, and the Jewish population there and thus somehow—it was not clear how—bringing about the collapse of Churchill's government. In the event, the East End would receive more bombs than the West End, in part because London's docks and warehouses were there, representing an immense target of undeniable military significance; and in part because the East End was easier for the bombers to reach by flying up the Thames estuary and easier to identify from the air by night or day because of the unmistakable bend of the Thames. But on the whole Londoners of every class and religion did not panic, and far from demanding a change in government remained united behind the one they had. (That is not to suggest that everybody behaved like a hero, but instances of panic or cowardice were few and isolated—most people behaved stoically.)

The notion that bombing would bring Londoners into the streets en masse in fear and panic, or that social collapse and class warfare would bring the duke of Windsor back to the throne to replace his younger brother, or David Lloyd George, now aged, decrepit, and discredited, back to the front benches of the House of Commons to replace Churchill as prime minister, was a fantasy; but very few of Germany's leaders had any personal experience of foreign countries, and Ribbentrop's appointment as German ambassador in Britain (which had begun badly when he insisted on greeting the king with a Nazi salute and a shout of *"Heil Hitler!"* on presenting his credentials), together with his mistaken belief that he understood the British upper classes (and that they admired him), compounded by his snobbery and tunnel vision, had given him a false sense of expertise on British life and politics. Such ideas about Britain as he passed on to the Führer were largely delusional. Göring, Goebbels, Himmler, and the other Nazi leaders, if they agreed on nothing else, detested Ribbentrop and paid no attention to his opinions. To be fair, Hitler was more realistic than his foreign minister—he listened to Ribbentrop, but somewhere at the back of his mind he now understood that the British would have to be confronted with a disaster before they gave in, whether it was bombing, an invasion, both, or something else.*

August 25 was a day of patchy, cloudy weather, with relatively few German air raids during the day. At night, however, there were large raids, mostly concentrated on the industrial targets of the Midlands. Although Field Marshal Kesselring was using 200 as the number of fighters the British had left, in fact Dowding started the day with 233 Spitfires and 416 Hurricanes. He lost a total of sixteen aircraft and ten pilots during the day; the RAF claimed forty-seven German aircraft, but in fact shot down twenty. British and German losses were getting alarmingly close in numbers.

The next day the weather was better, and the *Luftwaffe* went back to its previous strategy, which was to send large raids of more than

---

* "Something else" would prove to be Rommel's attempt to take Egypt and the Suez Canal, and the German invasion of the Soviet Union, intended to remove from the playing board Britain's last potential European ally (although it was not initially an ally the British particularly sought out or valued).

100 aircraft by day against No. 11 Group's major airfields, especially Kenley and Biggin Hill, and to raid widespread industrial targets by night. The Germans lost forty-one aircraft, but the British lost twenty-eight fighters, with four pilots and two air gunners killed or missing. This day, the 26th, also marked the beginning of a new British night-time strategy. Dummy airfields were built near the real ones (they were known as "Q airfields" after the navy's "Q ships," merchantmen armed with concealed heavy cannon and naval crews, intended to act as lethal decoys for German surface raiders and submarines), with a flare path lit up at night, which tricked a good many Germans into dropping their bombs on open fields. This was comforting, but to the statisticians of Fighter Command the day-by-day rate of attrition of British fighters showed that Dowding's reserves were being rapidly depleted—since August 10 the "wastage rate" of fighters was exceeding the number of new ones received, or of damaged ones repaired and returned. Here, it is worth pausing for a moment to consider what that meant. Dowding was never in danger of running out of fighters—on every day of the Battle of Britain he had at least as many fighters as the Germans did—but his reserves, representing the narrow margin of his superiority, were being reduced every day, and if losses continued at the same level would have been exhausted within three weeks. After that, Fighter Command would have been losing muscle, not fat. The lack of pilots was still the more critical factor, and the harder to deal with.

Haze and bad weather on the 27th led to a quiet day, so far as German attacks were concerned. But perhaps taking advantage of the momentary lull, Park unleashed, at last, an open though indirect attack on Leigh-Mallory. Park did this in a new set of instructions to his ground controllers,[7] expressing his satisfaction with the support he had received from No. 10 Group in protecting his airfields when his squadrons were fully engaged against the enemy, and contrasting that with No. 12 Group's apparent lack of interest. He pointed out that on at least two occasions when he had requested assistance from No. 12 Group in protecting his airfields, the aircraft never showed up, either because it took them too long to form up into big wings or because they were hunting for glory and easy pickings elsewhere over No. 11 Group's area instead of obeying his controllers' instructions. In the spirit of a man anxious to wash his hands of the whole business, he instructed his ground controllers to contact Fighter Command headquarters directly from now on in these circumstances, rather than deal with No. 12 Group's controller. In other words, he bumped the problem of Leigh-Mallory's lack of team spirit up to Dowding himself. It would be up to Fighter Command to order Leigh-Mallory to protect Park's airfields.

Park did not dwell on the "big wing" controversy—although that thorny subject would soon come to dominate the dispute between the two groups, and also between Leigh-Mallory and Dowding. But nobody reading Park's instructions to his controllers could have been in any doubt about his opinion or his anger, and news of the instructions soon spread in Fighter Command. Most of Park's airfields were too close to the coast to permit him the luxury of forming big wings, even if he had wanted to. The time it took for enemy aircraft to reach their targets in No. 11 Group was so short that Park was lucky when he could get one or two squadrons up to attack them, never mind having them "stooge about" in the sky trying to form a big wing. Being farther north, Leigh-Mallory had slightly more time to allow his squadrons to experiment with this tactic, but even then, Park thought it was a mistake, and events would subsequently prove that he knew what he was talking about. In the meantime, Leigh-Mallory's pilots raged at Park's implied criticism of them, and Bader in particular insisted on the merits of the big wing—an argument that by now had made its way up to the highest level at Air Ministry, where Dowding had few friends or admirers.

Through the rest of August, the Germans raids continued with increasing force, and the night bombing of certain cities—Portsmouth, because it was a naval base; Liverpool, because it was a vital port for convoys crossing the Atlantic; and Birmingham, because it was the largest industrial city within reasonable range of the German bombers—went from being a dangerous nuisance to becoming a major threat. The day raids continued to be aimed at major targets in No. 11 Group such as Biggin Hill, which was put out of action twice and suffered heavy casualties. The night raids on Birmingham damaged or destroyed various important targets, including the Castle Bromwich Spitfire factory, the Dunlop Rubber Company, "Humber Works, James' Cycle Works, BSA tools, Nuffield Factory, Daimler Works and Smith's Stamping Works." On August 31, Fighter Command suffered its greatest loss for any one day—thirty-nine fighters shot down and fourteen pilots killed, while the Germans lost forty-one aircraft. The RAF's superiority was being whittled away by huge numbers of attackers, constant waves of attacks, the loss of experienced pilots and sheer numbing exhaustion, particularly in the squadrons of No. 11 Group, whose airfields were continually under attack—on August 30 thirty-nine airmen and airwomen were killed and twenty-six wounded at Biggin Hill alone. Pilots were so tired that one of them landed, then fell forward and slumped over his controls—his ground crew assumed he was dead, but when they ran to his aircraft they discovered he had merely fallen asleep with the engine still running. Others slept curled up in armchairs in full flying kit, and had to be shaken awake to scramble. Ground personnel were numbed by the ceaseless bombing—ground crews refueled and rearmed their aircraft under fire, carrying on with their work even when bombs were exploding nearby; young women dragged unexploded or delayed-action bombs off the runways with tractors, apparently oblivious of the danger; tents were erected to replace destroyed sleeping quarters; mess kitchens were borrowed from the army to prepare food outdoors; airmen and airwomen slept in improvised quarters in nearby houses. Yet somehow the fighter squadrons kept flying, many of them now reduced to no more than a dozen pilots instead of the twenty-six they should normally have had. Improvisation was the order of the day in No. 11 Group, which was in effect under siege.

Air Vice-Marshal Park would later write,

> Contrary to general belief and official reports, the enemy's bombing attacks by day did extensive damage to five of our forward aerodromes and also to six of our seven sector stations. There was a critical period when the damage to sector stations and ground organization was having a serious effect on the fighting efficiency of the squadrons. . . . The absence of many essential telephone lines, the use of scratch equipment in emergency operations rooms, and the general dislocation of the ground organization, was seriously felt for about a week.[8]

As Park pointed out, the German attacks were now being delivered without any break or pause, giving neither the British fighter squadrons nor the ground organizations on which they depended time to recover. On September 1, in "glorious weather," at least 450 German aircraft attacked the British airfields again, at last destroying the Sector operations room at Biggin Hill. Two more WAAF NCOs there earned the Military Medal by continuing to work until a bomb blast finally shattered the building and severed the telephone cable; and a team of seven men from the GPO worked in a deep bomb crater under attack for hours to restore telephone service. The operations room was eventually, with heroic efforts, moved to a nearby village shop, but clearly no airfield could survive for long under these conditions or under such heavy bombing raids, which were repeated from September 2 through the 6th, and which were accompanied by heavy and increasingly accurate raids on aircraft factories. On September 1 and 3 RAF and *Luftwaffe* losses of aircraft were equal—an ominous sign.*

Thus, Fighter Command had approached the breaking point on September 6, and if the *Luftwaffe* had kept up the pressure on the airfields of No. 11 Group and the aircraft factories, history might have taken a different course. Of course we cannot know whether Hitler would have finally launched the invasion, or whether it would then have succeeded; but at last the Germans were in grasping distance of the first precondition for the invasion—the systematic destruction of Fighter Command's ability to maintain control of the airspace over the Channel, England south of the Thames, and Dover. Indeed Park's earlier order to his pilots not to pursue German aircraft over the Channel was the first sign that Fighter Command was being obliged by its losses to abandon part of the strategic area it needed to defend—a small step, admittedly, but a step down the slippery slope. British fighters shot down over the Channel were permanently lost, as, very often, was the pilot, whereas when they were shot down over land, there was a good chance that the aircraft

---

* An intriguing event was the capture of a German soldier dressed in civilian clothes and carrying a loaded pistol, a wireless set, a Swedish passport, and a forged British identity card; he had been dropped by parachute to report on the extent of damage to British airfields.

could be salvaged, and that the pilot could parachute safely and return to his squadron.

At this precise moment, however, the fatal decision of Hitler at his meeting with Göring in Berlin on August 30 took effect. On September 7, the brunt of the *Luftwaffe* attack was shifted decisively away from Park's airfields and the aircraft factories toward bombing London and other major cities. Although Dowding and Park had no way of knowing it, the tide of the battle and the conditions under which it was being fought were about to change dramatically. In a more sensible world than that of the Third Reich, the commander in chief of the air force ought to have warned Hitler that taking the pressure off Fighter Command was a fatal mistake, particularly at just the moment when the enormous efforts and sacrifices made by the *Luftwaffe* were about to pay off, but very fortunately for Britain, nothing of the sort happened. Indeed, Göring's own prestige and vanity were so wounded by the few British bombs that had fallen on Berlin the night of August 25 that he was not only willing but eager to undertake the bombing of London in revenge. Tellingly, Admiral Raeder, although he continued to go through the motions of gathering barges and ships for the invasion, constantly reminded everyone in the supreme command that he needed assurance from the *Luftwaffe* of full control of the air to have any hope of success. This fact was emphasized by RAF Bomber Command, which had succeeded in destroying the Dortmund-Ems ship canal in a daring daylight raid, thus slowing down the delivery of barges to the invasion ports, and forcing the OKW, the high command of the German armed forces, to delay the planned date for launching Operation Sea Lion to September 21, too late in the "invasion season" to count on good weather for the crossing. It was fourteen weeks later in the year than the period Eisenhower would later consider the ideal date for an invasion in the other direction. Had Göring kept on attacking Park's airfields and the factories that built British fighters for another three weeks with undiminished strength, September 21 might well have become a famous—or infamous—date in history, but it was not to be.

The Germans supposed that Dowding had stripped most of his forces from around the country to reinforce the squadrons south of London and protect the airfields there—indeed, part of the German calculation was that attacking the capital would force Fighter Command to defend it, and thus finally bring the last few remaining British fighters up in large numbers to be overwhelmed by superior German forces. But in fact Dowding's cautious strategy of holding back a large number of his squadrons to the north and west of No. 11 Group was about to pay off. Dowding had come in for much criticism, behind his back, because he was not using all his forces, but of course his responsibility was to protect the whole country, not just the area south of London, and he had stuck to his guns on this subject despite murmurings against him in the government, and of course from Sholto Douglas, Leigh-Mallory, and his detractors in the Air Ministry. By attacking London in large daylight raids, the *Luftwaffe* would now be exposed not just to No. 11 Group and a portion of No. 10 Group, but to No. 12 Group and No. 13 Group, which were relatively rested and intact. Leigh-Mallory's fighter pilots would get their chance to attack the enemy in full strength, instead of being used in small numbers (humiliatingly, in their view) merely to protect No. 11 Group's airfields, and Douglas Bader would have, at long last, his chance to put his "big wing" theory to the test of battle. Moreover, Dowding's squadrons would be flying from airfields that were no longer under attack. The *Luftwaffe*, contrary to expectations, was about to kick open a hornets' nest.

On neither side was there any doubt that full-scale air attacks on London would be deadly. Accurate bombing would no longer be of paramount importance—wherever the German bombers dropped their bombs over London, they would kill civilians in significant numbers. At the same time, Fighter Command could not possibly prevent the Germans from dropping bombs—the Greater London area was far too large to prevent the German raiders from getting through somewhere; all Dowding could do over time was to make the effort so costly to the Germans in terms of aircraft and aircrews that they would eventually have to stop, or change tactics. Those who wanted, or expected, a clear-cut moment of victory would be disappointed. The area of death and destruction would simply be shifted from the airfields of southern England and the major industrial cities of importance to the aircraft industry to the world's largest city.

On September 2 *Reichsmarschall* Göring had received the Führer's permission to begin large-scale day bombing of London (as well as continuing night bombing). He arrived at the Pas-de-Calais on September 7 in his luxurious private train to oversee the initial operation himself, and watch the big formations of both his air fleets' bombers and their escorting fighters heading toward the white cliffs of Dover in the afternoon and on to London. There were more than 300 bombers and 600 fighters, and the spectacle left most people who saw it speechless; translated into electronic blips and squiggles on a radar screen, it dismayed the RAF radar operators and controllers. This immense raid*—the largest so far in the history of air warfare—was far from being a military secret. It was watched by Göring and his staff as it flew overhead, in wave after wave, and was the subject of

---

* It would be dwarfed in 1942 when Air Chief Marshal Harris launched Millennium, the first 1,000-bomber raid, on the cathedral city of Cologne.

ecstatic reports on German radio at home as it took place. The radio reports were artfully orchestrated by Dr. Goebbels's staff, with awe-inspiring music and sound effects. Göring himself announced on the radio to the German people, "I have taken over personal command of the *Luftwaffe* in its war against England." Some people noted the strange implication that he had not hitherto been in command; others perhaps recalled that he had also promised that Berlin would never be bombed. But the tone of the day in the German media was not only optimistic but triumphalist, even orgiastic, in the tradition of Nazi propaganda. The British radar operators, who were not listening to Radio Berlin, were at first uncertain about what the Germans were planning to attack as they formed up in such large numbers over Calais, and jumped to the conclusion that Kenley and Biggin Hill would once again be the targets, as on previous days.

Fighter Command was, as a result, for once caught flat-footed. Some of the confusion was the result of Park's instructions to his controllers two days earlier. Although his criticism of Leigh-Mallory was what most of those who read the document noticed first, a second, and more important subject was his dissatisfaction with the way controllers were positioning No. 11 Group's fighter squadrons. To understand this, it is necessary to keep in mind that radar had originally been an unreliable indicator of height. Radar operators had therefore developed a habit of adding a few thousand feet to their estimate of height because their radar sets generally indicated a height they knew was too low. This technical problem had been largely corrected by August 1940, but many of the operators were still adding on a couple of thousand feet when they communicated their reading of the screen to the controllers. Unfortunately, the fighter pilots themselves usually added on another couple of thousand feet to the figure they were told, partly out of experience and habit and partly because fighter pilots always want to seek the advantage of height when attacking. The higher a pilot is, the better his view of the enemy, and, of course, for a pilot height also equals speed—diving at high speed on the enemy from above and behind was the best guarantee of making a kill and escaping alive. Since it took time for a Spitfire or a Hurricane to climb to a given altitude (about eleven minutes for the former to reach 25,000 feet), for obvious reasons the higher a squadron climbed, the longer it would take to get there. The result was that squadrons were often too late to attack the German bombers on their way in to their target and were attacking *after* the bombs had been dropped. One complaint about Dowding and Park was that however many German aircraft their pilots shot down, they were not doing enough to prevent the Germans from dropping bombs in the first place.

This was related to the second consequence of climbing to a higher altitude than was necessary—the higher British fighters climbed, the more likely they were to meet German fighter escorts, some of which, despite Göring's order to stick close to the bombers, still flew well above them (which was, of course, the only sensible way to protect them). This had the effect of increasing fighter-to-fighter combat, and of decreasing attacks on the bombers, which usually flew at least 4,000 to 5,000 feet lower. In theory, the Spitfire squadrons should have been taking on the German fighters high up, the Hurricane squadrons should have taken on the bombers lower down, since the Spitfire was faster and could reach a higher altitude than the Hurricane. But in practice this neat division of tasks was not happening, and the pilots were therefore not taking full advantage of each plane's particular characteristics—against the bombers, the Hurricane was a sturdy and rock solid "gun platform"; but the Spitfire was at its best at higher altitudes, where its speed, maneuverability, and tight turning circle allowed it to fight with the Bf 109 on equal terms, or better.

Adding to Fighter Command's difficulties that day, the arrival of large numbers of barges in the Belgian ports had led many to conclude that the German invasion might be imminent and that the big German raid building up was the opening move, thus further deflecting attention from what was actually happening. The German tactics were also designed to confuse the British. The huge bomber force crossed the coast to the southeast of London at a much higher altitude than usual, and at many different points, to confuse the radar operators about the direction of the attack. Then it reassembled at an altitude of about 16,000 feet and followed the Thames estuary directly toward RAF Kenley, Biggin Hill, and Croydon, which were in any case what Dowding and Park assumed were the targets; but having flown beyond Croydon it suddenly turned back toward London's East End. The approach to No. 11 Group's crucial Sector airfields was well protected, but the approach to London was not, and it was too late to change that—at first, Park could put in only four squadrons of fighters against the great mass of German bombers and fighters. Even veteran fighter pilots were amazed when they came into view of these aircraft. "It was a breathtaking sight," one of them commented later. "You couldn't help feeling you'd never again see anything as remarkable as that." Another said, "I'd never seen so many aircraft," and this was a common reaction among the pilots, the radar plotters, and the observers on the ground. Nobody had ever before seen so many aircraft gathered into one carefully organized formation, so numerous that they seemed unstoppable. As five o'clock in the afternoon approached, they were obviously headed for the East End of London, with its docks, warehouses, factories, endless rows of small homes, and sprawling tenements—perhaps the most densely populated urban target in the world.

The initial fighter attacks were pressed home with vigor, but there was no way that four squadrons of British fighters could deter or break up so big and well-defended a mass of aircraft, let alone prevent them from bombing. The best Fighter Command could do was to attack the Germans as they withdrew to the north over London, then turned east over the sea to fly back to their bases. Between four-twenty and five o'clock, Dowding managed to get twenty-one squadrons into the air, including Douglas Bader's controversial "Duxford Wing" of three squadrons, but the hard fighting did not begin until the bombs were already falling on the East End.

They fell on the London docks, Limehouse, Tower Bridge, Woolwich, Bermondsey, Tottenham, Barking, Hackney, Rotherhithe, and Stepney, they destroyed the Harland and Wolff factory, oil refineries, and warehouses; they damaged a gasworks, the Battersea Power Station, and the oil storage tanks at Thameshaven, which had been hit the day before; they forced "the entire population of Silvertown, surrounded by raging infernos . . . to be evacuated by water." By the end of the day 306 civilian Londoners were dead and 1,337 were seriously wounded; whole neighborhoods were turned into "raging infernos"; train lines, tram lines, gas and water mains, sewer lines, and electricity and telephone cables were cut all over east London; three main railway stations were seriously damaged and put out of operation; whole streets were reduced to rubble; buses and trams were crumpled sheet metal; and a dense pall of smoke, grit, and burned oil spread over all London, mixed with an occasionally more pungent smell as vast quantities of tobacco and liquor in the burning bonded warehouses by the docks went up in flames. Contrary to the predictions of von Ribbentrop, there was no sign of panic. Even so professional a judge of class warfare as Ivan Maisky, the Soviet ambassador to the United Kingdom, noted not only the scale of destruction but the calm behavior of those who were bombed. Stoically and patiently, East Enders, Jewish and gentile, abandoned their ruined homes and burning possessions, and threaded their way through the bomb craters and rubble to be looked after by organized volunteers.

During the night of September 7–8 the *Luftwaffe* came back, almost 300 bombers strong, and dropped more than 300 tons of high-explosive bombs and nearly 500 incendiary bombs on the already gutted neighborhoods of the East End, guided to their target by the flames still rising from the oil storage tanks, refineries, and broken gas mains. In the streets below, no fewer than nine "major conflagrations" were being battled by about 600 fire engines, and most of the firemen (and volunteer firemen)* and emergency workers of greater London.

That evening Göring called his wife, Emmy, in Berlin to tell her triumphantly, "London is in flames." A more perceptive comment came from the distinguished American journalist James Reston, then the correspondent of the *New York Times* in London, who cabled to his paper that night: "One simply cannot praise the average man here too highly. Out of history and environment of these past 1,000 years he has inherited a quality of courage which is a true inspiration. . . . One simply cannot convey the spirit of these people. Adversity only angers and strengthens them. They are tough in a way we Americans seldom understand. That curious gentility among their menfolk

---

* The volunteer firemen were often men who were medically unfit for the armed services. In the West End, as Evelyn Waugh pointed out, they included, among many others, a unit of book publishers, and famous poets, sculptors, novelists, and painters. Post-debutante volunteer drivers in the Motor Transport Corps helped remove the dead and wounded from the East End; these volunteers included Kay Summersby, who would later become General Eisenhower's driver and confidante, and the author's stepmother, Leila Hyde.

confuses us. We underestimate them. . . . The British people can hold out to the end."[9] Hitler had made the great mistake of choosing London as the target, instead of Fighter Command, and the result would be not only a propaganda victory for the British, who were suddenly proving to the world that they "could take it," but a real victory for Fighter Command.

That same night, while fires still blazed in London from the raid during the day, the Chiefs of Staff, after studying the photographs taken of the German barges and naval vessels and reviewing the latest intercepts of German radio and cable traffic, finally issued the dreaded code word "Cromwell"—the warning that an invasion was expected imminently. All over southern England, members of the Home Guard mustered and were issued live ammunition; the army was placed on full alert; church bells were rung; and in some places, with, to echo the words of Talleyrand, *trop de zèle*, roads were blocked, and a few strategic bridges were blown up by overenthusiastic sappers of the Royal Engineers.

But when morning came, the seas remained empty, the beaches were untouched by the boots of German infantry, and no swarms of parachute troops had landed at strategic points. Fighter Command had lost twenty-eight aircraft, with nineteen pilots killed or missing. The Germans had lost forty-one aircraft—thirty less than the RAF claimed, but still a substantial number, and a considerable improvement over the days earlier in the month when losses on both sides were about equal.

Seen from Bentley Priory, September 7 had been a victory, but seen from elsewhere, including the Air Ministry and 10 Downing Street, it was something short of Air Chief Marshal Dowding's "finest hour."

Despite the availability of twenty-one squadrons of fighters, Dowding had been unable to prevent the indiscriminate heavy bombing of London; his night fighters (hampered in part by the smoke over London) had brought down only one German bomber; and, at any rate to those in the know, he and Park had been caught napping, looking in the wrong direction for the target of the German attack. The fact that Bader's "Duxford Wing" had done well against the Germans (though only after the Germans had dropped their bombs and were on their way home) gave at least some credence to Leigh-Mallory's campaign for the "big wing" and his complaints that Dowding and No. 11 Group were stubbornly refusing to apply more up-to-date and effective tactics. Certainly, to those who did not understand the intricacies of radar and fighter control, or did not have the patience to delve into them, it did not seem too much to ask that Fighter Command should attack the enemy with its full strength *before* the Germans arrived over London to drop bombs, rather than afterward.

Those few who were in on the secret of airborne interceptor (AI) radar sets, which were being installed in twin-engine Blenheims, also felt that more might have been expected from the night fighters; but that reaction underrated the problems of new, untested equipment and neophyte airborne radar operators. At this time the airborne radar operators had not yet been made aircrew acting-sergeants or given flying badges, because of the secrecy of airborne radar. Eventually, the radar operator and the pilot would form a team, but for the moment the radar operator was merely an ordinary aircraftman, kneeling in front of a screen no larger than a saucer while being bounced around in pitch darkness at 15,000 feet with "friendly" anti-aircraft fire going off all around him and the pilot in front of him asking impatiently for a "fix" on an enemy bomber, so as to make a kill and go home to bed. Communication between the radar operators and controllers on the ground and the night fighters in the sky was uncertain, and the chance that the pilot would actually see the glow of an enemy aircraft's exhausts was slim. The AI set itself was unreliable and tended to drain the aircraft's batteries, so it limited the amount of time a night fighter could stay aloft. The entire idea of radar-equipped interceptors was in its infancy, and not until a year later would it mature into an effective weapon.

Thus the two major complaints that would form the basis for doubt (and a well-orchestrated whispering campaign) about the wisdom of Dowding and Park in conducting the battle were already in place on September 7, when it was becoming apparent that Dowding's strategy was succeeding. A more supple, more subtle man than Dowding might have tried to explain or justify his confidence in Park and his doubts about Leigh-Mallory's "big wing" or might have explained his larger strategy of using small numbers of squadrons to inflict a constant, and in the end unsupportable, rate of loss on the Germans, rather than risk losing a big, uncontrollable air battle. He might also have pointed out that just as ground radar had presented initial difficulties, which were eventually overcome, the successful use of airborne radar would take some time. He could also have made it clear that the air battle itself was secondary—as long as it continued and prevented the Germans from launching their invasion, it was saving Britain.

Being who he was, of course, Dowding did none of these things.

On the other side of the Channel the day had ended on a nastier and more public tone of anger and recrimination. Despite the vainglorious broadcasts of Radio Berlin, and his own triumphant telephone call to his wife, Göring was infuriated by the losses of the bomber force, for which he blamed his fighter pilots, and dismayed that Fighter

Command, whose demise he had repeatedly predicted, was apparently still able to put up significant numbers of squadrons. He ordered the fighter commanders to meet him at Kesselring's forward headquarters in the Pas-de-Calais, and there, standing on a windy field overlooking the Channel, he berated them for failing to protect the bombers, and even for cowardice. It was perhaps not the best way to greet commanders who had just returned from a furious battle in which they had lost many of their men, and their reaction, while respectful, was frosty. No doubt noticing this—he had after all been a fighter ace himself—Göring changed his tone to one of gruff paternalism, and made his way down the line of the commanders, as they stood rigidly to attention, asking each of them whether there was anything he needed. When Göring got to Adolf Galland, perhaps the most competent and respected fighter pilot in the *Luftwaffe* (and certainly the most outspoken), Galland blurted out, "I should like an outfit of Spitfires for my *Gruppe, Herr Reichsmarchall!*" [10]

With that, Göring, livid with rage, cut short the event, stamped back to his waiting Mercedes-Benz staff car, and departed for his private train, apparently relinquishing the personal command he had assumed over the attack on London only a few hours earlier, though once he had simmered down he would resume it. In the aftermath, Galland felt obliged to explain, many times over, what he had said to his commander in chief, though he never apologized for it, and he was soon forgiven by Göring. It has become one of the most famous remarks about the Battle of Britain—perhaps the most famous remark—particularly in Britain, where it is thought to be confirmation from an expert that the Spitfire was superior to the Messerschmitt; but the truth is that Galland thought then and always maintained after the war that the Messerschmitt Bf 109 was in fact a far better "fighting machine" than the Spitfire. What he had meant was that the

Bf 109 was wasted if it had to stick close to the slower bombers, an argument he had had with Göring before. The Bf 109 had been designed to attack, not to fly close escort; and for that purpose, he thought, though he had never flown one, that the more maneuverable Spitfire might be a better choice. (The RAF, though, never used it in such a role. Given its short range, it would have been even more at a disadvantage than the Bf 109.)

What Galland had in mind, or at any rate later decided he had had in mind, was that the *Luftwaffe* should have built big, heavily armed four-engine bombers, like the American B-17 and B-24, and the kind of long-range interceptor that could accompany them, like the later models of the North American P-51; but Göring had allowed Milch to quash the former because he didn't think they'd be needed, and the Bf 110 was intended to have been the latter. In short, Galland was saying to Göring, "If that's what you wanted, you should have given us a different kind of airplane, and very likely a different kind of fighter pilot," but this was to be wise after the event—nobody in Germany had ever given much thought to the strategic bombing of Britain, since it was always assumed that Britain wouldn't fight.* The failure, if the air war against Britain was going to prove a failure, could more reasonably be blamed on Hitler and von Ribbentrop than on Göring, despite his many character flaws and mistakes. Galland was not wrong—the *Luftwaffe* was poorly equipped for the task of battering the British into submission. Its bombers were too small and too lightly armed, and its fighter had a very limited range. But when

---

*Although both Heinkel and Junkers had produced a successful prototype four-engine bomber by 1937 (known as the *Uralbomber*, since it had to be capable of bombing beyond the Ural Mountains), the project fell victim to internal squabbles in the *Luftwaffe* high command, and to Göring's insistence on aircraft that could be produced in large quantity at once. With stronger engines, either of these prototypes would have given the *Luftwaffe* the equivalent of the American B-17 or the British Lancaster.

the larger British and American bomber forces tried to batter the Germans into submission, they too failed, although they had the right aircraft for the job. In the Pacific, even the B-29 raids, which burned most of Tokyo and other major Japanese cities to the ground, did not bring about the Japanese surrender in 1945—that would take the use of an entirely new and more terrifying weapon over Hiroshima and Nagasaki.

On both sides of the Channel, therefore, September 7 led to dissatisfaction and to reassessment of the situation. Dowding moved some of his more exhausted squadrons out of the first line of battle and replaced them with fresh ones; more significantly, he took the deeply unpopular but sensible step of dividing his fighter squadrons into three categories: A being those in No. 11 Group directly in the path of German air attacks, B those that could be used at short notice to replace them, and C those that were not yet ready for combat, except against small numbers of bombers or isolated bombers. In practice, this meant dividing the fighter squadrons into sheep and goats. The B squadrons felt slighted, and the C squadrons had their best pilots transferred to the hard-pressed A and B squadrons. Of course no pilot wanted to be relegated to a C squadron, so the categorization did nothing to increase Dowding's popularity with many of his pilots. The pilots not only found him a remote and "stuffy" figure but also blamed him for the many intricate plans—and the more irritating changes of plan—that made no sense to young men risking their lives or impatient to get into combat.

This scheme to stabilize the strength of the more experienced operational squadrons at the expense of the rest led to numerous complaints from pilots that they were being "buggered about," and tended to diminish squadron loyalty, which, like regimental loyalty in the army, was a real source of strength and morale—once a pilot found his place in a squadron, it was his home; the other pilots were his friends and comrades; and the ground crews were familiar faces. Being arbitrarily posted to another squadron was a serious matter for pilots clinging to an organizational unit small enough to give them a sense of identity and belonging; and remaining a pilot in a squadron that was downgraded to C was felt as a humiliation. This scheme did not endear the brass hats at Bentley Priory to their pilots. Dowding's decision of the same day to give up "standing patrols" over convoys also made sense, in that it conserved fighters and pilots, but it was of course resented by the Admiralty, and added fuel to a burning question in the minds of Dowding's critics: Just what could Fighter Command protect, if it couldn't protect major cities from being bombed by day or night, or aircraft factories, or, now, it seemed, vital convoys?

From the 8th through the 9th, the attacks on London continued, aided by "fair weather." The toll of civilian casualties also continued, vastly outstripping the number of pilots killed or missing. On September 8, day and night raids on London cost the lives of 412 civilians; on the 9th, despite strong attacks by No. 11 Group against the German formations, 370 civilian Londoners were killed and nearly 1,500 severely wounded. Cloudy weather, with some rain, diminished the German attacks and the civilian casualties on the 10th, but the 11th dawned fine and clear and was again a day of full-scale attacks, another of those days that stretched everybody's nerves to the breaking point on both sides of the Channel.

In Germany, the obvious fact that Fighter Command remained unbeaten and that the British were not yet cowed by the bombing of their cities caused Hitler to postpone giving the warning order for Operation Sea Lion again. The German navy needed at least two days of good weather and smooth seas to lay the long, intricately planned barriers of mines that would constitute its principal defense against British warships entering the Channel from the North Sea. Nobody was certain that the mines would deter the Royal Navy, but without them the invasion could be destroyed at sea by British cruisers and destroyers. On both sides there were those who remembered that Turkish minefields had prevented Admiral de Robeck from reaching Constantinople in 1915.

Reports of aerial mining of the sea off the French Channel ports, and of the movement of barges and German naval vessels observed by Photographic Reconnaissance Unit Spitfires, once again caused many people to conclude that the invasion was imminent—that the heavy bombing of London and, once again, of Park's crucial airfields could plausibly be interpreted as the opening moves of the invasion. Dowding did not appear to share this opinion—he stoutly, though unsuccessfully, resisted an order to transfer some of his precious Bofors antiaircraft guns to the army because the invasion was imminent. He argued that it was not imminent, even though the order came directly from the War Cabinet—but it must be borne in mind that his responsibility was for the air defense of *all* of Great Britain. If the invasion took place, he would have to use the squadrons of No. 10 Group to attack the enemy in the Channel and on the beaches, and to protect British warships as they engaged the invasion fleet; he could not ignore the possibility that *Luftflotte* 5 in Denmark and Norway would attack again once the invasion was launched, in which case he would need No. 13 Group to defend the north of England, Scotland, and the all-important naval base of the Home Fleet at Scapa Flow. Unlikely as the invasion might seem to him, he could not afford to concentrate all his strength on the defense of London.

The 11th was a day of intense air activity by nearly 500 German bombers, including large-scale raids on London, Portsmouth, and Southampton, followed by night raids by more than 200 bombers on London and Liverpool. The German fliers ran into more opposition than they had been told to expect—although Göring assumed that Fighter Command now had fewer than 200 fighters left, in fact Dowding had 214 serviceable Spitfires and 387 serviceable Hurricanes available at nine o'clock on the morning of the 11th, almost three times the latest estimate of Beppo Schmidt. This would not be much of a consolation to Dowding, however: by the end of the day his fighters had shot down twenty-five German aircraft, but his own losses came to twenty-nine fighters destroyed and seventeen pilots killed— Fighter Command's losses in aircraft were higher than those of the Germans, a very bad sign indeed. Even more threatening was the fact that the Germans had finally succeeded in partially jamming British radar, using specially made transmitters placed on the French coast. They were not as yet able to jam the radar completely, but they created enough electronic interference to make it difficult for the radar operators to interpret what appeared on the screens.

Perhaps the most notable building that was bombed on the 11th, surely not by accident, was Buckingham Palace. Six bombs struck the palace, two of them exploding less than twenty yards from where the king was talking with his private secretary, Alec Hardinge, in his "small sitting room." The royal family took the attack calmly, regarding it as a propaganda victory and a morale builder. The queen remarked, with evident relief, "Now we can look the people of the East End in the face," and she and the king were photographed examining the rubble and chatting amiably with the emergency workers. The king observed that the "aircraft was seen coming straight down the Mall below the clouds. . . . There is no doubt it was a direct attack on Buckingham Palace." However, it seems that this was not a matter of policy or deliberate frightfulness on the part of the German government or the *Luftwaffe*, but rather a result of high-spirited bomber crews' betting on which among them would be the first to score a hit on Buckingham Palace.

The City and the London docks were more seriously damaged, and fifty-three people were killed. Dover was not only bombed but also shelled, by German long-range coastal artillery; Kenley and Biggin Hill got another pasting; and the London–Brighton railway main line was closed for a time by unexploded or delayed-action bombs. Though he himself was as skeptical about the invasion as Dowding, Winston Churchill thought that apprehension about its imminence was sufficiently widespread that he should speak to the British people about it on the night of the 11th. This broadcast is not usually counted among his greatest war speeches, and though it was brief by his standards, it was masterly. He did not try to conceal or minimize the danger—indeed, he was very frank, telling almost as much as he knew, and drawing his listeners into his confidence. He pointed out firmly, "The effort of the Germans to secure daylight mastery of the air over England is of course the crux of the whole war," one of the rare points on which he and Hitler were in full agreement. Then he went on to say that preparations for "invasion on a great scale," were nevertheless "going forward steadily," and to predict that it would be, for the enemy, "a very hazardous undertaking," as was certainly true. He made it clear that if the invasion was to take place, it must be very soon, since the weather would break at any time—something of which Hitler was also acutely conscious. Then, in words that still ring with optimism, he drew on two stories of English victories over powerful continental enemies, stories with which everybody in Britain, irrespective of education or class, was familiar: "We must regard the next week or so as a very important period in our history. It ranks with the days when the Spanish Armada was approaching the Channel, and Drake was finishing his game of bowls; or when Nelson stood between us and Napoleon's Grand Army at Boulogne."[11] He had placed the Battle of Britain firmly in the minds of his listeners among the greatest heroic victories of the past—the Armada and Trafalgar—striking exactly the patriotic note that was most likely to appeal to them, and increasing their resolution for whatever the next few days would bring.

From September 12 to September 14, the German attacks slackened off a bit, in part because of "unsettled weather," in part because the Germans were rethinking their own bombing tactics. They were using more frequent attacks by smaller units, rather than a single big raid, and sending over masses of fighters to keep the radar operators guessing (and to keep Fighter Command busy). Increasingly, German bomber units returning from London flew a course that took them through their own "stream of bombers" flying toward London, since air traffic flying in opposite directions on a parallel course tended to confuse the British radar operators. On the 12th, in one of the most dramatic episodes of the Blitz, a very heavy delayed-action bomb fell close to Saint Paul's Cathedral in London, and the bomb disposal unit had to dig down nearly thirty feet to disarm and remove it before it could destroy one of London's most famous and cherished historical landmarks. On the 13th central London was hit badly again, with bombs falling on Downing Street, Trafalgar Square, and Buckingham Palace. On the 14th, London was bombed in a day of confused and widespread fighting, which ended in the loss of fourteen aircraft on each side, and from which the Germans drew the impression that Fighter Command was at last beginning to weaken.

Although in Britain the invasion was now expected at any moment, in Berlin there was still hesitation. Hitler gathered his service chiefs for a conference, and once again postponed Operation Sea Lion. The intention was to give the *Luftwaffe* a chance to complete the destruction of the British fighter force, on which the navy continued to insist, as well as an uninterrupted four to five days of good weather and calm seas (only a few days ago the German navy had asked for just two days of good weather). The bombing raids on London during the night of September 14–15 were noticeably less strong than they had been over the past few days, causing many people in the RAF to wonder if the Germans might be preparing something special for September 15.

This, as it happened, was a good guess—September 15 would turn out to be the decisive day of the Battle of Britain, and indeed very possibly the decisive day of the war.

A prediction (for once accurate, despite some early-morning mist) of almost perfect weather for September 15, coupled with a general feeling in the *Luftwaffe* high command that the RAF was weakening, made it certain that the Germans would undertake a major effort. It was not attended by all the fanfare of Eagle Day, especially since that had been so disappointing, but both air fleets were under strict orders to produce a maximum effort for the day. Two separate attacks were planned: one in the late morning, consisting of more than 250 aircraft; the next in the early afternoon, consisting of nearly 300 aircraft (to be followed by a night attack). Each would take place in two separate waves, but perhaps out of overconfidence, no fancy tactics were planned—there were no sweeps of German fighter aircraft, and no attempts to deceive the RAF about the direction of the attacks. This was to be a trial of brute force and numbers, with London as the principal target. The *Luftwaffe* formed up over France in full view of British radar operators, who had, for once, ample time to take a careful count and warn Fighter Command of what was in store. This time even Douglas Bader's Duxford big wing would have time to form up and hit the Germans before they bombed. Well before noon, Air Vice-Marshal Park had twenty-one squadrons of fighters in the air to attack the German formations as they crossed the Kent coastline, from Biggin Hill, Northolt, Kenley, Hendon, Hornchurch, Middle Wallop, and Duxford. For once, the quarrel between Park and Leigh-Mallory did not affect operations; nor were there any arguments about the "big wing." Ground controllers had ample time to form big wings, even in No. 11 Group, and by the time the massive force of German aircraft was over Kent, it was attacked from every quarter.

It should not be thought that at the outset either side regarded Sunday, September 15, as a "historic" day. Certainly, Göring had hopes of striking a knockout blow that would fatally cripple Fighter Command and demoralize Londoners, but by now many of his aircrews—not to speak of their commanders—were disillusioned and exhausted. On the British side, it merely looked like another brutal day of battle, and the British had experienced such days before. The invasion scare had spread to the newspapers, where there was much speculation on the subject, to which the Ministry of Information responded sternly by announcing that if an invasion were to take place, the public would be informed of the fact on the BBC. ("Only in England!") Pilots, as they woke before dawn on the 15th, were warned there was "a flap on." This warning made many of them assume that the invasion was taking place, whereas all that was happening was the intrusion of German reconnaissance aircraft into British airspace—almost always the precursor of a major effort on the part of the *Luftwaffe*. (One of the German early-morning reconnaissance aircraft was shot down by an RAF pilot who had taken off in his pajamas, before even drinking his morning cup of tea.)

Churchill had an infallible sense of timing for the historic moment, and the good weather prompted him to visit Park's headquarters at Uxbridge after breakfast on Sunday morning. He and Mrs. Churchill were driven over from Chequers, the prime minister's country residence, and arrived at Uxbridge at eleven in the morning. Rather to his disappointment, Churchill found that nothing much was happening. "I don't know whether anything will happen today," Park told him. "At present all is quiet."

Churchill took a seat in what he called the "dress circle" (in American theaters, this is the most expensive front-row seats in the balcony) of No. 11 Group Operations Room. "Below us," he wrote later, "was the large-scale map-table, around which perhaps twenty highly-trained young men and women, with their telephone assistants, were assembled. Opposite to us, covering the entire wall, where the theatre curtain would be, was a gigantic blackboard divided into six columns with electric bulbs, for the six fighter stations, each of their squadrons having a sub-column of its own, and also divided by lateral lines."[12]

At No. 11 Group the "dress circle" balcony from which the battle was directed was separated from the big map table on the floor below by a modernistic curved glass wall, which made looking down into the "orchestra pit" where the action was going on a little like being in an aquarium. The object had been to isolate the decision makers above from the inevitable hubbub and excitement below. The prime minister had only fifteen minutes to wait there before the plotters began to move around the map table, marking raids with their long croupier's sticks, and the lamps on the big wall "tote board" began to light up one after another. German raids of "forty-plus" and even "eighty-plus" were forming up over Dieppe, Calais, and Boulogne until more than 250 approaching enemy aircraft were being plotted on the table, and very shortly Park had sixteen squadrons of his own, plus five from No. 12 Group, in the air to meet them. Between the German attackers and the British defenders there would soon be more than 500 aircraft in the small airspace over Kent, most of them between 15,000 and 20,000 feet high. The German formations were attacked all the way from the beach to the suburbs of London, and inevitably their neat formations broke up. This breakup on the one hand allowed RAF fighters to pick off the stragglers, but on the other hand allowed some of the German bombers to slip through singly and drop their bombs on London. Before noon bombs had fallen on "Westminster, Lambeth, Lewisham, Battersea, Camberwell, Crystal Palace, Clapham, Tooting, Wandsworth and Kensington," as well as "the Queen's private apartments at Buckingham Palace."

Had the German bombers been able to stay in close formation and concentrate on a few strategic targets, they might have done more serious damage, but with one British fighter in the air for every German aircraft, there was no chance of this, as the German formations of bombers broke up under relentless attack. Dropping a bomb on the queen's apartments or near the palace of the archbishop of Canterbury, and scattering them around the London suburbs, was not going to bring the British to their knees, as Göring had promised. Of course from the point of view of those who were bombed, this was no consolation, even had they known it. For hundreds of thousands of people, life was suddenly and savagely disrupted. A Dornier crashed into Victoria Station, and its crew landed by parachute in a famous

London cricket pitch, the Oval; bombs and British and German aircraft fell all over the Greater London area. The Strand (one of London's famous shopping streets, and home to many clubs and the Savoy Hotel) was bombed, and the Gaiety Theatre was almost destroyed. Guys and Lambeth hospitals were badly hit. Water and gas mains, railway and tube lines were broken or destroyed; electricity generating plants were put out of commission; and fires started everywhere. But serious as all this was, it was a long way from a Wellsian vision of total urban destruction and collapse.

From Park's Operations Room, where the prime minister sat, the danger was in the sky, not in the streets of London. By noon all of Park's squadrons were in the air, and "some had already begun to return for fuel. . . . There was not one squadron left in reserve." Park requested another three squadrons from No. 12 Group to patrol over his airfields while his squadrons landed for fuel and ammunition, and this was done, for once, with no hesitation or complaint. "I became conscious of the anxiety of the Commander, who now stood behind his subordinate's chair," Churchill wrote. "Hitherto I had watched in silence. I now asked, 'What other reserves have we?' 'There are none,' said Air Vice-Marshal Park. In an account which he wrote about it afterward he said that at this I 'looked grave.' Well I might. What losses would we not suffer if our refueling planes were caught on the ground by further raids of '40 plus' or '50 plus'! The odds were great: our margins small; the stakes infinite."[13]

Churchill, with his usual perspicacity, had understood what Göring apparently failed to think about in advance—in order to win, the *Luftwaffe* needed to be able to catch Park's squadrons on the ground as they refueled, and deal them a smashing blow, but for that the Germans needed better intelligence and a perfect sense of timing. At two o'clock in the afternoon, they were to send another 150 aircraft in three waves against central London, but if instead they had sent those same aircraft against Park's airfields at noon, just as his fighter squadrons were landing, No. 11 Group might well have been wiped out. It was the critical moment of the battle, perhaps the one point at which victory was almost within Göring's grasp. But the German morning raid fled home in disorder, having suffered heavy losses—some of the German bombers actually turned back, having lost faith in their own fighter escorts and in their commanders' promises that Fighter Command was all but defeated—and by the time the afternoon raid formed up, Park's squadrons were refueled, rearmed, and waiting for them.

Again, in the afternoon, No. 11 Group broke up the German formations, so instead of a concentrated raid, the bombers, fiercely attacked by fighters, dropped their bombs indiscriminately all over the London suburbs, in places like Woolwich, Stepney, and Hackney, killing people; destroying homes, shops, schools, and small factories; disrupting train service; but not in any way seriously threatening the continued existence of Britain's capital, or—more important still—the fighting capacity of No. 11 Group.

Seldom has so rich an opportunity been wasted by lack of forethought and planning. The Germans were certainly not short of aircraft or aircrews—that night they sent another large raid of nearly 200 aircraft against London, and Southampton, Portland, and Cardiff were also attacked. But the opportunity for the really damaging blow that Göring expected his forces to deliver had been missed at noon, and would never recur.

At eight o'clock in the evening, when Churchill, exhausted by the day's drama, woke from a nap, he rang for his principal private secretary, John Martin, who brought him the latest news. "This had gone wrong here; that had been delayed there; an unsatisfactory answer had been received from so-and-so; there had been bad sinkings in the Atlantic. 'However,' said Martin, as he finished this account, 'all is redeemed by the air. We have shot down one hundred eighty-three for a loss of under forty.'"[14]

In fact the Germans had lost only sixty aircraft—in the chaos of battle the claims of pilots (and antiaircraft gunners on the ground) tended to overlap. Still, the *Luftwaffe* had made its maximum effort, and had lost sixty aircraft to twenty-six British fighters destroyed and thirteen pilots killed. The *Daily Telegraph*'s subhead on Monday, September 16, got the facts right: "Massed Day Attack on London Smashed."[15]

More important still—more important than anything else—on the next day, September 17, Hitler sent a signal postponing Operation Sea Lion "indefinitely." The continuing heavy losses of German aircraft and the evident survival of Fighter Command, meant that the precondition of the German navy for the invasion of England—control of the air—could not be met, and with the autumn weather approaching it was useless to keep up the pretense.

Very soon, the great fleet of barges would be dispersed back to their ports, canals, and rivers, and the Führer's attention would be drawn east toward the Soviet Union. The worst of the Blitz was still to come, the night fighters' problem had still not been solved, and the British Army still patrolled the beaches of southern England just in case Hitler changed his mind; but Dowding's strategy had worked. The invasion would never come, Fighter Command had never lost control of the air for even a single moment, and "the Few" had won one of the four most crucial victories in British history—the Armada, Trafalgar, Waterloo, and the Battle of Britain.

Perhaps without even realizing it, in mid-September 1940 Hitler lost the war, defeated by the efforts of perhaps 1,000 young men. Unable to invade and conquer Britain, he would turn against the Soviet Union, sacrificing the German army, and thereby prolonging his war until, at last, the Americans were dragged into it by the Japanese attack on Pearl Harbor, pitting Germany against three of the most powerful industrial countries in the world.

All this was to come, and nobody, not even Churchill, could foretell it in the autumn of 1940, when Britain still stood alone. But Dowding and "his chicks" had prevailed, and it is perfectly fitting that September 15 should be celebrated every year as "Battle of Britain Day."

CHAPTER 10

The Turning Point

Napoleon's comment that no moment in war is more dangerous than that of victory was perfectly illustrated by the events that followed September 15. First of all, on the British side there was no immediate recognition that a great victory had been won—the *Luftwaffe* kept on bombing, though increasingly it did so at night, thus inevitably drawing attention to the weakness of Dowding's night fighters. The worst of the Blitz would begin in the autumn, with night after night of sustained bombing that would eventually cost the lives of more than 50,000 British civilians. As the days grew shorter, however, and the autumn storms began to lash the seas in the Channel, it began to dawn on most people that invasion was no longer an immediate prospect, if indeed it was still a prospect at all. To those in the know, the fact that the barges and tugs so painstakingly assembled in the Channel ports for Operation Sea Lion were being dispersed back to where they had come from was a certain sign that Hitler had changed his mind, if he had ever been serious about invading. As far as the public and the armed forces were concerned, it was thought more prudent not to dismiss the threat of an invasion, for fear that complacency would replace alertness, so the Home Guard and most of the British Army in the United Kingdom continued to go through the motions of patrolling the beaches and preparing for invasion long after the threat had ceased to exist.

In the air the glamour of the fighter pilots was rapidly eclipsed by that of night fighter aces such as "Cat's Eyes" John Cunningham, and by the need to place greater emphasis on Bomber Command, as it took the first steps toward paying back the enemy in kind. Soon the bomber crews got the lion's share of the publicity, leaving the fighter pilots with an ever diminishing role. (Despite contemporary retroactive angst in the English-speaking world about the "strategic" bombing of Germany in World War II, much of it centered on the firebombing of Hamburg in 1943 and the destruction of Dresden in 1945, it would be difficult to overstate the enthusiasm of the British public for giving the Germans a taste of their own medicine after the Blitz began in earnest in the autumn of 1940 and the winter of 1941.) Fighter Command took to making "sweeps" over occupied France, bringing the *Luftwaffe* fighter squadrons up to fight in strength—a strategy that was as costly for the British as it was for the Germans, if not more so.

A long grim period in the war began for the British after September 15, obscuring to some degree the magnitude (and permanence) of their victory. At sea, losses of shipping to the ubiquitous U-boats (which benefited now from the fact that French ports on the Atlantic were in German hands) soared. Initial successes against the Italians in North Africa would soon be followed by

calamitous and even shameful defeats in Greece and Crete and by
the arrival in Libya of the first elements of General Erwin Rommel's *Deutsche Afrika Korps.* At home, the British became accus-
tomed to the dreary rigors of rationing (one egg a month, and only
a few ounces of doubtful meat), the blackout, and the bombing.
Clothing was rationed; electric heaters glowed a dull red because
of the reduced wattage; coal and coke were rationed; the whole nation darned, mended, patched, did without, and shivered. The
British had faced Hitler down and given him his first military defeat, but until June 1941, when he attacked the Soviet Union, they
stood alone, facing an occupied continent and a determined enemy. Quite apart from the feeling of many people in Britain (outside the extreme left) that Stalin and communism were not much
better than Hitler and Nazism, the Russians did not at first seem
like promising allies. The Soviet Union rapidly lost its entire air
force, all of western Russia and the Ukraine, and millions of troops
as the German armies advanced toward Moscow. At the same time,
it made imperious demands in terms of aid and supplies that the
British could not possibly provide, given the precariousness of
their own situation and the perils of sending shipping to the Soviet
Union through seas dominated by German U-boats and aircraft
from Norway. Even to the optimists, there was still no sign that the
United States would ever enter the war, despite the flow of Lend-
Lease supplies across the Atlantic to an increasingly impoverished
Britain, which had long since exhausted its dollar reserves and its
credit to buy arms.

Precisely because the world around them looked so grim in the
winter of 1940 and the spring of 1941, with no end to the war in sight,
and with diminishing resources forcing people whose belts were already pulled tight to tighten them some more, Britons were already

looking back at the warm summer of 1940 as a moment of triumph, when the "fighter boys" in their Spitfires and Hurricanes had gained a glorious victory in the clear blue sky above Kent. The Battle of Britain was already becoming a patriotic myth before it was even over. No time was required to turn it into a legend, or to transform the pilots into airborne knights of the Round Table, reminders of the days when the British public had thought of itself as heroic, rather than merely alone and beleaguered.

In the remembered glow of those summer days, much of the pain and bitterness of the Battle of Britain was eventually suppressed in favor of a more glamorous picture. That picture did not necessarily include the young WAAFs in the operations rooms listening to the screams of pilots trapped in the cockpits of flaming airplanes plunging to the ground. Nor did it include the faces of the "guinea pigs," so called in RAF slang not just because they were the subjects of experimental burn surgery, but also because someone whose lips, nose, and ears had been burned off had the smooth, featureless face of a guinea pig—until the surgeons began a long, excruciatingly painful series of operations to graft on some semblance of features. (Even less could be done about hands that were burned to shriveled claws.)* The picture also left out the rows of dead WAAFs in improvised mortuaries on the badly bombed airfields of No. 11 Group; the pilots who died at sea, bobbing in their inflated Mae Wests in sight of the white cliffs of Dover as hypothermia overcame them; and the aircraftmen of the ground crews who died of shrapnel wounds or machine-gun fire while rearming "their" aircraft during a German low-level bombing attack rather than take shelter. In

---

* The RAF had prudently set up special burns units in anticipation of such casualties. The presiding genius of burn rehabilitation was the plastic surgeon Archibald McIndoe, of Queen Victoria Hospital, in East Grinstead.

much the same way, the discharged legless or armless sailors begging on the docks of Portsmouth or Plymouth after the Armada or
the Battle of Trafalgar were soon expunged from the patriotic myth—
it has always been so.

The Battle of Britain rapidly developed its own mythology, with
the result that in many people's minds the Spitfires, the Hurricanes,
and radar appeared spontaneously in 1940, rather than as a result of
decisions made by the two principal appeasers of prewar British political history, Stanley Baldwin and Neville Chamberlain. But without their determination to provide Britain with a modern, credible
fighter defense, and without the immense amounts of public money
needed to build the aircraft and the factories that would produce
them (and the Rolls-Royce Merlin engine) in quantity, Britain would
have been overwhelmed after Dunkirk. Whatever their other shortcomings as prime ministers, Baldwin and Chamberlain were responsible for the creation of Dowding's Fighter Command—often against
the advice of (and despite dire warnings from) the Air Ministry, where
the cult of the bomber as the only reliable deterrent against attack
remained unshaken until events in 1940 suddenly, unexpectedly, and
briefly made the fighter the all-important weapon on which Britain's
survival depended.

There is also a tendency today toward retroactive complacency:
historians look at the numbers of aircraft the British were producing,
compare them with production in the German aircraft industry, and
conclude that the outcome was never in doubt—that the margin was
never as slim as people thought at the time. But this, too, is an illusion. Certainly, the output of the German aircraft industry in 1940
ought to have been higher—neither Hitler nor Göring had expected
or prepared for a long war with Great Britain—and, like the British,
the Germans produced too many aircraft that were inappropriate

and ineffective for the kind of air war they found themselves in.*
Nevertheless, time and time again the *Luftwaffe* came very close to
crippling Fighter Command. Had the Germans been able to follow
August 18 with another couple of days of attack on the airfields of
No. 11 Group on the same scale and at the same level of intensity, the
story might have ended quite differently. True, the Germans would
have stood a better chance of winning if Göring had not canceled
the four-engine bomber program in 1937, and if a rush program had
been instituted in 1939 to enable the Bf 109 to carry an external jet-
tisonable fuel tank (this was a problem shared by the Spitfire and the
Hurricane). However, the *Luftwaffe* was defeated not because of its
technical shortcomings but because of poor intelligence work, a fatal
tendency to bomb the wrong targets, and the severe underestima-
tion of the importance to Fighter Command of the radar stations and
the interlocking series of operations rooms to which the radar stations fed information. Had the Germans known which building at
Biggin Hill contained the Sector operations room and destroyed it,
they might have come very much closer to paralyzing No. 11 Group,
at least for a time. But fortunately, they had no idea—the real culprits
of the Germans' failure, if there were culprits, were General Martini,
the commander of the *Luftwaffe* signals force; and Colonel Schmidt,
whose intelligence reports on Fighter Command were hopelessly
flawed.

Of course the most important culprit was Göring, whose self-
indulgence, short attention span, arrogance, overconfidence, and
failure to institute (or respect) a disciplined and well-organized chain
of command, rather than ruling the *Luftwaffe* by a combination of
cronyism and a calculated policy of divide and conquer, doomed the

---

* The *Luftwaffe* was not alone. British bombers in 1940 were inadequate, the Defiant was
a disaster, and the RAF would have no specially built night fighter until later in 1941.

air attack against Britain from the start. Had Göring been willing to delegate the air war against Britain to a single commander, and back him up—Kesselring would have been an obvious choice for the role—the Germans might have succeeded. But giving that kind of authority to anyone other than himself would have gone against Göring's instinct for self-preservation, and against his inflated pride and his self-image as Germany's first soldier and airman. There was simply no place in the *Luftwaffe* for a man with the untrammeled authority that Air Chief Marshal Sir Arthur "Bomber" Harris would have over Bomber Command from 1942 on, or that Dowding had as Commander-in-Chief, Fighter Command, during the Battle of Britain. Still less, of course, was there any possibility of putting one determined man in charge of every aspect of Operation Sea Lion, the army, the *Luftwaffe*, and the navy, and giving him full authority to get on with it—a German equivalent of Eisenhower in 1944. The only person who could play this role, to the extent that it existed, was Hitler himself. But quite apart from his lack of interest in naval matters and his delegation of the air war to Göring, his ability to command Sea Lion was destroyed by his never altogether banished hope that in the end it wouldn't be necessary, that the mere threat of an invasion might be enough to bring the British to their senses and make them recognize that they had been defeated.

Perhaps for no one did the Battle of Britain have a more unexpected end than for Dowding himself. As the battle continued throughout the rest of September, and the German aircraft ranged farther north over London, instead of concentrating their attacks against No. 11 Group's airfields south of the capital, Leigh-Mallory's No. 12 Group was drawn increasingly into the fighting, rather than being used merely when Park called for fighter protection over his Sector airfields. A consequence of this change in the balance of

British forces was that Douglas Bader's "big wing" began to play a larger role in the battle, despite Park's doubts about its wisdom and his preferences for "squadron strength" attacks, which had in any case hitherto been accepted dogma for fighter operations. Bader did not hide his anger at Park's reluctance to use his big wing as he saw fit, and one of his pilots, who happened to be a member of Parliament, passed this growing dispute about Fighter Command tactics on to the Undersecretary of State for Air and, more disturbingly, to the prime minister. The fat was now in the fire, and with a politician's natural sense of self-preservation when faced with a sharp difference of opinion between senior officers of any service in wartime, Churchill urged the Chief of the Air Staff to arrange for a meeting of the interested parties and discuss "Major Day Tactics in the Fighter Force." Since Churchill was more than capable of intervening directly in service matters when he wanted to, he was clearly throwing a hot potato back to the air force. That there was no urgency to the matter in his mind is proved by the fact that it did not take place until October 17, more than a month after the greatest and most successful day of the battle.

Much has been made of this meeting by those who see it as a trap carefully set and baited by Air Marshal Sholto Douglas and Air Vice-Marshal Leigh-Mallory to catch Air Chief Marshal Dowding and Air Vice-Marshal Park; and there is no doubt, even in supposedly objective accounts, that it reflects one element in a very determined campaign on the part of Dowding's many enemies in the Air Ministry to get rid of him. Dowding's supporters—and there is no lack of them decades after the fact—tend to portray him as an innocent victim of backstairs intrigue and jealousy, but he had not reached the rank of Air Chief Marshal and Commander-in-Chief, Fighter Command, without some natural political instincts of his own, and a large part of his career had been spent amid the intrigues and cabals of the Air Ministry. He was, in fact, a skilled infighter himself, when it came to the Air Ministry and the Cabinet; and if he had a lot of enemies, it has to be said that he had made many of them himself, by his brusque manner, his impatience with those who disagreed with him, and his aloof, distant, eccentric personality.

It may be that Dowding was simply too tired by October 1940 to perceive that he was walking into a trap, or that he put too much reliance on Churchill's promises of support (though given his long experience with politicians that seems unlikely); or perhaps he had simply had enough of repeatedly being given new dates for his retirement. Certainly, he can have had no illusions about the meeting; nor can Park—it was a grim, hanging jury of his peers that he was facing, barely disguised as an impartial inquiry into the facts. His old rival Newall, the Chief of the Air Staff, was too ill to attend, and this ought to have been a warning, since he was replaced at the meeting by Sholto Douglas, now the Deputy Chief of the Air Staff, with whom Dowding had clashed many times before. Douglas was younger than Dowding, sleeker, an altogether jollier and more outgoing personality, at least on the surface, a decorated war hero, happily married, and a good mixer, and he had set his eyes long since on Dowding's job. The presence of Leigh-Mallory cannot have surprised Dowding—the whole purpose of the meeting was ostensibly to thrash out the differences between Park and Leigh-Mallory—but it must have come as a shock to realize that Leigh-Mallory had brought Bader along to represent the views of the fighter pilots. That Sholto Douglas had allowed Leigh-Mallory to introduce into the meeting a mere squadron leader (the equivalent of a major), however highly decorated and celebrated, to dispute the views of the Air Officer Commanding-in-

Chief, Fighter Command, and of Air Vice-Marshal Park, who commanded No. 11 Group, would have been enough to tell Dowding that his neck was on the block.

Nothing of this is reflected in the minutes of the meeting—it took place in England, after all. Everybody gave his point of view politely, making full allowance for the other fellow's point of view. Park conceded that there was something to be said for the big wing, Leigh-Mallory admitted that there were occasions when an attack by one or two squadrons might be called for, and even Bader was restrained in front of his superiors. Sholto Douglas gave an impartial summing up, and Dowding promised to increase cooperation between the two groups, though he did not suggest how he hoped to achieve this. It was all very polite and English, but there is no question that his failure to get his two principal subordinate commanders to cooperate with each other was being criticized, with some reason.

Reading between the lines in Churchill's history of World War II, it is possible to wonder if matters regarding Dowding had gone farther—or faster—than Churchill had ever intended. He almost certainly assumed that whatever happened, Dowding could be brought into line, as could his fellow air marshals—Churchill always thought he could deal with senior officers the way he did with politicians, smoothing things over with a strong dose of flattery, a new appointment, or, when all else failed, an emotional appeal to their sense of duty or friendship. It was a mistake he had already made during World War I, with his friend Admiral of the Fleet Lord Fisher and with that more remote potentate Field Marshal Lord Kitchener of Khartoum. Every great man has his faults, and among Churchill's was the belief that his powers of persuasion were unlimited, and that when he had concluded an argument he had invariably changed the other person's mind. He consistently underrated the stiff neck of most senior officers

in the armed forces, a mistake he was to make again with Generals
Auchinleck and Wavell in the Western Desert, in 1941. Though he
had been a cadet at Sandhurst and had begun his adult life as a professional soldier, Churchill was a born politician, not necessarily a born
military man, and he never fully understood that whereas politicians
could differ and remain friends, or quarrel in public and make up in
private, admirals, generals, and air marshals were cut from different
cloth—they believed in rank, duty, and what we would now call the
chain of command. This was perhaps the one area of statecraft in
which Churchill's wisdom was exceeded by that of George VI, who
was constitutionally the head of the armed forces and took seriously
the opinion of their senior officers, most of whom he knew.*

In the end, what brought Dowding down was not the "big wing"
controversy but the poor performance of his night fighters. As the
Luftwaffe moved from day bombing to night bombing, it became increasingly (and embarrassingly) clear that Dowding's night fighters,
for the most part, remained unable to find enemy planes, let alone
shoot them down. Politically, this was unacceptable to the prime
minister, who not unreasonably felt that the British deserved and
expected something better from Fighter Command while bombs
and incendiaries fell on them every night. Another committee was set
up to examine the matter, this time under the leadership of Marshal
of the Royal Air Force Sir John Salmond, another longtime adversary
of Dowding's. Salmond accepted the recommendation of Sholto
Douglas that some of Dowding's fighter squadrons, with their single-

* George VI—like his father, George V (and unlike his older brother, Edward VIII)—took
a personal, proprietary interest in the opinions and careers of his senior officers. Because
he had been educated as a naval officer (and had fought at the Battle of Jutland in 1916 as
a midshipman), this was an area in which the king was never a rubber stamp for his prime
minister, and had strong opinions and preferences of his own.

engine Spitfires and Hurricanes, should be retrained to fight at night, and that the centralized fighter control system, which Dowding had installed at such pains at Fighter Command headquarters, and which had been one of the principal factors in winning the Battle of Britain, should now be decentralized, to give each Group more direct control over its own fighters. (This was both a blow against Park's conduct at No. 11 Group and a gesture of support for Leigh-Mallory's opinions.)

Dowding vigorously resisted both these directives, and wrote a letter to the prime minister rebutting them in detail, which was surely a mistake, since although Churchill wanted results, the last thing he wanted was to be drawn into a technical dispute between feuding air marshals. Dowding certainly understood at once that decentralizing Fighter Command's operations center was an attempt to take control of the fighter squadrons out of his hands, and he rightly predicted that to send up Hurricanes and Spitfires at night in any meaningful quantity would merely be to sacrifice pilots and aircraft for no purpose, and that nothing useful could be accomplished until Fighter Command received a new twin-engine aircraft—the Bristol Beaufighter, which was still being flight-tested—suitable for night fighting, and equipped with an improved AI set, as well as a quantity of trained aircrew radar operators, to form a two-man team with the pilot. The solution to the problem of the night fighters depended, therefore, on three things that were still in development: the Beaufighter, the new AI set, and the fully trained pilot–radar operator two-man crew. There was no way to rush any one of these, or to put one into service without the others.

Although Dowding was absolutely right, the notion that, for the present, nothing could be done about a serious military problem was not one that Churchill would have accepted tamely from any senior officer. He was not about to tell the British people that they should wait quietly and patiently until Fighter Command eventually received the right equipment and revised its training procedures, while in the meantime their homes were being blown up or burned night after night. There is no doubt that he was made aware of this new controversy between Dowding and the Air Ministry—it was the job of Churchill's old friend Sir Archibald Sinclair, Secretary of State for Air, to keep him informed, and even had Sinclair not done so, Sholto Douglas and numerous other people would have found ways to let the prime minister know what was going on at the "Night Air Defence Committee." In the circumstances, it took no great effort to float the suggestion in high quarters that Dowding was too old for the job and out of touch with the latest technology, not to speak of being tired, stubborn, difficult, and hostile to new ideas.

In any case, Dowding had been commanding Fighter Command for four years, during which he had frequently had to fight off attempts to retire him, and for five months he had been fighting—and winning—the greatest and the most crucial air battle of history to date. It is hardly surprising, then, that not only his enemies assumed he was past his prime, and felt it was time for a change—even his own authorized biographer and those historians of the Battle of Britain sympathetic to him (as most are) take this view. He had been put on notice in August, at the height of the battle, that his retirement date would be postponed to November, and this time it was not extended. On November 25 he at last gave up his beloved command and retired, having been informed rather abruptly that there was no further post available for an officer of his seniority. Those who favor the conspiracy theory of history have, in this case, felt their view to be justified by the fact that

Sholto Douglas replaced Dowding at Fighter Command, and that Leigh-Mallory replaced his own antagonist, Park, at No. 11 Group—thus the "anti-Dowding" faction finally won.

In the event, Dowding had a brief, though unhappy, comeback. He was persuaded by the prime minister to take a position of great importance: trying to get "American war aviation developed on the right lines, and lines parallel to ours," a task for which he warned the prime minister he was completely unsuited. One senses, in Churchill's note on the matter to Sinclair, a rare tone of guilt and embarrassment. Churchill had neither forgotten nor forgiven Dowding's attempt at the War Cabinet to stop him from sending more fighters to France, but he recognized that the country owed Dowding a great debt. He managed to overcome Dowding's objections to this new post (and Sinclair's doubts about the wisdom of sending him to America), because the assignment was intended to postpone his retirement from the RAF. In the end, however, Dowding was right—hardly anybody could have been less well suited to bringing the Americans a message which they did not want to hear and which they would in any case ignore. He arrived bearing a personal message from the prime minister to President Roosevelt, which the latter received with his usual affability, but neither Dowding's personality nor his mission was much appreciated by Americans—he had, after all, the uncongenial task of telling them that what they were building was all wrong, and that they would do better to follow the British example. He made the situation worse by warning the Americans against building day bombers at all, although day bombers were the heart of their planning for war if or when it came. He had also been charged with persuading the Americans to build the new Napier "Sabre" aircraft engine and use it in their new aircraft—a lost cause, since the Sabre was troublesome and difficult to manufacture, and turned out to be inferior to the aircraft engines the Americans already had on the drawing board. Dowding's eccentric remarks in public about other problems in the Anglo-American relationship caused so much bad feeling that Lord Halifax, the British ambassador to the United States, felt obliged to complain about him to the Foreign Office; and Air Commodore Sir John Slessor wrote from Washington to the new Chief of the Air Staff Air Chief Marshal Sir Charles Portal, "I hate writing like this about a very senior officer, but in the national interest I must express the fervent hope that you will get him out of this country before he does much more harm."[1]

It has to be said in Churchill's favor that his sense of guilt was strong enough for him to intervene several times more on Dowding's behalf—Dowding was selected to write the official *Despatch* on the Battle of Britain; Churchill recommended him, in vain, to head Army Cooperation Command;[2] then Dowding was appointed to the thankless task of touring RAF commands to suggest economies, a job in which his seniority, high rank, and growing status as a national hero made his suggestions about where and how money could be saved all the less welcome. Unsurprisingly, the latter job finally caused Dowding himself to put in for retirement in the summer of 1942, and by that time he was as happy to go as Churchill was, no doubt, happy to be relieved of the thankless task of finding further employment for him in the RAF.

Dowding's supporters (who grew in number as the Battle of Britain receded) complained that he was not promoted to Marshal of the Royal Air Force (the equivalent of a British Field Marshal or an American five-star general) on retirement; but the custom was then that this rank should be reserved for officers who had served as Chief of the Air Staff, as Dowding had not, and even the king, who was a

Marshal of the Royal Air Force himself, was unable to persuade the Air Ministry to make an exception for Dowding.*

Dowding remarried, happily; and, after some initial bitterness at the way he had been dismissed from Fighter Command, he mellowed, took up the cause of spiritualism, and following the example of his wife, vegetarianism, as well as that of a single universal human language. In compensation for not having been raised to the rank of Marshal of the Royal Air Force, he was made Lord Dowding of Bentley Priory in 1943, and awarded the Grand Cross of the Victorian Order, one of the few honors that remain entirely within gift of the sovereign.

When the official history of the Battle of Britain was published (it sold more than 6 million copies), Dowding's name was not mentioned in it.[†]

Dowding's biographer Basil Collier called him a "prophet." Collier was placing Dowding, oddly enough, among such religious cult figures as Madame Blavatsky, the founder of the Theosophical Society, and Mary Baker Eddy, the founder of Christian Science, no doubt because he had in mind Dowding's preoccupation with spiritualism, which became stronger as he grew older.

But in fact Dowding was a prophet of a very different sort. Almost alone, he had prophesied, correctly, the form air warfare would take; and almost without help, indeed against determined opposition, he

---

* The tradition was eventually altered in 1945 because the newly elected Labour government was unwilling to raise Air Chief Marshal Sir Arthur Harris, the outspoken commanding officer of Bomber Command, to the peerage. A peerage might have implied their approval of the bombing of Dresden, among other things. The goverment raised him to the rank of Marshal of the Royal Air Force instead.

[†] Leading Churchill to minute Sinclair, "This is not a good story. . . . The jealousies and cliquism which have led to the committing of this offence are a discredit to the Air Ministry"(Gilbert, *Finest Hour*, page 1061).

had invented the means with which to defend Britain against attack from the air, right down to the smallest item. Not only did he prophesy the nature of the attack; he prophesied the kind of tools that would be needed to defeat it—radar, the single-engine monoplane fighter, the centralized operations room—and by a miracle of vision and obstinacy managed to put it all in place by 1940, just when it was needed.

Few prophets have ever had a clearer picture of what was to come—or what to do about it.

ACKNOWLEDGMENTS

For their help and advice in researching the story of the Battle of Britain I am indebted to Len Deighton, whose own book *Fighter* remains the benchmark for anybody writing about these events; to Tim Staples of Diverse Images, whose detailed knowledge of British and German aircraft of the period and enthusiasm were invaluable; to Sir Martin Gilbert, the fount of all wisdom on the subject of Winston Churchill, for his painstaking reading of the manuscript; to my neighbor Alex Kollmar, a pilot who generously refreshed my memory of the many things I have forgotten about airplanes since I left the Royal Air Force in 1953; and to Geoff Simpson, editor of *1940*, the magazine of the Friends of the Few. I am also very grateful indeed to my friends Winston S. Churchill and Sir Alistair Horne, CBE, for their careful reading of the manuscript, and for their numerous corrections and suggestions. Any remaining errors are, of course, my own.

I would like to express my very special gratitude to Dawn Lafferty, my assistant, for her help in preparing the manuscript; to the invaluable Mike Hill for his dedicated research skills; to Kevin Kwan for photo research; and to Barry Singer, of Chartwell Books, for his uncanny ability to lay his hands on books that have been out of print for decades.

I would never have written this book without the encouragement of my dear agent Lynn Nesbit and my good friend and fellow history lover Morton Janklow, or without the patience and sound editorial judgment of my editor Hugh Van Dusen, and the help of his assistant Rob Crawford, as well as the advice of the incomparable Gypsy Da Silva, whose ambition it turned out to be to go up in a Spitfire one of these days. (This is not an impossible dream—there are at least two Spitfires converted to two-seater trainers for the Irish Air Force still flying, one of them in California.)

Above all, I thank my wife, Margaret, for her patience in putting up with yet another long task of reading and research on my part, and for collecting yet another huge pile of books that fills a room in our house and strains the floorboards.

BIBLIOGRAPHY

Addison, Paul, and Jeremy A. Crang (eds.). *The Burning Blue*. London: Pimlico, 2000.

Battle of Britain Campaign Diary. Royal Air Force, 1940.

Bickers, Richard Townsend. *The Battle of Britain*. London: Salamander, 1990.

Brickhill, Paul. *Reach for the Sky: The Story of Douglas Bader, Legless Ace of the Battle of Britain*. Annapolis, Md.: Naval Institute Press, 2001.

"Cato." See Owen, Frank.

Churchill, Winston S. *Into Battle: Speeches*. London: Cassell, 1941.

———. *Never Give In!: The Best of Winston Churchill's Speeches*. New York: Hyperion, 2003.

———. *The Second World War*, Vol. II, *Their Finest Hour*. London: Cassell, 1949.

Clayton, Tim, and Phil Craig. *Finest Hour: The Battle of Britain*. New York: Simon and Schuster, 1999.

Collier, Basil. *Leader of the Few*. London: Jarrolds, 1957.

Collier, Richard. *Eagle Day: The Battle of Britain, August 6–September 15, 1940*, 2nd ed. New York: Dutton, 1980.

Deighton, Len. *Fighter: The True Story of the Battle of Britain*. London: Cape, 1977.

Faber, Harold (ed.). *Luftwaffe: A History*. New York: Times Books, 1977.

Fisher, David E. *A Summer Bright and Terrible: Winston Churchill, Lord Dowding, Radar, and the Impossible Triumph of the Battle of Britain*. Berkeley, Calif.: Shoemaker and Hoard, 2005.

Flint, Peter. *Dowding and Headquarters Fighter Command*. London: Airlife, 1986.

Fozard, John W. (ed.). *Sydney Camm and the Hurricane: Perspectives on the Master Fighter Designer and His Finest Achievement*. Washington, D.C.: Smithsonian Institution Press, 1991.

Freiden, Seymour, and William Richardson (eds.). *The Fatal Decisions*. New York: Berkley, 1968.

Fuchser, Larry William. *Neville Chamberlain and Appeasement: A Study in the Politics of History*. New York: Norton, 1982.

Galland, Adolf. *The First and the Last*. Bristol: Cerberus, 2001.

Gallico, Paul. *The Hurricane Story: How a Great Plane Saved a War*. New York: Doubleday, 1960.

Gilbert, Martin. *Finest Hour*. London: Heinemann, 1983.

———. *Never Surrender. The Churchill Papers*, Volume II. New York: Norton, 1995.

Green, William. *Augsburg Eagle: The Story of the Messerschmitt 109*. New York: Doubleday, 1971.

Grinsell, Robert. *Messerschmitt Bf 109*. New York: Crown, 1980.

Hillary, Richard. *The Last Enemy*. London: Macmillan and Co., 1942.

Hough, Richard, and Denis Richards. *The Battle of Britain*. New York: Norton, 1989.

Ismay, H. L. *The Memoirs of General Lord Ismay*. New York: Viking, 1960.

Jenkins, Roy. *Churchill: A Biography*. New York: Farrar, Straus and Giroux, 2001.

Jones, R. V. *Most Secret War: British Scientific Intelligence, 1939–1945*. London: Coronet, 1978.

Kaplan, Philip, and Richard Collier. *The Few: Summer 1940—The Battle of Britain*. London: Seven Dials, 1989.

Kens, Karlheinz, and Heinz J. Nowarra. *Die deutschen Flugzeuge 1933–1945*. Munich: Lehmanns Verlag, 1964.

Kurowski, Franz. *Luftwaffe Aces*. Canada: Fedorowicz, 1996; Mechanicsburg, Pa.: Stackpole, 2002.

Mason, Herbert Molloy, Jr. *The Rise of the Luftwaffe*. New York: Dial, 1973.

Morgan, Eric B., and Edward Shacklady. *Spitfire: The History*. Stamford, Conn.: Key, 1987.

Mosley, Leonard. *The Reich Marshal: A Biography of Hermann Goering*. New York: Doubleday, 1974.

Nesbit, Roy Conyers. *The Battle of Britain*. Stroud, U.K.: Sutton, 2000.

Nicolson, Harold. *Diaries and Letters, 1930–1939,* Nigel Nicolson, ed. New York: Atheneum, 1966.

Overy, Richard. *The Battle of Britain: The Myth and the Reality*. New York: Norton, 2000.

Owen, Frank ("Cato"). *Guilty Men*. London: Penguin, 1998.

Parkinson, Roger. *Summer of 1940: The Battle of Britain*. New York: David McKay, 1977.

Price, Alfred. *The Battle of Britain: The Hardest Day*. London: MacDonald and Jane's, 1979.

——. *The Spitfire Story*. London: Arm and Armour, 1982.

Richards, Denis. *Royal Air Force 1939–1945,* Vol. I, *The Fight at Odds*. London: Her Majesty's Stationery Office, 1953.

Rigg, Bryan Mark. *Hitler's Jewish Soldiers: The Untold Story of Nazi Racial Laws and Men of Jewish Descent in the German Military*. Lawrence: Univ. of Kansas Press, 2002.

Robertson, Bruce. *Spitfire—The Story of a Famous Fighter*. Letchworth, U.K.: Harleyford, 1960.

Robinson, Derek. *Invasion 1940: The Truth about the Battle of Britain and What Stopped Hitler*. New York: Carroll and Graf, 2005.

Sarkar, Dilip. *Group Captain Sir Douglas Bader: An Inspiration in Photographs*. Worcester, U.K.: Ramrod, 2001.

Terraine, John. *The Right of the Line*. London: Hodder and Stoughton, 1985.

Townsend, Peter. *Duel of Eagles*. New York: Simon and Schuster, 1970.

Wellum, Geoffrey. *First Light*. London: Penguin/Viking, 2002.

Wood, Derek, and Derek Dempster. *The Narrow Margin: The Battle of Britain and the Rise of Air Power 1930–1949*. Barnsley, U.K.: Pen and Sword, 2003.

Young, G. M. *Stanley Baldwin*. London: Rupert Hart-Davis, 1952.

NOTES

CHAPTER 1

1. Young, *Stanley Baldwin*, 174.
2. Jenkins, *Churchill*, 608.
3. Rigg, *Hitler's Jewish Soldiers*, 21–22.
4. "Cato" (Frank Owen), *Guilty Men*.

CHAPTER 2

1. Young, *Stanley Baldwin*, 61.
2. Churchill, *Never Give In!* 106.
3. Nicolson, *Diaries and Letters*, 129.
4. Young, *Stanley Baldwin*, 174.
5. Ibid., 179.
6. Ibid., 182.
7. Ibid.

CHAPTER 3

1. For the best and most comprehensive account of Dowding's creation of the Fighter Command Headquarters, and its ramifications for the air defense of the United Kingdom, I am indebted to Peter Flint's *Dowding and Headquarters Fighter Command*.
2. Ibid., 4.

3. Price, *The Spitfire Story*, 11.
4. See www.rjmitchell-spitfire.co.uk: click on Schneider Trophy, "History of the Contest," October 2, 2006, 1.
5. Price, *The Spitfire Story*, 16.
6. Deighton, *Fighter*, 77.
7. Price, *The Spitfire Story*, 67. See also Robertson, *Spitfire*, 18.
8. Gallico, *The Hurricane Story*, 22–23.
9. Ibid., 36.

CHAPTER 4

1. See www.fiskes.co.uk/billy_fiske.htm.
2. Grinsell, *Messerschmitt Bf109*, 306.
3. Kens and Nowarra, *Die deutschen Flugzeuge, 1933–1945*, 275–78.
4. Deighton, *Fighter*, 80–81.
5. Ibid., 81.

CHAPTER 5

1. The best and most detailed account of the differences between the Bf 109 and the Spitfire and Hurricane is to be found in Green, *Augsburg Eagle*. I have relied heavily (and gratefully) on his expertise.
2. Deighton, *Fighter*, 131.
3. Churchill, *The Second World War*, Vol. II, *Their Finest Hour*, 38.
4. Ibid., 42.
5. Ibid., 46.
6. Richards, *Royal Air Force, 1939–1945*, Vol. II, *The Fight at Odds*, 109.
7. Flint, *Dowding*, 53.
8. Richards, *Royal Air Force, 1939–1945*, 120.
9. Flint, *Dowding*, 73.
10. Churchill, *The Second World War*, Vol. II, *Their Finest Hour*, 38.
11. Ibid., 46.
12. Collier, *Leader of the Few*, 192–94.
13. Flint, *Dowding*, 149.

CHAPTER 6

1. Gilbert, *The Churchill War Papers*, Vol. II, *Never Surrender*, 582.

CHAPTER 7

1. Wood and Dempster, *The Narrow Margin*, 321.
2. Bickers, *The Battle of Britain*, 37.
3. Ibid., 120.
4. Gilbert, *Finest Hour*, 766.
5. Flint, *Dowding*, 93.
6. Gilbert, *The Churchill War Papers*, Vol. II, *Never Surrender*, 472.
7. Ibid., 472.
8. Fisher, *A Summer Bright and Terrible*.

CHAPTER 8

1. The numbers of aircraft available at the beginning and end of each day, as well as RAF losses and RAF civilian casualties, are from *The Battle of Britain Campaign Diary*.
2. Brickhill, *Reach for the Sky*, 146.
3. Ibid., 173.
4. Ibid., 164.
5. Collier, *Eagle Day*, 83.
6. Hough and Richards, *The Battle of Britain*, 184.
7. Hillary, *The Last Enemy*, 101–2.
8. Gilbert, *The Churchill War Papers*, Vol. II, *Never Surrender*, 700–1.
9. Gilbert, *Finest Hour*, 824.
10. Ibid., 673–74.

CHAPTER 9

1. Nigel Rose's letters quoted in Addison and Crang, *The Burning Blue*, 145.
2. Ibid.
3. Ismay, *Memoirs*, 181–82.
4. Gilbert, *The Churchill War Papers*, Vol. II, *Never Surrender*, 235.
5. Gilbert, *Finest Hour*, 658.
6. The best account of this meeting is in Jones, *Most Secret War*, 109–8.
7. Hough and Richards, *The Battle of Britain*, 316.
8. Ibid., 237.
9. James Reston, "Can Britain Hold Out?" *New York Times*, September 8, 1940.

10. Galland, *The First and the Last*, 59.
11. Churchill, *Into Battle*, 273.
12. Churchill, *The Second World War*, Vol. II, *Their Finest Hour*, 294–97.
13. Ibid., 296.
14. Ibid., 297.
15. Hough and Richards, *The Battle of Britain*, 293.

CHAPTER 10

1. Hough and Richards, *The Battle of Britain*, 322.
2. Gilbert, *Finest Hour*, 1040.

INDEX

Grateful acknowledgment is made to the following for the images in the inserts:

COLOR INSERT

Page 1: From the painting *The American Friend* by John Howard Worsley
Pages 2–3: Imperial War Museum, Negative No. IWM ART LD 1550
Page 4: Her Majesty's Stationery Office
Page 5: Her Majesty's Stationery Office
Pages 6–7: From *The Battle of Britain*, by Richard T. Bickers (Salamander Books, 1990), page 42
Page 8: From the painting *Achtung Spitfire!* by Charles J. Thompson, G.Av.A: A.S.A.A.

BLACK-AND-WHITE INSERT

Page 1: *top*: Imperial War Museum, Negative No. D1417; *bottom*: Time & Life Pictures/Getty Images
Page 2: *top*: Fox Photos/Hulton Archive/Getty Images; *bottom*: Hulton-Deutsch Collection/Corbis
Page 3: *top*: Royal Aeronautical Society Library; *bottom*: from *Spitfire: The Story of a Famous Fighter*, by Bruce Robertson (Harleyford Publications, 1960), page 9
Page 4: *top*: Imperial War Museum, printed in *Eagle Day*, by Basil Collier (E. P. Dutton, 1966), page 161; *bottom*: Bob Thomas/Popperfoto/Getty Images
Page 5: *top left*: Corbis; *top right*: Getty Images; *bottom*: From *The Battle of Britain*, by Richard T. Bickers (Salamander Books, 1990), page 69
Page 6: *top*: Imperial War Museum, Negative No. C1870; *bottom*: Imperial War Museum, Negative No. CH7698
Page 7: *top and bottom left*: Bettmann/Corbis; *bottom right*: Bundesarchiv
Page 8: cartoons by Ernst "Udlinger" Udet
Page 9: *top*: Imperial War Museum, Negative No. CM5663; *bottom*: Imperial War Museum, Negative No. CH11943
Page 10: *top*: Imperial War Museum, Negative No. CH1233; *middle and bottom*: Bettmann/Corbis